"十四五"普通高等教育精品系列教材

U0519445

Introduction to Financial Reporting

财务报告导论

（第二版）

▶ 薄　澜　张微微◎编著

西南财经大学出版社

中国·成都

图书在版编目（CIP）数据

财务报告导论＝Introduction to Financial Reporting：英文/薄澜，张微微编著．—2 版．—成都：西南财经大学出版社，2024.2
ISBN 978-7-5504-6099-7

Ⅰ.①财…　Ⅱ.①薄…②张…　Ⅲ.①会计报表—会计分析—高等学校—教材—英文　Ⅳ.①F231.5

中国国家版本馆 CIP 数据核字（2024）第 020363 号

Introduction to Financial Reporting

财务报告导论（第二版）

CAIWU BAOGAO DAOLUN

薄　澜　张微微　编著

策划编辑：孙　婧
责任编辑：孙　婧
责任校对：廖　韧
封面设计：墨创文化
责任印制：朱曼丽

出版发行	西南财经大学出版社（四川省成都市光华村街 55 号）
网　址	http：//cbs. swufe. edu. cn
电子邮件	bookcj@ swufe. edu. cn
邮政编码	610074
电　话	028-87353785
照　排	四川胜翔数码印务设计有限公司
印　刷	郫县犀浦印刷厂
成品尺寸	185mm×260mm
印　张	20. 875
字　数	640 千字
版　次	2024 年 2 月第 2 版
印　次	2024 年 2 月第 1 次印刷
印　数	1— 2000 册
书　号	ISBN 978-7-5504-6099-7
定　价	52. 00 元

▶▶ 第二版序言

　　《财务报告导论》自 2021 年出版以来,在中外合作办学商科专业财务会计教学中得到了广泛应用,作为重要成果之一获得了 2022 年辽宁省本科教学成果奖。依托该教材的课程——"初级财务会计(英文)"获批辽宁省线上线下混合式一流课程和辽宁大学思政示范课程。在两年四学期的教学应用中,该教材的慕课资源使用人数达到千余人次。此次再版除对书中的错误进行更正外,还删改了部分难度较大的习题,并结合学生课堂反馈补充了关于 Events after the reporting period(IAS 10) 的相关知识点与习题。

　　本次教材修订第 1 章至第 7 章由张微微副教授负责,第 8 章至第 14 章由薄澜教授负责。我们希望通过此次《财务报告导论》第二版的修订出版,能够为读者提供质量更高的教材,也欢迎各位读者对本教材不吝批评指正,以便我们不断修改和完善该教材,为提高中外合作办学的会计教学质量而努力。

编者

2023 年 7 月

▶▶ 序言

2006年,财政部发布了中国企业会计准则,实现中国企业会计准则与国际财务报告准则(IFRSs)的实质性趋同。2010年,为响应二十国集团(G20)关于建立全球统一的高质量会计准则的倡议,推进中国企业会计准则与国际财务报告准则的持续全面趋同,财政部发布了《中国企业会计准则与国际财务报告准则持续趋同路线图》。从2014年至今,财政部发布了一系列新制定或修订的企业会计准则,以保持中国企业会计准则与国际财务报告准则的持续趋同。当前,在经济全球化及国内外形势深刻变化的背景下,掌握国际会计准则和提高会计信息质量是中国企业走向海外、节约成本和增强国际竞争力的基本要求,而为中国企业培养与输送具有国际化专业素养的会计人才就成为国内高等会计教育的重要任务。

在教育部的大力倡导下,近年来高校中外合作办学项目发展趋势良好,会计专业的双语教学也在持续发展,而高质量的英文会计教材是满足合作办学与双语教学的根本保障。目前国内高校使用的英文会计教材多为引进的国外原版教材。原版教材具有为国外教学量身定制的特点,如篇幅较大、体系庞杂且具有一定难度,尤其是许多内容紧密结合国外的经济、法律和文化背景,不适合国内教学采用,这也成为国内会计专业全英文或双语教学的制约因素。因此,对符合国情且适合国内教师与学生使用的会计学英文教材的开发与编写具有现实的必要性和迫切性。

本教材——Introduction to Financial Reporting(《财务报告导论》)遵循"十四五"规划期间教育部对高校本科教材建设的总体指导方针,坚持以习近平新时代中国特色社会主义思想为指导,落实《全国大中小学教材建设规划(2019—2022年)》和《普通高等学校教材管理办法》,力求满足普及化阶段高等教育人才培养的需要。

本教材是以国际会计准则(IAS)为基础,由浅入深讲解编制个体经营者、股份公司财务报表的全英文教材。全书共14章,知识点分三大部分:

第一部分(1~3章)为个体经营者的收益表及资产负债表的编制;

第二部分(4~10章)为报表编制调整项目——存货的计量(IAS 2)、坏账及可疑账的计提、折旧的计提(IAS 16)、应计及预付调整、预计负债和或有事项(IAS 37)、固定资产的重估与处置(IAS 16)及无形资产的界定和披露(IAS 38);

第三部分(11~14章)为股份公司收益表、资产负债表、所有者权益变动表(IAS 1)和现金流量表(IAS 7)的编制,以及财务报表分析。

本教材的大纲设计与内容编写均依托于辽宁大学新华国际商学院与英国德蒙福特大学莱斯特商学院合作办学会计专业项目,授课对象为本科二年级学生。该项目经过17年实践检验。本教材具有以下特点:

1. 英文专业术语规范,符合最新国际会计准则要求

本教材英文专业术语准确规范,报告编制方法反映了国际会计准则的最新变化,例如,根据《国际会计准则第18号——收入》(IAS 18 Revenue)的最新修订,购货折扣(discounts received)的抵减位置和原有规定相比发生了较大的变化,因此教材在例题和习题的设计上及时跟进了该准则的最新要求。此外,规范和准确的英文会计教材不仅能提高学生的专业知识,也能提高学生的英语阅读能力。

2. 体系完整、简繁得当、符合国情

本教材建立了财务报告的基本体系,涵盖了财务会计的基础内容及报表编制的核心内容。本教材的基本素材筛选自英文原版教材,在传统财务报告教学体系基础上,吸收国际会计研究理论和实务的精髓,结合国内学生的学习特点,有重点地对符合国际财务报告准则的报表编制方法进行了介绍。教材内容做到了通俗易懂、由浅入深、逐层提高,表述形式与习题设计更符合国内学生的思维习惯、价值观念与文化特征。

3. 慕课配套、注重实训、习题丰富

本教材按照50~70课内学时,课内、外学时比为1∶1设计教学与习题内容。本教材在阐述会计理论与实务方法时,既注重会计理论的深度与广度,又强调会计实务的操作方法与应用。例题讲解思路清晰,便于理解,注重实训,具有较强的实践指导性。此外,本教材配有慕课资源"Introduction to Financial Accounting and Reporting"(在线教学资源详情请咨询辽宁大学新华国际商学院 http://swibs.lnu.edu.cn),方便学生预习与复习。每一章的配套练习题,类型丰富齐全,难度适中。其中带"＊"的习题配套答案由出版社向任课教师提供,方便教师对课外作业或考试进行设计安排。

本教材的适用对象为高等院校经济学类、管理学类本科生,尤其是会计学、财务管理、金融学等专业的本科生,以及经济管理类低年级学术型硕士研究生、国内留学生、MBA(工商管理硕士)学生、备考ACCA(国际注册会计师)的学生等。

本教材第1章至第7章由张微微副教授编著,第8章至第14章由薄澜副教授编著。全书由薄澜副教授进行统稿。在本书的编著过程中,参考了 *Frank Wood's Business Accounting Volume 1*(Pearson,2019)、*Financial Accounting*(Routledge,2014)、*Financial Accounting*, *Reporting and Analysis*(Oxford University Press,2017)等多本教材与资料(书目与资料列于每章的参考文献中)。在此向有关作者和出版社表示衷心感谢。此外,本书的出版得到了辽宁大学新华国际商学院、"辽宁省兴辽英才计划"(项目编号:XLYC2002116)的经费支持和西南财经大学出版社的鼎力帮助,在此一并致谢。

由于水平有限,书中定有疏漏之处,恳请读者批评指正。

编者

2021年6月

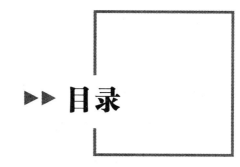

▶▶ 目录

Chapter 1   Statements of Profit or Loss: Sole Traders

目录

Answers

Chapter 1

Statements of Profit or Loss: Sole Traders

■Learning Objectives

· Explain the purpose and structure of statement of profit or loss.

· Calculate cost of goods sold, gross profit, and net profit.

· Explain the relationship between the trading account and the profit and loss account.

· Explain how the trading account and the profit and loss account fit together to create the statement of profit or loss.

· Explain how to deal with closing inventory when preparing the trading account section of a statement of profit or loss.

· Close down the appropriate accounts and transfer the balances to the trading account.

· Close down the appropriate accounts and transfer the balances to the profit and loss account.

· Prepare a statement of profit or loss from information given in a trial balance.

· Make appropriate double entries to incorporate net profit and drawings in the capital account.

1.1   Introduction to the Statement of Profit or Loss

The statement of profit or loss provides a summary of the results of a business's trading activities during a given accounting year. It shows the profit or loss for the year. The calculation of such profits and losses is probably the most important objective of the accounting function. The owners will want to know how the actual profits compare with the profits they had hoped to make. Knowing what profits are being made helps businesses to do many things, including:

· Planning ahead.

· Obtaining loans from banks, from other businesses, or from private individuals.

· Telling prospective business partners or someone who may be interested in buying the business how successful the business is.

· Used to determine the amount of taxation on the profit.

The basic format of the statement of profit or loss is shown in Exhibit 1.1. You will learn how to prepare it in the following section.

Exhibit 1.1

ABC		
Statement of profit or loss for the year ended 20×1		
	£	£
Revenue		XX
Less cost of sales		XX
Gross profit		<u>XX</u>
Less other expenses		
Selling and distribution costs	X	
Administrative expenses	X	
Interest payable on loans	<u>X</u>	<u>X</u>
Net Profit/(Loss)		<u>X/(X)</u>

1.2   Gross Profit and Net Profit

One of the most important uses of statements of profit or loss is that of comparing the results obtained with the results expected. We will see the profit calculated is split into two sections—one in which the gross profit is found and the next section in which the net profit is calculated.

1. Gross Profit

The first stage in the determination of the profit for the year involves calculating gross profit. The gross profit for a given period is computed by subtracting the cost of goods sold (or cost of sales) from sales revenue. Gross profit is calculated as:

Gross Profit = Sales − Cost of Goods Sold
Cost of Goods Sold = Opening Inventory + Purchases − Closing Inventory

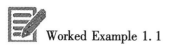

Worked Example 1. 1

Calculate the gross profit or gross loss of each of the following businesses in Exhibit 1. 2:

Exhibit 1. 2

Business	Cost of goods purchased	Sales	Gross profit/(Gross loss)
	£	£	£
A	9,820	10,676	
B	7,530	14,307	
C	10,500	19,370	
D	9,580	9,350	
E	8,760	17,200	

Solution

Sales−Cost of goods=Gross profit/(Gross loss)

Business A:£10,676 − £9,820 = £856

Business B:£14,307 − £7,530 = £6,777

Business C:£19,370 − £10,500 = £8,870

Business D:£9,350 − £9,580 = £(230)

Business E:£17,200 − £8,760 = £8,440

It is important to appreciate that the cost of goods sold is not usually the same as the amount of purchases. This is because most businesses will have purchased goods that are unsold at the end of the accounting period. These goods are referred to as **inventory.**The cost of inventory unsold is carried forward into the next accounting period to be matched against the income that it generates (matching concept), by being transferred to the statement of financial position at the end of the year.

A manufacturing business will have a number of different types of inventories. However, for simplicity, the following exposition is confined to non-manufacturing businesses whose inventory consists of goods purchased for resale that have not undergone any further processing by the entity.

2. Net Profit

Net profit, found in the profit and loss account section of the statement of profit or loss, consists of the gross profit plus any revenue other than that from sales, such as rents received or commissions earned, less the total costs used up during the period other than those already included in the 'cost of goods sold'. Where the costs used up exceed the gross profit plus other revenue, the result is said to be a net loss.Net profit is calculated as:

Net Profit = Gross Profit + Other Revenues − all other Expenses

Worked Example 1. 2

Using the answer of example 1.1, calculate the net profit/loss in Exhibit 1.3:

Exhibit 1. 3

Business	Other revenues	Expenses	Net profit/ (Net loss)
	£	£	£
A	–	2,622	
B	4,280	2,800	
C	500	2,500	
D	–	1,780	
E	3,260	2,440	

Solution

Gross profit/ (Gross loss) + Other revenues − Expenses = Net profit/ (Net loss)

Business A:£856 − £2,622 = £(1,766)

Business B:£6,777 + £4,280 − £2,800 = £8,257

Business C:£8,870 + £500 − £2,500 = £6,870

Business D:£(230) − £1,780 = £(2,010)

Business E:£8,440 + £3,260 − £2,440 = £9,260

1. 3   Preparation of a Trading and Profit and Loss Account

When a trading and profit and loss account is shown in details rather than in summary form (as is the case for the published statements of profit or loss of companies), it contains two accounts. One is called the **trading account.**The trading account is prepared in order to arrive at a figure for **gross profit.**Below the trading account is shown a summary of another account—the **profit and loss account.**It is these two accounts that together comprise the statement of profit or loss.

This profit and loss account should not be confused with the 'statement of profit **OR** loss'. The profit **AND** loss account is prepared so as to arrive at the figure for **net profit.**It is these two accounts that together comprise the statement of profit or loss. The basic format of the Trading and Profit and Loss account is shown in Exhibit 1. 4. The trading account is combined with the profit and loss account. Both the trading account and the profit and loss account are part of the double entry system. At the end of a financial period, they are closed off. They are then summarised and the information they contain is then copied into a statement of profit or loss.

Exhibit 1. 4

Trading and profit and loss account for the year ended 31 March 20X1				
	£		£	
Inventory of 1 Apr 20X0	xxx	Sales revenue	xxx	Trading
Purchases	xxx	Inventory of 31 Mar	xxx	
Carriage inwards	xxx			
Gross profit c/d	xxx		——	Account
	xxx		xxx	
Carriage outwards	xxx	Gross profit b/d	xxx	
Wages and salaries	xxx	Other revenue	xxx	
Rent	xxx			Profit and
Light and heat	xxx			
Telephone and postage	xxx			Loss Account
Net profit	xxx		——	
	xxx		xxx	

Note:

· The trading account shows the gross profit (or loss) that the company has made. The gross profit is the difference between the two sides of the trading account and must be brought down to the opposite side of the profit and loss account.

· The profit and loss account shows the net profit (or loss) made. Net profit is the difference between the two sides of the profit and loss account. This is recorded by debiting the profit and loss account and crediting the capital account. The reason is because the profit belongs to the owner and it increases the amount of capital he or she is entitled to withdraw from the business.

· If the debit side of the profit and loss account exceeds the credit side, this is shown as a net loss on the credit side and debited to the capital account.

Before drawing up a statement of profit or loss you should prepare the trial balance. This contains nearly all the information needed (Later on in this book you will see that certain adjustments have to be made, but we will ignore these at this stage).

We now look at the trial balance of G. John (Exhibit 1. 5), drawn up as on 31 December 20×1 after the completion of his first year in business.

Exhibit 1. 5

G. John		
Trial balance as at 31 December 20×1		
	Dr	Cr
	£	£
Sales		38,500
Purchases	29,000	
Rent	2,400	
Lighting expenses	1,500	
General expenses	600	
Fixtures and fittings	5,000	
Accounts receivable	6,800	
Accounts payable		9,100
Bank	15,100	
Cash	200	
Drawings	7,000	
Capital		20,000
	67,600	67,600

There are goods unsold at the end of the period. However, there is no record in the accounting books of the value of this unsold inventory. The only way that John can find this figure is by checking his inventory at the close of business on 31 December 20×1.

To do this he would have to make a list of all the unsold goods and then find out their value. The value he would normally place on them would be the cost price of the goods, i.e. what he paid for them. Let's assume that this is £3,000.

Note: To make this easier to follow, we shall assume that purchases consist of goods that are resold without needing any further work. You'll learn later that these are known as 'finished goods' but, for now, we'll simply refer to them as 'goods'.

Firstly, we have to calculate the cost of goods sold as follows:

		£
What John bought in the period:	Purchases	29,000
Less Goods bought but not sold in the period:	(Closing Inventory)	(3,000)
	= Cost of Goods Sold	26,000

Based on the sales revenue of £38,500 the gross profit can be calculated:

Sales−Cost of Goods Sold = Gross Profit

£38,500−£26,000 = £12,500

We now have the information we need to complete the trading account section of the statements of profit or loss. Next, the following four steps should be followed when preparing the **trading account**:

Step 1

The balance of the sales account is transferred to the trading account by:

DEBIT	Sales account (thus closing it)	X	
CREDIT	Trading account		X

Step 2

The balance of the purchases account is transferred to the trading account by:

DEBIT	Trading account	X	
CREDIT	Purchases account (thus closing it)		X

Step 3

Account for the closing inventory in the double entry accounts by:

DEBIT	Closing inventory account	X	
CREDIT	Trading account (thus completing the double entry)		X

Step 4

Carry the gross profit (or gross loss) figure from the trading account part down to the profit and loss part by:

DEBIT	Trading account	X	
CREDIT	Profit and loss account		X

We now close off the trading account in the normal way. In this case, revenues exceed costs so we describe the balance as 'gross profit'. The double entry transactions for the above transfers are shown as follows:

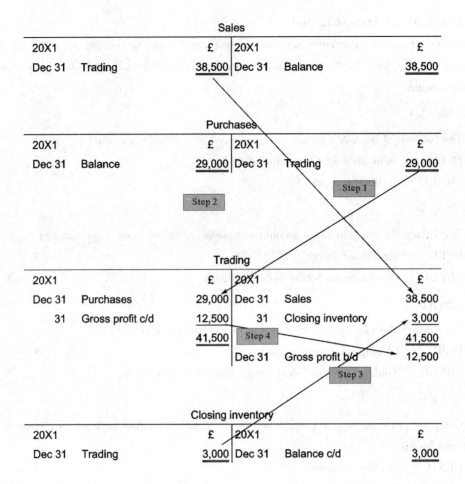

Sales

20X1		£	20X1		£
Dec 31	Trading	38,500	Dec 31	Balance	38,500

Purchases

20X1		£	20X1		£
Dec 31	Balance	29,000	Dec 31	Trading	29,000

Step 1

Step 2

Trading

20X1		£	20X1		£
Dec 31	Purchases	29,000	Dec 31	Sales	38,500
31	Gross profit c/d	12,500	31	Closing inventory	3,000
		41,500			41,500
			Dec 31	Gross profit b/d	12,500

Step 4

Step 3

Closing inventory

20X1		£	20X1		£
Dec 31	Trading	3,000	Dec 31	Balance c/d	3,000

Note:

· The balance shown on the trading account is described as 'gross profit' rather than being described as a balance.

· The balance (i.e. the gross profit) is not brought down to the next period.

· The entry of the closing inventory on the credit side of the trading account is a deduction from the purchases on the debit side.

· After the trading account has been completed, there are no balances remaining in the sales and purchases accounts. These accounts are now said to be 'closed off'.

We can now draw up a profit and loss account. The gross profit has been transferred from the trading account to the credit of the profit and loss account. Next, any revenue account balances, other than sales (which have already been dealt with in the trading account), are transferred to the credit of the profit and loss account. Typical examples are commissions.

To calculate net profit and record it

$$\text{Gross profit} - \text{Expenses} = \text{Net profit}$$
$$£12,500 - £4,500 = £8,000$$

The double entries needed to transfer the expense accounts to the profit and loss account, and the net profit to the capital account, are as follows:

The profit and loss account will now appear as follows:

Rent expense

20X1		£	20X1		£
Dec 31	Balance	2,400	Dec 31	Profit and loss	2,400

Lighting expenses

20X1		£	20X1		£
Dec 31	Balance	1,500	Dec 31	Profit and loss	1,500

General expenses

20X1		£	20X1		£
Dec 31	Balance	600	Dec 31	Profit and loss	600

Step 1

Profit and loss

20X1		£	20X1		£
Dec 31	Rent	2,400	Dec 31	Gross profit b/d	12,500
31	Lighting expenses	1,500			
31	General expenses	600			
31	Net profit	8,000			
		12,500			12,500

Step 2

Capital

20X1		£	20X1		£
			Dec 31	Profit and loss	8,000

Step 1

Transfer the debit balances on expenses accounts to the debit of the profit and loss account.

DEBIT	Profit and loss account	X	
CREDIT	Expenses accounts		X

Step 2

Transfer the net profit, when found, to the capital account to show the increase in capital.

DEBIT	Profit and loss account	X	
CREDIT	Capital account		X

The fact that a separate drawings account has been in use can now also be seen to have been in keeping with the policy of avoiding unnecessary detail in the capital account. There

will, therefore, only be one figure for drawings entered in the debit side of the capital account
— the total of the drawings for the whole of the period.

To increase the capital account and record it

$$\text{Old Capital} + \text{Net Profit} - \text{Drawings} = \text{New Capital}$$
$$£20,000 + £8,000 - £7,000 = £21,000$$

The capital and drawings account will now appear as follows:

Capital

20×1		£	20×1		£
Dec 31	Drawings	7,000	Dec 1	Balance b/d	20,000
Dec 31	Balance c/d	21,000	Dec 31	Profit and loss	8,000
		28,000			28,000

Drawings

20×1		£	20×1		£
Dec 31	Balance	7,000	Dec 31	Capital	7,000

1.4   Preparation of a Statement of Profit or Loss

The trading and profit and loss account is a **horizontal format** to demonstrate how the double entry system works. The statement of profit or loss is a **vertical format** for the trading and profit and loss account as you've seen in section 1.1. You now have all the information you need in order to prepare G. John's statement of profit or loss for the year ending 31 December 20×1. It is shown in Exhibit 1.6:

Exhibit 1.6

G. John		
Statement of profit or loss for the year ending 31 December 20×1		
	£	£
Sales		38,500
Less Cost of goods sold		
Purchases	29,000	
Less Closing inventory	(3,000)	(26,000)
Gross profit		12,500
Less Expenses		
Rent	2,400	
Lighting expenses	1,500	
General expenses	600	(4,500)
Net profit		8,000

You can see that the figures used are exactly the same using either the horizontal or vertical format. The vertical format is more widely used today since it is intended to make accounts easier to read and shows a more modern method of presentation. We will use it in future in this book.

You should note that not all the items in the trial balance have been used in the statement of profit or loss. The remaining balances in Exhibit 1. 7 are assets or liabilities or capital, they are not expenses or revenue. These will be used later when a statement of financial position is drawn up.

Exhibit 1. 7

G. John		
Trial balance as at 31 December 20×1		
	Dr	Cr
	£	£
Fixtures and fittings	5,000	
Accounts receivable	6,800	
Accounts payable		9,100
Inventory	3,000	
Bank	15,100	
Cash	200	
Capital		21,000
	30,100	30,100

Summary
· One of the main uses of the trading and profit and loss account is to provide information on the profit/losses made in the period and compare these figures with previous year's results.

· Calculate the cost of goods sold, gross profit and net profit.

· Close off the sales, purchases and relevant expense accounts at the end of a period and post the entries to the trading and profit and loss account.

· Transfer the net profit and drawings to the capital account at the end of a period.

· The double entries required in order to close off the relevant expense and revenue accounts at the end of a period and post the entries to the trading account and to the profit and loss account.

· Any balances still remaining in the books of account after preparation of the trading and profit and loss account represent assets, liabilities and capital. These balances are entered into the statement of financial position (see Chapter 2) and then carried forward to the next accounting period.

Exercise

1. 1 Which of the following is the correct formula for cost of sales? (　　)

　　A.Opening inventory − purchases + closing inventory

　　B.Purchases − closing inventory + sales

　　C.Opening inventory + closing inventory − purchases

　　D.Opening inventory − closing inventory + purchases

1. 2 If an owner takes goods out of inventory for their own use, how is this dealt with?
(　　)

　　A.Credited to drawings at cost

　　B.Credited to drawings at selling price

　　C.Debited to drawings at cost

　　D.Debited to drawings at selling price

1. 3 A business starts trading on 1 September 20×0. During the year, it has sales of
£500,000, purchases of £250,000 and closing inventory of £75,000. What is the gross profit
for the year? (　　)

　　A.£175,000

　　B.£250,000

　　C.£325,000

　　D.£675,000

1. 4 Using the information in Question 1. 3 above, what is the figure for total assets?
(　　)

　　A.£179,000

　　B.£169,000

　　C.£129,000

　　D.£5,000

1. 5 In a period, sales are £140,000, purchases £75,000 and other expenses £25,000.
What is the figure for net profit to be transferred to the capital account? (　　)

　　A.£40,000

　　B.£65,000

　　C.£75,000

　　D.£140,000

1. 6 The balance on an expense account will go to the P/L account. However, the balance on a liability account is written off to capital.

Is this statement correct? (　　)

　A.Yes

　B.No

1. 7 Net assets at the beginning of 20×7 were£101,700. The proprietor injected new capital of £8,000 during the year and took drawings of £2,200. Net assets at the end of 20×7 were £180,000.

What was the profit earned by the business in 20×7? (　　)

　A.£72,500 profit

　B.£88,300 profit

　C.£84,300 profit

　D.£(84,100) loss

1. 8 Mr Harmon does not keep full accounting records, but the following information is available in respect of his accounting year ended 31 December 20×9.

	£
Cash purchases in year	3,900
Cash paid for goods supplied on credit	27,850
Trade payables at 1 January 20×9	970
Trade payables at 31 December 20×9	720

In his trading account for 20×9, what will be Harmon's figure for purchases? (　　)

　A.£31,500

　B.£31,750

　C.£27,850

　D.£33,440

1. 9 Anchor is preparing his financial statements. After transferring the balances on all the income and expense ledger accounts to the profit and loss ledger account, the total credits in the profit and loss ledger account exceed the total debits by£4,000.

Which two of the following statements about Anchor Ltd are correct? (　　)

　A.Anchor Ltd has made a loss for the year of £4,000.

　B.Anchor Ltd has made a profit for the year of £4,000.

　C.To begin to calculate the closing capital account balance, Anchor Ltd should credit the capital account and debit the profit and loss ledger account with £4,000.

　D.The opening balance on the profit and loss ledger account for the next reporting period is £4,000 credit.

E. The closing balance on the profit and loss ledger account of £4,000 should be deducted from the capital account to give the profit for the year.

1. 10 Which of the following statements concerning preparation of financial statements is true? (　　)

A. The balances on income and expense accounts are brought down at the end of the accounting period to be carried forward to the next accounting period.

B. The balances on asset and liability accounts are summarized in an additional ledger account known as the statement of financial position ledger account.

C. The statement of profit or loss is a list of all the balances extracted from the business's accounts.

D. Loss for the year is a credit entry in the statement of profit or loss.

1. 11 At 31 December 20×6 Richard's total assets are £20,376 and his non-current liabilities are £10,000. If his current liabilities are £6,290 then his capital balance at 31 December 20×6 must be (　　).

A. £4,086

B. £16,666

C. £24,086

D. £36,666

1. 12 Jude's profit and loss ledger account shows total entries on the debit side of £57,390 and total entries on the credit side of £84,928. What entry would Jude make in the profit and loss ledger account to transfer the profit or loss for the period to capital? (　　)

A. Credit the profit and loss ledger account by £27,538 and credit the capital account by the same amount

B. Credit the profit and loss ledger account by £27,538 and debit the capital account by the same amount

C. Debit the profit and loss ledger account by £27,538 and debit the capital account by the same amount

D. Debit the profit and loss ledger account by £27,538 and credit the capital account by the same amount

1. 13 A business has opening payables of £75,000 and closing payables of £65,000. Cash paid to suppliers was £65,000 and discounts received were £3,000. What is the figure for purchases? (　　)

A. £58,000

B. £78,000

C.£52,000

D.£55,000

1. 14 A business has net assets of £70,000 at the beginning of the year and £80,000 at the end of the year. Drawings were £25,000 and a lottery win of £5,000 was paid into the business during the year. What was the profit for the year? (   )

　　A.£10,000 loss

　　B.£30,000 profit

　　C.£10,000 profit

　　D.£30,000 loss

1. 15 A sole trader who does not keep full accounting records wishes to calculate her sales revenue for the year. The information available is：

1 Opening inventory £17,000

2 Closing inventory £24,000

3 Purchases £91,000

4 Standard gross profit percentage on sales revenue 40%.

Which of the following is the sales figure for the year calculated from these figures? (   )

　　A.£117,600

　　B.£108,000

　　C.£210,000

　　D.£140,000

1. 16 A business has compiled the following information for the year ended 31 October 20×2：

	£
Opening inventory	386,200
Purchases	989,000
Closing inventory	422,700

The gross profit as a percentage of sales is always 40%.

Based on these figures, what is the sales revenue for the year? (   )

　　A.£1,333,500

　　B.£1,587,500

　　C.£2,381,250

　　D.The sales revenue figure cannot be calculated from this information

1. 17 From the following details of Lucy Chan (Exhibit 1. 8), draw up her trading and profit and loss account for the year ended 31 December 20×0, this being her first year of trading:

Exhibit 1. 8

Extract of Lucy Chan's Trial Balance	
Year to 31 December 20×0	
	£
Purchases	84,665
Sales	133,770
Rent	4,595
Wages and salaries	28,865
Printing and stationery	2,940
Electricity expenses	2,485
General expenses	1,295

Note: At 31 December 20×0, the inventory was valued (at cost) at £15,085.

1. 18 From the following trial balance of I. Lamb (Exhibit 1. 9), extracted after one year's trading, prepare a statement of profit or loss for the year ending 31 October 20×6.

Exhibit 1. 9

I. Lamb		
Trial balance as at 31 October 20×6		
	Dr	Cr
	£	£
Sales		100,250
Purchases	60,400	
Salaries	29,300	
Motor expenses	1,200	
Rent	950	
Insurance	150	
General expenses	85	
Premises	47,800	
Motor vehicles	8,600	
Accounts receivable	13,400	
Accounts payable		8,800
Cash at bank	8,200	
Cash in hand	300	

Exhibit 1. 9(continued)

Drawings	4,200	
Capital	____	65,535
	174,585	174,585

Inventory at 31 October 20×6 was £ 15,600. (Retain your answer—it will be used later in Exercise 2. 18).

1. 19 From the following trial balance of E. David (Exhibit 1. 10), extracted after one year's trading, prepare the statement of profit or loss for the year ended 31 December 20×1.

Exhibit 1. 10

E. David		
Trial Balance as at 31 December 20×1		
	Dr	Cr
	£	£
Sales		73,848
Purchases	58,516	
Wages	8,600	
Motor expenses	2,080	
Rates	2,680	
Insurance	444	
General expenses	420	
Buildings	20,000	
Motor vehicle	12,000	
Accounts receivables	7,800	
Accounts payables		6,418
Cash at bank	6,616	
Cash in hand	160	
Drawings	8,950	
Capital	____	48,000
	128,266	128,266

Inventory at 31 December 20×1 was valued at £ 10,192. (Retain your answer—it will be used later in Exercise 2. 19).

1. 20 * From the following trial balance of G. Foot (Exhibit 1. 11) after his first year's trading, you are required to draw up a statement of profit or loss for the year ending 30

June 20×7.

Exhibit 1. 11

G. Foot		
Trial balance as at 30 June 20×7		
	Dr	Cr
	£	£
Sales		266,000
Purchases	154,000	
Rent	3,800	
Lighting and heating expenses	700	
Salaries and wages	52,000	
Insurance	3,000	
Buildings	84,800	
Fixtures	2,000	
Accounts receivable	31,200	
Sundry expenses	300	
Accounts payable		16,000
Cash at bank	15,000	
Drawings	28,600	
Vans	16,000	
Motor running expenses	4,600	
Capital		114,000
	396,000	396,000

Inventory at 30 June 20×7 was £18,000. (Retain your answer—it will be used later in Exercise 2. 20).

1. 21 * From the following trial balance of F. Dover (Exhibit 1. 12) drawn-up on conclusion of his first year in business, draw up a statement of profit or loss for the year ending 31 May 20×7.

Exhibit 1. 12

F. Dover		
Trial balance as at 31 May 20×7		
	Dr	Cr
	£	£

Exhibit 1. 12(continued)

General expenses	610	
Business rates	4,800	
Motor expenses	1,820	
Salaries	79,120	
Insurance	2,480	
Purchases	242,080	
Sales		471,624
Car	8,600	
Accounts payable		22,400
Accounts receivable	42,160	
Premises	106,000	
Cash at bank	5,430	
Cash in hand	650	
Capital		46,526
Drawings	46,800	
	540,550	540,550

Inventory at 31 May 20×7 was £28,972. (Retain your answer—it will be used later in Exercise 2.21).

1. 22 * Extract a statement of profit or loss for the year ending 30 June 20×8 for G. Graham. The trial balance as at 30 June 20 × 8 after his first year of trading was shown in Exhibit 1. 13:

Exhibit 1. 13

G. Graham		
Trial balance as at 31 May 20×8		
	Dr	Cr
	£	£
Equipment rental	940	
Insurance	1,804	
Lighting and heating expenses	1,990	
Motor expenses	2,350	
Salaries and wages	48,580	
Sales		382,420
Purchases	245,950	
Sundry expenses	624	
Lorry	19,400	

Exhibit 1. 13(continued)

Accounts payable		23,408
Accounts receivable	44,516	
Fixtures	4,600	
Shop	174,000	
Cash at bank	11,346	
Drawings	44,000	
Capital		194,272
	600,100	600,100

Inventory at 30 June 20×8 was £29,304. (Retain your answer—it will be used later in Exercise 2. 22).

1. 23 * On 1 June 20×5, Jock Heiss commenced trading as an ice cream salesman, using a van. He borrowed £2,000 from his bank, and the interest cost of the loan was £25 per month.

(1) He rented the van for £1,000 for three months. Running expenses for the van averaged £300 per month.

(2) He hired an assistant for £100 per month.

(3) His main business was to sell ice cream to customers in the street, but he also did special catering for business customers, supplying ice creams for office parties. Sales to these customers were usually on credit.

(4) For the three months to 31 August 20×5, his total sales were as follows.

· Cash sales £8,900

· Credit sales £1,100

(5) He purchased his ice cream from a local manufacturer, Floors Co. The purchase cost in the three months to 31 August 20×5 was £6,200, and at 31 August he had sold every item. He still owed £700 to Floors Co for unpaid purchases on credit.

(6) He paid telephone fee £250 for three months in cash.

(7) He used his own home for his office work. Postage expenses for the three months to 31 August were £150, which he paid in cash.

(8) During the period he paid himself £300 per month.

Requirement

Prepare a statement of profit or loss for the year ended 31 August 20×5.

Reference

1. Alan Sangster, Frank Wood's Business Accounting Volume 1(2019), Pearson.

2. Andrew Thomas and Anne Marie Ward. Introduction to Financial Accounting (2019), McGraw-Hill Education.

3. ACCA FA Financial Accounting/FIA FFA Interactive Text 2020, BPP Learning Media.

4. ACCA FA Financial Accounting/FIA FFA Practice & Revision Kit 2020, BPP Learning Media.

5. Accounting (Study Manual 2020), The Institute of Chartered Accountants in England and Wales.

6. Accounting (Question Bank 2020), The Institute of Chartered Accountants in England and Wales.

Chapter 2

Statement of Financial Position

┌───┐
│ ■Learning Objectives
│   · Define a statement of financial position.
│   · Understand that a statement of financial position is prepared from the remaining
│ balances in the trial balance after preparation of the trading and profit and loss account
│ (the statement of profit or loss).
│   · Explain the meaning of the terms: non-current assets, current assets, current lia-
│ bilities, and non-current liabilities.
│   · Know which items appear in the owner's capital account.
│   · Prepare a statement of financial position using two structures of presentation.
└───┘

2.1   Contents of the Statement of Financial Position

The statement of financial position provides information about the resources and debts of the reporting entity. It enables users of financial statements to evaluate the entity's financial position, in particular whether the business is likely to be unable to pay its debts. The statement of financial position is like a photograph of the financial state of affairs of a business at a specific time.

A statement of financial position comprises those accounts with balances that were not included in the statement of profit or loss. All these accounts that continue to have balances must be assets, capital or liabilities. Because it is these balances that are entered in the statement of financial position, it used to be called the 'balance sheet'. You should be aware of this: you may meet this term in an examination question or in a textbook—many people still use the old term.

Statements of financial position contain five groups of items, as follows.

1. Assets

We are going to show the assets under two headings, non-current assets and current assets.

· Non-current assets

These are items not specifically bought for resale but to be used in the production or distribution of those goods normally sold by the business. They are utilised to generate economic inflows to the entity. Non-current assets are durable goods that usually last for several years, and are normally kept by a business for more than one accounting year.

Examples of non-current assets are buildings, machinery, motor vehicles, fixtures and fittings. These are tangible assets. The different types are recorded in separate ledger accounts with the balances on each account being disclosed in the statement of financial position.

Non-current assets are listed first in the statement of financial position starting with those the business will keep the longest, down to those which will not be kept so long, For instance:

Non-current assets
1. Land and buildings
2. Fixtures and fittings
3. Machinery
4. Motor vehicles

· Current assets

These are items that are normally kept by a business for less than one accounting year. Indeed, the composition of each type of current asset is usually continually changing. Examples include inventories, accounts receivable, cash in the bank, and cash in hand.

These are listed in increasing order of liquidity—that is, starting with the asset furthest away from being turned into cash, and finishing with cash itself. For instance:

Current assets
1. Inventory
2. Accounts receivable
3. Cash at bank
4. Cash in hand

2. Liabilities

There are two categories of liabilities, current liabilities and non-current liabilities.

· Current liabilities

These are debts owed by a business that are payable within one year (often considerably less) from the date of the statement of financial position.

Examples include bank overdrafts, accounts payable resulting from the purchase on credit of goods for resale.

· **Non-current liabilities**

These are debts owed by a business that are not due until after one year (often much longer) from the date of the statement of financial position.

Examples include bank loans, loans from other businesses and mortgages.

3. Capital

This refers to the amount of money invested in the business by the owner(s). This can take the form of cash introduced or profits not withdrawn.

This is the proprietor's or partners' account with the business. It will start with the balance brought forward from the previous accounting period, to which is added any personal cash introduced into the business and the net profit made by the business in this accounting period. Deducted from the capital account will be amounts drawn from the business and any loss made by the business. The final balance on the capital account should equal the net assets or net liabilities figure. Exhibit 2. 1 gives the standard format.

Exhibit 2. 1

Capital Account		
	£	£
Balance b/d		X
Add Cash introduced	X	
Net profit for the period	<u>X</u>	X
Less Drawings	(X)	
Net loss for the period	<u>(X)</u>	<u>(X)</u>
		<u>X</u>

It is important to note that the statement of financial position shows the balances of the business at one point in time: the statement of financial position date, for example, 'as at 31 December 20×1'. It is like taking a snapshot of the business at one moment in time. On the other hand, the statement of profit or loss account shows the profit/loss of that business for a period of time (normally a year), i.e. 'for the year ended 31 December 20×1'.

2. 2　Format of the Statement of Financial Position

The format of the statement of financial position follows the basic accounting equation. Both a net asset and a total asset presentation are allowed.

Net asset presentation states that 'Assets − Liabilities = Capital', where net assets equal total capital. This format is shown in Exhibit 2. 2.

Exhibit 2. 2

ABC
Statement of financial position as at ...
Non-current assets
+
Current assets
−
(Current liabilities
+
Non-current liabilities)
=
Net assets
‖
Total capital

Total asset presentation states that 'Assets = Capital + Liabilities', where total assets e-qual capital plus total liabilities. This format is shown in Exhibit 2. 3. Note that the items shown in bold are subtotals or totals that should be shown on the statement of financial position.

Exhibit 2. 3

ABC
Statement of financial position as at ...
Non-current assets
+
Current assets
=
Total assets
Capital
+
Non-current liabilities
+
Current liabilities
=
Total capital and liabilities

2.3　No Double Entry in Statements of Financial Position

It may seem strange to you to learn that statements of financial position are not part of the double entry system. When accounts such as the cash account, rent account, sales account, trading and profit and loss account and so on are drawn up, entries are made on the debit and credit side of these accounts since they are part of the double entry system.

When preparing a statement of financial position, no entries are made in any of the various accounts. We do not actually transfer the 'Fixtures and fittings balance' or the 'Accounts receivable balance', or any of the other accounts, to the statements of financial position. All that is necessary is to list the balances for assets, capital and liabilities to form a statement of financial position. This means that none of these accounts have been closed off. Nothing is entered in the accounts.

When the next accounting period starts, these accounts contain balances which are brought forward as 'opening balances'. During the next accounting period, business transactions are then entered into these accounts as part of the normal double entry system.

If you see the word 'account', you will know that what you are looking at is part of the double entry system and will include debit and credit entries. If the word 'account' is not used, it is not part of double entry. For instance, the following items are not 'accounts', and are therefore not part of the double entry:

· Trial balance: this is a list of the debit and credit balances in the accounts.

· Statement of profit or loss: this is a list of revenues and expenditures arranged so as to produce figures for gross profit and net profit for a specific period of time.

· Statement of financial position: this is a list of balances arranged according to whether they are assets, capital or liabilities and so depict the financial situation on a specific date.

2.4　Drawing up a Statement of Financial Position

In practice and in examinations, it is usual to prepare final financial statements from the information given in the trial balance. Let's look again at the post—statement of profit or loss trial balance of G. John in Exhibit 2.4, and prepare the statement of financial position.

Exhibit 2.4

G. John		
Trial balance as at 31 December 20×1		
	Dr	Cr
	£	£
Fixtures and fittings	5,000	

Exhibit 2. 4(continued)

Accounts receivable	6,800	
Accounts payable		9,100
Inventory	3,000	
Bank	15,100	
Cash	200	
Capital	___	21,000
	30,100	30,100

The statement of financial position for G. John as at 31 December 20×1, using **net asset presentation** is shown in Exhibit 2. 5.

Exhibit 2. 5

G. John		
Statement of financial position as at 31 December 20×1		
	£	£
Non-current assets		
Fixtures and fittings		5,000
Current assets		
Inventory	3,000	
Accounts receivable	6,800	
Bank	15,100	
Cash	200	
		25,100
Total assets		30,100
Current liabilities		
Accounts payable		(9,100)
Net assets		21,000
Capital		
Cash introduced		20,000
Add Net profit for the year		8,000
		28,000
Less Drawings		(7,000)
		21,000

Note:

(a) There are four categories of entries shown in this statement of financial position. In practice, the fifth, non-current liabilities, often appears. It is positioned after the current liabilities; and its total is added to the total of current liabilities to get the figure for total liabilities.

(b) The figure for each item within each category should be shown and a total for the category produced is shown below them. An example of this is the £25,100, total of current assets.

(c) The total for non-current assets is added to the total for current assets and the total is labelled 'total assets'.

(d) The total for current liabilities is added to the total for non-current liabilities and the total is labelled 'total liabilities'.

(e) The total liabilities amount is subtracted from the total assets to get an amount labelled 'net assets'. This amount will be the same as the total capital (which, in company financial statements, is called 'total equity').

(f) You do not write the word 'account' after each item.

(g) The owners will be most interested in their capital and the reasons why it has changed during the period. To show only the final balance of £21,000 means that the owners will not know how it was calculated. So we show the full details of the capital account.

(h) The difference between current assets and total liabilities is known as 'net current assets' or 'working capital' and is the amount of resources the business has in a form that is readily convertible into cash. This figure is not shown in the statement of financial position but is easy to produce from a completed statement of financial position.

The statement of financial position for G. John as at 31 December 20×1, using **total asset presentation** is shown as Exhibit 2.6. It also shows where this would be if G. John had any non-current liabilities.

Exhibit 2.6

G. John		
Statement of financial position as at 31 December 20×1		
	£	£
Non-current assets		
Fixtures and fittings		5,000
Current assets		
Inventory	3,000	
Accounts receivable	6,800	
Bank	15,100	
Cash	200	

Exhibit 2. 6(continued)

		25,100
Total assets		30,100
Capital and liabilities		
Capital		
Cash introduced		20,000
Add Net profit for the year		8,000
		28,000
Less Drawings		(7,000)
		21,000
Current liabilities		
Accounts payable	9,100	
		9,100
Total capital and liabilities		30,100

Summary

· All balances remaining on a trial balance after the statement of profit or loss for a period has been drawn up are displayed in a statement of financial position dated 'as at' the last day of the period.

· The meanings of the terms non-current asset, current asset, current liability, and non-current liability.

· List non-current assets in descending order starting with those that will remain in use in the business for the longest time.

· List current assets from top to bottom in increasing order of liquidity, with cash as the final item.

· There are two categories of liabilities, current liabilities and non-current liabilities.

· Current assets less current liabilities are known as 'net current assets' or 'working capital'.

· Capital refers to the amount of money invested in the business by the owner(s). This can take the form of cash introduced or profits not withdrawn.

· The statement of financial position follows the basic accounting equation. It can be presented in different format.

· The statement of financial position is not part of double entry.

Exercise

2. 1 Which of the following statements is incorrect? (   )

    A.Assets − Capital = Liabilities

    B.Liabilities + Capital = Assets

    C.Liabilities + Assets = Capital

    D.Assets − Liabilities = Capital

2. 2 Which of the following is incorrect? (   )

	Assets £	Liabilities £	Capital £
A.	7,850	1,250	6,600
B.	8,200	2,800	5,400
C.	9,550	1,150	8,200
D.	6,540	1,120	5,420

2. 3 Which of the following statements is correct? (   )

		Effect upon	
		Assets	Liabilities
A.	We paid a creditor by cheque	− Bank	− Accounts payable
B.	A debtor paid us £90 in cash	+ Cash	+ Accounts receivable
C.	J. Hall lends us £500 by cheque	+ Bank	− Loan from Hall
D.	Bought goods on credit	+ Inventory	+ Capital

2. 4 Given the following, what is the amount of Capital? Assets: Premises £20,000; Inventory £8,500; Cash £100. Liabilities: Accounts payable £3,000; Loan from A. Adams £4,000(   )

    A.£21,100

    B.£21,600

    C.£32,400

    D.£21,400

2. 5 Which of the following is correct? (   )

    A.Profit does not alter capital

    B.Profit reduces capital

    C.Capital can only come from profit

    D.Profit increases capital

2. 6 Which of the following are correct? (   )

	Account to be debited	Account to be credited
① Received commission by cheque	Bank	Commission received
② Paid rates by cash	Rates	Cash
③ Paid motor expenses by cheque	Motor expenses	Bank
④ Received refund of insurance by cheque	Insurance	Bank

    A.① and ② only

    B.①, ② and ③ only

    C.②, ③ and ④ only

    D.①, ② and ④ only

2. 7 Of the following, which are incorrect? (   )

	Account to be debited	Account to be credited
① Sold van for cash	Cash	Sales
② Bought stationery by cheque	Stationery	Bank
③ Took cash out of business for private use	Cash	Drawings
④ Paid general expenses by cheque	General expenses	Bank

    A.② and ④ only

    B.① and ② only

    C.① and ③ only

    D.② and ③ only

2. 8 Which of the following would be classified as a non-current asset? (   )

    A.Cash

    B.Prepayments

    C.Land

    D.Receivables

2. 9 Which two of the following types of account would normally appear on the debit side of the initial trial balance? (   )

    A.Asset

    B.Liability

    C.Income

    D.Expense

    E.Capital

2. 10 Alpha has the following opening balances on its ledger accounts.

	£
Fixtures	5,000
Trade accounts receivable	2,000
Bank account	1,000
Loan	3,000

What is the total assets figure? (   )

A.£6,000

B.£5,000

C.£8,000

D.£3,000

2. 11 Following question 2. 10 above, what is the opening figure for capital? (   )

A.£6,000

B.£5,000

C.£8,000

D.£3,000

2. 12 A sole trader had trade receivables of £2,700 at 1 May and during May made cash sales of £7,200, credit sales of £16,500 and received £15,300 from his credit customers. The balance on his trade receivables account at the end of May was(   ).

A.£1,500

B.£3,900

C.£8,700

D.£11,100

2. 13 In double-entry bookkeeping, which of the following statements is true? (   )

A.Credit entries decrease liabilities and increase income

B.Debit entries decrease income and increase assets

C.Credit entries decrease expenses and increase assets

D.Debit entries decrease expenses and increase assets

2. 14 A debit balance of £3,000 brought down on A Ltd's account in B Ltd's books means that B Ltd owes A Ltd £3,000. (   )

A.True

B.False

2. 15 The owner's drawings are shown on the initial trial balance. (   )

    A.True

    B.False

2. 16 The closing inventory balance is included in the final trial balance. (   )

    A.True

    B.False

2. 17 * A business has been trading for one year. Please draw a statement of profit or loss and a statement of financial position as at the year ended 31 December 20×1 for D. Brown from the following trial balance (Exhibit 2. 7). Inventory at 31 December 20×1 was £0.

Exhibit 2. 7

D. Brown		
Trial Balance as at 31 Dec 20×1		
	Dr	Cr
	£	£
Sales		5,800
Purchases	4,300	
Non-current assets	1,500	
Trade receivables	2,600	
Trade payables		700
Bank overdraft		800
Other expenses	900	
Capital		2,000
	9,300	9,300

2. 18 Return to exercise 1. 18 and prepare a statement of financial position as at 31 October 20×6 for I. Lamb.

2. 19 Return to exercise 1. 19 and prepare a statement of financial position as at 31 December 20×1 for E.David.

2. 20 * Return to exercise 1. 20 and prepare a statement of financial position as at 30 June 20×7 for G.Foot.

2. 21 * Return to exercise 1. 21 and prepare a statement of financial position as at 31 May

20×7 for F. Dover.

2. 22* Return to exercise 1. 22 and prepare a statement of financial position as at 30 June 20×8 for G. Graham.

2. 23 A business has been trading for one year. Please prepare a statement of profit or loss for the year and a statement of financial position as at the year ended 31 March 20×1 for T.Leung from the following trial balance (Exhibit 2. 8).

Exhibit 2. 8

T.Leung		
Trial Balance as at 31 March 20×1		
	Dr	Cr
	£	£
Rent and rates	6,708	
Insurance	1,312	
Electricity expenses	2,219	
Motor expenses	2,429	
Salaries and wages	26,855	
Sales		153,080
Purchases	133,171	
General expenses	3,466	
Motor van	15,050	
Accounts payables		13,975
Accounts receivables	29,283	
Equipment	17,028	
Buildings	120,400	
Cash at bank	4,876	
Drawings	16,994	
Capital		212,736
	379,791	379,791

Note: Inventory at 31 March 20×1 was £42,828.

Reference

1. Alan Sangster, Frank Wood's Business Accounting Volume 1(2019), Pearson.

2. Andrew Thomas and Anne Marie Ward. Introduction to Financial Accounting (2019),

McGraw-Hill Education.

3. ACCA FA Financial Accounting/FIA FFA Interactive Text 2020, BPP Learning Media.

4. ACCA FA Financial Accounting/FIA FFA Practice & Revision Kit 2020, BPP Learning Media.

5. Accounting (Study Manual 2020), The Institute of Chartered Accountants in England and Wales.

6. Accounting (Question Bank 2020), The Institute of Chartered Accountants in England and Wales.

Chapter 3

Statements of Profit or Loss and Statements of Financial Position: Further Considerations

```
┌─────■Learning Objectives ───────────────────────────────────┐
      · Explain the terms returns inwards, returns outwards, carriage inwards and carriage
  outwards.
      · Record returns inwards and returns outwards in the statement of profit or loss.
      · Explain the difference between the treatment of carriage inwards and carriage out-
  wards in the statement of profit or loss.
      · Explain why carriage inwards is treated as part of the cost of purchasing goods.
      · Explain why carriage outwards is not treated as part of the cost of purchasing goods.
      · Prepare an inventory account showing the entries for opening and closing inventory.
      · Prepare a statement of profit or loss and a statement of financial position containing
  the appropriate adjustments for returns, carriage and other items that affect the calculation
  of the cost of goods sold.
      · Explain why the costs of putting goods into a saleable condition should be charged
  to the trading account.
└──────────────────────────────────────────────────────────────┘
```

3.1 Returns Inwards and Returns Outwards

In this chapter, the idea of different accounts for different movements of goods was intro-duced. The sales account and the returns inwards account deal with goods sold and goods re-turned by customers. The purchases account and the returns outwards account deal with goods purchased and goods returned to the supplier respectively. In our first look at the preparation of a trading account in Chapter 1, returns inwards and returns outwards were omitted. This was done deliberately, so that your first sight of statements of profit or loss would be as straightforward as possible.

Returns inwards, alternatively called sales return. Referred to goods which had been previously sold to customers are now returned to the business. This could be for various reasons such as:

- You sent goods of the wrong size, the wrong color or the wrong model.
- The goods may have been damaged in transit.
- The goods are of poor quality.

Returns outwards, alternatively called purchases return. Referred to goods which had been previously bought are returned by the business to suppliers.

Just as you may have done yourself, a large number of businesses return goods to their suppliers(returns outwards) and will have goods returned to them by their customers (returns inwards). When the gross profit is calculated, these returns will have to be included in the calculations. Let's look at the first two lines of the trial balance in Exhibit 3.1 as you saw in Section 1.3 from Chapter 1:

Exhibit 3.1

G. John(extract)		
Trial balance as at 31 December 20×1		
	Dr	Cr
	£	£
Sales		38,500
Purchases	29,000	

Now, suppose that in the trial balance of G. John, rather than simply containing a sales account balance of £38,500 and a purchases account balance of £29,000 the balances included those for returns inwards and outwards, the balances in Exhibit 3.2 showing goods movement had been:

Exhibit 3.2

G. John		
Trial balance as at 31 December 20×1		
	Dr	Cr
	£	£
Sales		40,000
Purchases	31,200	

Exhibit 3. 2(continued)

Returns inwards	1,500	
Returns outwards		2,200

If we compare the two trial balances above, the gross profit amount will be exactly the same. Sales in Exhibit 3. 1 were £38,500, while in Exhibit 3. 2 the sales returns is deducted from sales as follows:

	£
Sales	40,000
Less Sales returns	1,500
Net sales	38,500

Purchases in Exhibit 3. 1 were shown as £29,000 but in Exhibit 3. 2 purchase returns will need to be deducted from purchases to ascertain the amount of goods retained by the business as shown below:

	£
Purchases	31,200
Less Purchases returns	2,200
Net Purchases	29,000

Comparing these two calculations reveals that they amount to the same thing so far as gross profit is concerned. Sales were £38,500 in the original example because returns inwards had already been deducted in arriving at the amount. In the amended version, returns inwards should be shown separately in the trial balance and then deducted on the face of the statement of profit or loss to get the correct figure for goods sold to customers and kept by them. In the new version, returns outwards should be deducted to get the correct figure of purchases kept by G. John. Both the returns accounts are included in the calculation of gross profit, which now becomes:

(Sales less Returns Inwards) – (Cost of Goods Sold less Returns Outwards) = Gross Profit

The gross profit is therefore unaffected and is the same as in Chapter 1: £12,500. The trading account section of the statement of profit or loss will appear as shown in Exhibit 3. 3:

Exhibit 3. 3

G. John		
Trading account section of the statement of profit or loss for the year ending 31 December 20×1		
	£	£
Sales		40,000
Less Returns inwards		(1,500)
		38,500
Less Cost of goods sold		
Purchases	31,200	
Less Returns outwards	(2,200)	
	29,000	
Less Closing Inventory	(3,000)	
		(26,000)
Gross profit		12,500

You may have difficulty deciding whether sales returns should be deducted from sales or purchases figures and vice versa. The same applies to the purchase returns figure. The following illustration in Exhibit 3. 4 shows that the returns are always deducted from the figure on the opposite side so forming an 'X' in the trial balance:

Exhibit 3. 4

G. John		
Trial balance as at 31 December 20×1		
	Dr	Cr
	£	£
Sales		40,000
Purchases	31,200	
Returns inwards	1,500	
Returns outwards		2,200

3. 2 Carriage Inwards and Carriage Outwards

When a business buys goods from a supplier the cost of delivering or transporting the goods also has to be paid. In accountancy terms, this cost of transport is often referred to as ' **carriage**'.

Carriage charges for transporting goods purchased into a business is known as **carriage inwards**. When goods are purchased one supplier may include carriage within the purchase cost whilst another may charge separately for carriage. For example, suppose your business was buying exactly the same goods from two suppliers. One supplier might sell them for £100 and not charge anything for carriage. Another supplier might sell the goods for £95, but you would have to pay £5 to a courier for carriage inwards, i.e. a total cost of £100. In both cases, the same goods cost you the same total amount. It would not be appropriate to leave out the cost of carriage inwards from the 'cheaper' supplier in the calculation of gross profit, as the real cost to you having the goods available for resale is £100. When this happens the carriage inwards charge is always added to the cost of purchases in the trading account.

Carriage outwards is the cost of delivering the goods to the business's customers. It is an expense and not part of the selling price of the goods. Carriage outwards is always charged as an expense in the profit and loss account. It is never included in the calculation of gross profit.

Suppose that in the illustration shown in this chapter, the goods had been bought for the same total figure of £31,200 but, in fact, £29,200 was the figure for purchases and £2,000 for carriage inwards. The trial balance extract would appear as below in Exhibit 3.5.

Exhibit 3.5

G. John		
Trial balance as at 31 December 20×1		
	Dr	Cr
	£	£
Sales		40,000
Purchases	29,200	
Returns inwards	1,500	
Returns outwards		2,200
Carriage inwards	2,000	

Considering this carriage inwards, the trading account section of the statement of profit or loss would then be as shown in Exhibit 3.6.

Exhibit 3.6

G. John		
Trading account section of the statement of profit or loss for the year ending 31 December 20×1		
	£	£
Sales		40,000
Less Returns inwards		(1,500)

Exhibit 3. 6(continued)

		38,500
Less Cost of goods sold		
Purchases	29,200	
Less Returns outwards	(2,200)	
	27,000	
Carriage inwards	2,000	
	29,000	
Less Closing Inventory	(3,000)	
		(26,000)
Gross profit		12,500

3. 3　The Second Year of a Business

Continuing with the example of G. John, at the end of his second year of trading, on 31 December 20×2, he draws up another trial balance (Exhibit 3. 7).

Exhibit 3. 7

G. John		
Trial balance as at 31 December 20×2		
	Dr	Cr
	£	£
Sales		67,000
Purchases	42,600	
Lighting and heating expenses	1,900	
Rent	2,400	
Wages: shop assistant	5,200	
General expenses	700	
Carriage outwards	1,100	
Buildings	20,000	
Fixtures and fittings	7,500	
Accounts receivable	12,000	
Accounts payable		9,000
Bank	1,200	

Exhibit 3. 7(continued)

Cash	400	
Drawings	9,000	
Capital		31,000
Inventory (at 31 December 20×1)	3,000	
	107,000	107,000

1. Adjustments Needed for Inventory

So far, we have been looking at new businesses only. When a business starts, it has no inventory brought forward. G. John started in business in 20×1. Therefore, when we were preparing John's statement of profit or loss for 20×1, there was only closing inventory to worry about. When we prepare the statement of profit or loss for the second year we can see the difference. If you look back to the statement of profit or loss in previous sections, you can see that there was closing inventory of £3,000. This is, therefore, the opening inventory figure for 20×2. We will need to incorporate it in the trading account. It is also the figure for inventory that you can see in the trial balance as at 31 December 20×2.

Remember:The closing inventory for one period is always brought forward as the opening inventory for the next period.

G.John checked his inventory at 31 December 20×2 and valued it at that date at £5,500. We can summarise the opening and closing inventory account positions for John over the two years as shown in Exhibit 3. 8.

Exhibit 3. 8

Trading account for the period	Year ending 31 December 20×1	Year ending 31 December 20×2
Opening inventory 1. 1. 20×1	None	
Closing inventory 31. 12. 20×1	£3,000	
Opening inventory 1. 1. 20×2		£3,000
Closing inventory 31. 12. 20×2		£5,500

2. Ledger Accounting for Inventory

To enable you to understand the double entry aspect of inventory, both the inventory account and the trading account for G. John for the year ended 31 December 20×2 are shown below:

Inventory Account

20X1	£	20X1	£
Dec 31 Trading a/c	3,000	Dec 31 Balance c/d	3,000
20X2		20X2	
Jan 1 Balance b/d	3,000	Dec 31 Trading a/c (opening inv.)	3,000
Dec 31 Trading a/c (closing inv.)	5,500	Dec 31 Balance c/d	5,500
	8,500		8,500

Trading and Profit and Loss Account for the year ended 31 December 20X2

	£		£
Opening Inventory	3,000	Sales	67,000
Purchases	42,600	Closing Inventory	5,500
Gross profit c/d	26,900		
	72,500		72,500

You can see that in 20×2 there is both a debit and a credit double entry made at the end of the period to the trading account. First, the inventory account is credited with the opening inventory amount of £3,000 and the trading account is debited with the same amount. The entries above show how this has been recorded using double entry:

		£	£
DEBIT	Trading account	3,000	
CREDIT	Inventory account		3,000

Then, the inventory at 31 December 20×2 is £5,500 and had not been entered into the accounts previously. The entries above show how this has been recorded using double entry:

		£	£
DEBIT	Inventory account	5,500	
CREDIT	Trading account		5,500

Thus, while the first year of trading only includes one inventory figure in the trading account, for the second year of trading both opening and closing inventory figures will be in the calculations. Let's now calculate the cost of goods sold for 20×2:

	£
Inventory of goods at start of year	3,000
Add Purchases	42,600
Total goods available for sale	45,600
Less What remains at the end of the year (i.e. closing inventory)	(5,500)
Therefore the cost of goods that have been sold is	40,100

Cost of Goods Sold=	Opening Inventory+Purchases	–	Closing–Inventory

| | Inventory available for sale | | Unsold inventory |

The gross profit can now be found by taking into consideration the effect the closing inventory has on the gross profit. Remember that sales less cost of goods sold equals gross profit, therefore:

	£
Sales	67,000
Less Cost of goods sold (see above)	40,100
Gross profit	26,900

Now the statement of profit or loss and the statement of financial position can be drawn up, as shown below in Exhibit 3. 9 and Exhibit 3. 10:

· 44 ·

Exhibit 3. 9

G. John		
Statement of profit or loss for the year ending 31 December 20×2		
	£	£
Sales		67,000
Less Cost of goods sold		
Opening inventory	3,000	
Add Purchases	42,600	
	45,600	
Less Closing inventory	(5,500)	
		(40,100)
Gross profit		26,900
Less Expenses		
Wages	5,200	
Lighting and heating expenses	1,900	
Rent	2,400	
General expenses	700	
Carriage outwards	1,100	
		(11,300)
Net profit		15,600

Exhibit 3. 10

G. John		
Statement of financial position as at 31 December 20×2		
	£	£
Non-current assets		
Buildings		20,000
Fixtures and fittings		7,500
		27,500
Current assets		
Inventory	5,500	
Accounts receivable	12,000	
Bank	1,200	
Cash	400	
		19,100
Total assets		46,600
Current liabilities		
Accounts payable		(9,000)
Net assets		37,600
Capital		
Balance at 1 January 20×2		31,000
Add Net profit for the year		15,600
		46,600
Less Drawings		(9,000)
Total capital		37,600

Financial statements is the term given to all the summary statements that accountants produce at the end of reporting periods. They are often called '**final accounts**', but this term is quite misleading (as none of the financial statements are 'accounts' in the accounting sense). Nevertheless, some people do still refer to them as the 'final accounts' or simply as **the accounts** of a business. You therefore, will, need to be aware of these terms, just in case you read something that uses these terms, or your teacher or lecturer, or an examiner, uses them at some time.

3. Other Expenses in the Trading Account

You already know that carriage inwards is added to the cost of purchases in the trading account. You also need to add to the cost of goods in the trading account any costs incurred in converting purchases into goods for resale. In the case of a trader, it is very unusual for any additional costs to be incurred getting the goods ready for sale.

For goods imported from abroad it is usual to find that the costs of import duty and insurance are treated as part of the cost of the goods, along with any costs incurred in repackaging the goods. Any such additional costs incurred in getting goods ready for sale are debited to the trading account.

Some of you often find it difficult to remember how to treat returns and carriage when preparing the statement of profit or loss. You need to be sure to learn and remember that all returns, inwards and outwards, and carriage inwards appear in the calculation of gross profit. All the costs of putting goods into a saleable condition should be charged to the trading account. Carriage outwards appears as an expense in the profit and loss account section of the statement of profit or loss.

Some students lose a lot of marks on the topics covered in this chapter because they assume that the topics are easy and unlikely to be things that they will forget. Unfortunately, they are fairly easy to understand, and that is why they are easily forgotten and confused. You would be wise to make sure that you have understood and learnt everything presented to you in this chapter before you go any further in the book.

Summary

· Returns inwards should be deducted from sales in the trading account.

· Returns outwards should be deducted from purchases in the trading account.

· Carriage inwards is shown as an expense item in the trading account.

· Carriage outwards is shown as an expense in the profit and loss account.

· Inventory account carries forward the balance from one period to the next.

· In the second and later years of a business, both opening and closing inventory are brought into the trading account.

· It is normal practice to show cost of goods sold as a separate figure in the trading account.

· A statement of profit or loss that includes the adjustments for carriage inwards and both opening and closing inventory in the trading section and carriage outwards as an expense in the profit and loss section.

· That expense items concerned with getting goods into a saleable condition are charged in the trading account.

· That where there is import duty or insurance charged on goods purchased, these costs are treated as part of the cost of goods sold.

Exercise

3. 1 Which of the following would be a credit balance in the trial balance? (   )

    A. Bank overdraft

    B. Drawings

    C. Purchases

    D. Carriage outwards

3. 2 A business has opening inventory of £7,200 and closing inventory of £8,100. Purchases for the year were £76,500, carriage inwards was £50 and carriage outwards was £180. The figure for cost of sales is(   ).

    A. £75,550

    B. £75,650

    C. £75,830

    D. £77,450

3. 3 Muse began trading on 1 January 20×8 and had zero inventories at that date. During 20×8 it made purchases of £455,000, incurred carriage inwards of £24,000, and carriage outwards of £29,000. Closing inventories at 31 December 20×8 were £52,000.

In the statement of profit or loss for the year ended 31 December 20×8, the cost of sales figure is(   ).

    A. £456,000

    B. £427,000

    C. £432,000

    D. £531,000

3. 4 Indicate whether the following statements (3. 4 & 3. 5) are true or false.(   )

A van for sale by a dealer is shown as a non-current asset in its statement of financial position.

    A. True

    B. False

3. 5 Import duties may be included in the cost of inventory.(   )

    A. True

    B. False

3. 6 For the year ended 31 October 20×3 a company did a physical count of inventory on 4 November 20×3, leading to an inventory cost at this date of £483,700.

Between 1 November 20×3 and 4 November 20×3 the following transactions took place:

1 Goods costing £38,400 were received from suppliers.

2 Goods that had cost £14,800 were sold for £20,000.

3 A customer returned, in good condition, some goods which had been sold to him in October for £600 and which had cost £400.

4 The company returned goods that had cost £1,800 in October to the supplier, and received a credit note for them.

What figure should be shown in the company's financial statements at 31 October 20×3 for closing inventory, based on this information? (   )

    A.£458,700

    B.£505,900

    C.£508,700

    D.£461,500

3. 7 The cost of inventory in the financial statements of Quebec Ltd for the year ended 31 December 20×4 of £836,200 was based on an inventory count on 4 January 20×5. Between 31 December 20×4 and 4 January 20×5, the following transactions took place:

	£
Purchases of goods	8,600
Sales of goods (cost is 70% on sales)	14,000
Goods returned by Quebec Ltd to a supplier	700

What adjusted figure should be included in the financial statements for inventories at 31 December 20×4? (   )

    A.£838,100

    B.£842,300

    C.£818,500

    D.£834,300

3. 8 A statement of financial position is best described as(   ).

    A.A snapshot of the entity's financial position at a particular point in time

    B.A record of an entity's financial performance over a period of time

    C.A list of all the income and expenses of the entity at a particular point in time

    D.A list of all the assets and liabilities of the entity over a period of time

3. 9 Which of the following calculations could produce an acceptable figure for a trader's net profit for a period if no accounting records had been kept? (　　)

　　A.Closing net assets plus drawings minus capital introduced minus opening net assets

　　B.Closing net assets minus drawings plus capital introduced minus opening net assets

　　C.Closing net assets minus drawings minus capital introduced minus opening net assets

　　D.Closing net assets plus drawings plus capital introduced minus opening net assets

3. 10 A sole trader fixes his prices to achieve a gross profit percentage on sales revenue of 40%. All his sales are for cash. He suspects that one of his sales assistants is stealing cash from sales revenue. His trading account for the month of June 20×3 is as follows:

	£
Recorded sales revenue	181,600
Cost of sales	114,000
Gross profit	67,600

Assuming that the cost of sales figure is correct, how much cash could the sales assistant have taken? (　　)

　　A.£5,040

　　B.£8,400

　　C.£22,000

　　D.It is not possible to calculate a figure from this information

3. 11 Aluki fixes prices to make a standard gross profit percentage on sales of 20%. The following information for the year ended 31 January 20×3 is available to compute her sales total for the year.

	£
Inventory: 1 February 20×2	243,000
31 January 20×3	261,700
Purchases	595,400
Purchases returns	41,200

What is the sales figure for the year ended 31 January 20×3? (　　)

　　A.£669,375

　　B.£702,600

　　C.£772,375

　　D.£741,480

3. 12 Wanda keeps no accounting records. The following information is available about her position and transactions for the year ended 31 December 20×4:

	£
Net assets at 1 January 20×4	210,000
Drawings during 20×4	48,000
Capital introduced during 20×4	100,000
Net assets at 31 December 20×4	400,000

Based on this information, what was Wanda's profit for 20×4? (　　)

A.£42,000

B.£242,000

C.£138,000

D.£338,000

3. 13 The following information is available for a sole trader who keeps no accounting records:

	£
Net business assets at 1 July 20×4	186,000
Net business assets at 30 June 20×5	274,000

During the year ended 30 June 20×5	
Cash drawings by proprietor	68,000
Additional capital introduced by proprietor	50,000
Business cash used to buy a car for the proprietor's wife, who takes no part in the business	20,000

Using this information, what is the trader's profit for the year ended 30 June 20×5? (　　)

A.£126,000

B.£50,000

C.£86,000

D.£90,000

3. 14 The following information is available about the transactions of Razil, a sole trader who does not keep proper accounting records:

	£
Opening inventory	77,000
Closing inventory	84,000
Purchases	763,000
Gross profit as a percentage of sales 30%	

Based on this information, what is Razil's sales revenue for the year? (   )

    A.£982,800

    B.£1,090,000

    C.£2,520,000

    D.£1,080,000

3. 15 Prepare the statement of profit or loss for the year ended 31 July 20×1, in respect of T. Mann, from the following details in Exhibit 3. 11:

Exhibit 3. 11

Balances of T. Mann as at 31 July 20×1	
	£
Sales returns	1,029
Purchase returns	1,176
Purchases	65,100
Sales	110,859
Inventory 1 August 20×0	11,949
31 July 20×1	8,883
Carriage inwards	3,570
Salaries and wages	10,521
Rent	3,066
Motor expenses	6,552
General expenses	882
Carriage outwards	1,659

3. 16 From the following trial balance of G. Still (Exhibit 3. 12), draw up a statement of profit or loss for the year ending 30 September 20×7, and a statement of financial position as at that date.

Exhibit 3. 12

G. Still		
Trial Balance as at 30 September 20×7		
	Dr	Cr
	£	£
Inventory: 1 October 20×6	41,600	
Carriage outwards	2,100	
Carriage inwards	3,700	
Returns inwards	1,540	
Returns outwards		3,410
Purchases	188,430	
Sales		380,400
Salaries and wages	61,400	
Warehouse rent	3,700	
Insurance	1,356	
Motor expenses	1,910	
Office expenses	412	
Lighting and heating expenses	894	
General expenses	245	
Premises	92,000	
Motor vehicles	13,400	
Fixtures and fittings	1,900	
Accounts receivable	42,560	
Accounts payable		31,600
Cash at bank	5,106	
Drawings	22,000	
Capital		68,843
	484,253	484,253

Note: Inventory at 30 September 20×7 was £44,780

3. 17 From the following trial balance of S. Shah (Exhibit 3. 13), draw up a statement of profit and loss for the year ended 30 June 20×1 and statement of financial position as at that date.

Exhibit 3. 13

S. Shah		
Trial Balance as at 30 June 20×1		
	Dr	Cr
	£	£
Inventory 1 July 20×0	22,733	
Carriage outwards	1,920	
Carriage inwards	2,976	
Sales returns	1,968	
Purchase returns		3,091
Purchases	113,990	
Sales		178,560
Salaries and wages	37,075	
Rent and rates	2,918	
Insurance	749	
Motor expenses	4,250	
Telephone and internet	4,198	
Electricity	1,594	
General expenses	3,014	
Buildings	80,000	
Motor vehicles	17,280	
Accounts receivables	37,402	
Computer equipment	3,360	
Accounts payables		32,618
Cash at bank	4,627	
Drawings	11,520	
Capital		137,305
	351,574	351,574

Note: Inventory at 30 June 20×1 was £28,320.

3. 18 The following is the trial balance of T. Owen as at 31 March 20×6 (Exhibit 3. 14).
Draw up a set of financial statements for the year ended 31 March 20×6.

Exhibit 3. 14

T. Owen		
Trial Balance as at 31 March 20×6		
	Dr	Cr
	£	£
Inventory 1 April 20×5	52,800	
Carriage outwards	5,840	
Carriage inwards	1,350	
Purchase returns		2,408
Purchases	141,300	
Sales		276,400
Salaries and wages	63,400	
Business rates	3,800	
Insurance	1,830	
Communication expenses	714	
Commissions paid	1,930	
Sundry expenses	208	
Buildings	125,000	
Fixtures	1,106	
Accounts receivable	45,900	
Accounts payable		24,870
Cash at bank	31,420	
Cash in hand	276	
Drawing	37,320	
Capital		210,516
	514,194	514,194

Note: Inventory at 31 March 20×6 was £58,440.

3. 19 * F. Brown drew up the following trial balance as at 30 September 20×5 (Exhibit
3. 15). You are to draft the statement of profit or loss for the year ending 30 September 20×5
and a statement of financial position as at that date.

Exhibit 3. 15

F. Brown		
Trial Balance as at 30 September 20×5		
	Dr	Cr
	£	£
Capital		49,675
Drawing	28,600	
Cash at bank	4,420	
Cash in hand	112	
Accounts receivable	38,100	
Accounts payable		26,300
Inventory: 30 September 20×4	72,410	
Van	5,650	
Office equipment	7,470	
Sales		391,400
Purchases	254,810	
Returns inwards	2,110	
Carriage inwards	760	
Returns outwards		1,240
Carriage outwards	2,850	
Motor expenses	1,490	
Rent	8,200	
Telephone charges	680	
Wages and salaries	39,600	
Insurance	745	
Office expenses	392	
Sundry expenses	216	——
	468,615	468,615

Note: Inventory at 30 September 20×5 was £89,404.

Reference

1. Alan Sangster, Frank Wood's Business Accounting Volume 1(2019) , Pearson.

2. Andrew Thomas and Anne Marie Ward. Introduction to Financial Accounting (2019) , McGraw-Hill Education.

3. ACCA FA Financial Accounting/FIA FFA Interactive Text 2020, BPP Learning

Media.

4. ACCA FA Financial Accounting/FIA FFA Practice & Revision Kit 2020, BPP Learning Media.

5. Accounting (Study Manual 2020), The Institute of Chartered Accountants in England and Wales.

6. Accounting (Question Bank 2020), The Institute of Chartered Accountants in England and Wales.

Chapter 4

Inventory

┌─── ■Learning Objectives ───┐

· Understand the definition of inventory and its components.

· Recognise which costs should be included in valuing inventories.

· Understand the IFRS requirements for valuing inventories.

· Understand the use of continuous and period-end inventory records.

· Calculate the value of closing inventory using first in, first out (FIFO) and average cost (AVCO)—both periodic weighted average and continuous weighted average.

· Understand the impact of accounting concepts on the valuation of inventory.

· Identify the impact of inventory valuation methods on profit and on assets.

· Understand the difference between margin and mark-up.

└──┘

4.1   IAS 2 Inventories

This is the first time that you will be required to consider the impact of the relevant International Financial Reporting Standards (IFRSs) on the valuation and presentation of an item in the accounts: IAS 2 Inventories. Although you are not required to prepare financial statements for listed companies until Chapter 12, you will begin to study the requirement of IFRSs gradually from this chapter. IAS 2 Inventories lays out the required accounting treatment for inventory.

Inventory is one of the most important assets in a company's statement of financial position. IAS 2 Inventories gives the following important definitions.

Inventories are assets:

· Held for sale in the ordinary course of business.

· In the process of production for such sale.

· In the form of materials or supplies to be consumed in the production process or in the rendering of services.

Inventories may include any of the following:

· **Goods purchased and held for resale.**

· **Finished goods** which have been made by the business but not yet sold.

· **Work in progress** being produced (part completed items).

· **Raw materials** or components bought from suppliers.

4.2   Cost of Goods Sold

So far we have come across opening inventory in the preparation of a simple statement of financial position in Chapter 2 and have learned closing inventory, carriage inwards and outwards in chapter 3. They all relate to the calculation of cost of goods sold, which sometimes can be stated as 'cost of sales'. Here we will do some recap first and then explore more details of the cost of goods sold.

1. Recap

You already know how to calculate the cost of goods sold for a retailing company. If we consider the case of a manufacturing company, a more general formula for cost of goods sold is found as below.

Cost of Goods Sold	£
Opening inventory value	X
Add Cost of purchase (or, for a manufacturing company, the cost of production)	X
Add Carriage inwards	X
Less Closing inventory value	(X)
	X

To match 'sales' and the 'cost of goods sold', it is necessary to adjust the cost of goods manufactured or purchased to allow for increases or decrease in inventory levels during the period.

2. Inventories Written off or Written down

A trader might be unable to sell all the goods that they purchase, because a number of things might happen to the goods before they can be sold. For example:

· Goods might be lost or stolen.

· Goods might be damaged, become worthless and so be thrown away.

• Goods might become obsolete or out of fashion; These might be thrown away, or sold off at a very low price in a clearance sale.

When goods are **lost, stolen or thrown away** as worthless, the business will make a loss on those goods because their '**sales value**' **will be nil.**

Similarly, when goods lose value because they have become **obsolete** or out of fashion, the business will **make a loss** if their clearance sales value is less than their cost. For example, if goods which originally cost £500 are now obsolete and could only be sold for £150, the business would suffer a loss of £350.

If, at the end of an accounting period, a business still has goods in inventory which are either worthless or worth less than their original cost, the value of the inventories should be **written down** to:

 • Nothing, if they are worthless.

 • Their net realisable value(we will discuss this concept in section 4.3), if this is less than their original cost.

This means that the loss will be reported as soon as the loss is foreseen, even if the goods have not yet been thrown away or sold off at a cheap price. This is an application of the prudence concept.

The costs of inventory written off or written down should not usually cause any problems when calculating the gross profit of a business, because the cost of goods sold will include the cost of inventories written off or written down, as the following example shows.

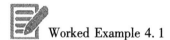 Worked Example 4. 1

W. Lucas, trading as Fairlock Fashions, ends his financial year on 31 March. At 1 April 20×5 he had goods in inventory valued at £8,800. During the year to 31 March 20×6, he purchased goods costing £48,000. Fashion goods which cost £2,100 were still held in inventory at 31 March 20×6, and W. Lucas believes that these could only now be sold at a sale price of £400. The goods still held in inventory at 31 March 20×6 (including the fashion goods) had an original purchase cost of £7,600. Sales for the year were £81,400.

Requirement

Calculate the gross profit of Fairlock Fashions for the year ended 31 March 20×6.

Solution

Initial calculation of closing inventory values:

	At cost	Realisable value	Amount written down
	£	£	£
Fashion goods	2,100	400	1,700
Other goods (balancing figure)	5,500	5,500	————
	7,600	5,900	1,700

Gross profit calculation is shown in Exhibit 4.1:

Exhibit 4.1

Gross profit calculation		
	£	£
Sales		81,400
Less Cost of goods sold		
Opening inventory	8,800	
Add Purchases	48,000	
	56,800	
Less Closing inventory	(5,900)	
		50,900
Gross profit		30,500

By using the figure of £5,900 for closing inventories, the cost of goods sold automatically includes the inventory written down of £1,700.

3. Inventory Destroyed or Stolen and Subject to an Insurance Claim

Where a **material** amount of inventory has been stolen or destroyed, including their cost in gross profit will give a very distorted idea of the business's basic profitability:

· Purchases will include the cost of goods that could not be sold, so the accrual principle is broken, yet they are not in closing inventory either, so it will look as if the business's gross margin on sales has fallen catastrophically.

· There may be an amount of income as a result of an insurance claim, which cannot be included in cost of sales.

These problems are overcome by taking the cost of goods stolen or destroyed **out of purchases**, and including it under **expenses.** An insurance claim is treated as **other income** in calculating net profit; if it has not yet been received in the form **of cash** it is disclosed as '**other receivables**' on the statement of financial position. It should only be recorded if it is reasonably certain that the amount will be received, which will be evidenced by having a valid insurance policy and confirmation from the insurer that the claim will be settled.

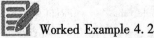 Worked Example 4.2

Farita had £15,000 of inventory as at 1 January 20×2. During the year to 31 December 20×2 she purchased inventory for £98,000, incurring carriage inwards of £150. She made sales of £150,000, incurring carriage outwards to her customers of £2,400. At 31 December 20×2 she realises that she has inventory costing only £200 left; goods costing £18,000 have been stolen.

Requirement

Prepare Farita's statement of profit or loss assuming:

Scenario 1: Farita has relevant insurance and her insurer has agreed to pay her claim for 75% of the cost.

Scenario 2: Farita does not have any insurance.

Solution

Farita's statement of profit or loss under scenario 1 & 2 is shown in Exhibit 4. 2.

Exhibit 4. 2

Farita's statement of profit or loss for the year ended 31 December 20×2				
	Scenario 1		Scenario 2	
	£	£	£	£
Revenue		150,000		150,000
Cost of goods sold				
Opening inventory	15,000		15,000	
Purchases	98,000		98,000	
Carriage inwards	150		150	
Inventory stolen	(18,000)		(18,000)	
Less Closing inventory	(200)		(200)	
		(94,950)		(94,950)
Gross profit		55,050		55,050
Other income (18,000 × 75%)		13,500		
Less expenses				
Cost of goods stolen		(18,000)		(18,000)
Carriage outwards		(2,400)		(2,400)
Net profit		48,150		34,650

4. Counting Inventory

Business trading is a continuous activity, but accounting statements must be drawn up at a particular date. In preparing a statement of financial position it is necessary to 'freeze' the activity of a business to determine its assets and liabilities at a given moment. This includes establishing the quantities of inventories on hand.

In simple cases, usually when a business holds easily counted and relatively small amounts of inventory, quantities of inventories on hand at the reporting date can be determined by physically counting them in an **inventory count** at that date. This kind of system is known as 'periodic inventory valuation' system.

In more complicated cases, where a business holds considerable quantities of varied inventory, an alternative approach to establishing quantities is to maintain **continuous inventory records.** This means that the accounting system keeps a record for each line of inventory item, showing purchases and issues from the stores, and a running total. A few inventory line items are counted each day to make sure their record cards are correct—this is called a 'continuous' count because it is spread out over the reporting period rather than completed in one count at a designated time. This kind of system is also known as 'perpetual inventory records' system.

5. Accounting for Opening and Closing Inventories

If a business adopts 'periodic inventory valuation' system, it usually keeps an inventory account. This inventory account is only ever used **at the end of an accounting period,** when the business counts up and values the inventory in hand. Let's recap the ledger entries for opening and closing inventories.

(1) **When an inventory count is made,** the business will have a value for its **closing inventory,** and the double entry is:

		£	£
DEBIT	Inventory account (closing inventory value)	X	
CREDIT	Trading account		X

However, rather than show the closing inventory as a 'plus' value in the trading account (by adding it to sales) it is usual to show it as a 'minus' figure in arriving at cost of goods sold (therefore, in some textbooks, the credit entry goes to Cost of Goods Sold account). This is illustrated in Chapter 3. The debit balance on inventory account represents an asset, which will be shown as part of current assets in the statement of financial position.

(2) Closing inventory at the end of one period becomes **opening inventory** at the start of the next period. The inventory account remains unchanged until the end of the next period, when the value of opening inventory is taken to the trading account.

		£	£
DEBIT	Trading account	X	
CREDIT	Inventory account (value of opening inventory)		X

4.3 Measurement of Inventories

Inventory is normally measured at its historical cost, at which the inventory was originally bought. The only time when historical cost is not used is when cost needs to be reduced to net realisable value. **Net realisable value** (NRV) is the estimated selling price in the ordinary course of business less the estimated costs of completion and the estimated costs necessary to make the sale. In other words, net realisable value is the expected selling price, less any costs still to be incurred in getting the inventory ready for sale. IAS 2 states that inventory should be stated at the lower of cost and NRV, as we will see below. This is an important rule and one which you should learn by heart.

1. Applying the Lower of Cost and NRV

If a business has many inventory items on hand, the comparison of cost and NRV should theoretically be carried out for each item separately. It is not sufficient to compare the total cost of all inventory items with their total NRV. An example will show why.

Suppose a company has four items of inventory on hand at the end of its accounting period. Their cost and NRVs are shown in Exhibit 4. 3.

Exhibit 4. 3

Applying the lower of cost and NRV			
Inventory item	Cost	NRV	Lower of cost/NRV
	£	£	£
1	27	32	27
2	14	8	8
3	43	55	43
4	29	40	29
	113	135	107

It would be incorrect to compare total costs (£113) with total NRV (£135) and to state inventories at £113 in the statement of financial position. The company can foresee a loss of £6 on item 2 and this should be recognised. If the four items are taken together in total, the loss on item 2 is masked by the anticipated profits on the other items. By performing the cost and NRV comparison for each item separately the prudent valuation of £107 can be derived. This is the value which should appear in the statement of financial position.

However, for a company with large amounts of inventory, this procedure may be impracticable. In this case it is acceptable to group similar items into categories and perform the comparison of cost and NRV category by category, rather than item by item.

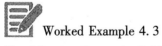 Worked Example 4. 3

The following figures in Exhibit 4. 4 relate to inventory held at the year end.

Exhibit 4. 4

Inventory information			
	Item A	Item B	Item C
	£	£	£
Cost	20	9	12
Selling price	30	12	22

Exhibit 4. 4(continued)

Modification cost to enable sale	–	2	8
Marketing costs	7	2	2
Units held	200	150	300

Requirement

Calculate the value of inventory for inclusion in the financial statements.

Solution

The comparison of cost and NRV for each item is shown in Exhibit 4. 5.

Exhibit 4. 5

Comparison of cost and NRV for item A, B & C					
Item	Cost	NRV	Valuation	Quantity	Total value
	£	£	£	Units	£
A	20	23	20	200	4,000
B	9	8	8	150	1,200
C	12	12	12	300	3,600
					8,800

So have we now solved the problem of how a business should value its inventories? It seems that all the business has to do is choose the lower of cost and NRV. This is true as far as it goes, but there is one further problem, perhaps not so easy to foresee: for a given type of inventory, **what was the cost?**

2. Determining the Cost of Inventory

IAS 2 states cost of inventories should include all:

· Costs of purchases.

· Costs of conversion.

· Other costs incurred in bringing the inventories to their present location and condition.

Cost of purchase includes: The purchase price, import duties and other non-recoverable taxes, transport, handling and other costs directly attributable to the acquisition of finished goods and materials.

Cost of conversion includes: Any costs involved in converting raw materials into final product, including labour, expenses directly related to the product and an appropriate share of production overheads (but not sales, administrative or general overheads).

Other costs: Any other costs should only be recognised if they are incurred in bringing the inventories to their **present location and condition.**

In other words, the total cost of an item of inventory includes all costs of purchase, of conversion and of other in bringing the items to their saleable condition.

 Worked Example 4. 4

A business has the following details relating to production and sales for a reporting period:

Sales: 900 units at £600 each

1,000 units are produced with the following costs being incurred:

Opening inventory of raw materials: 200 units at £100 each

Purchases of raw materials: 1,050 units at £100 each

Closing inventory of raw materials: 250 units at £100 each

Production wages: £150,000

Production overheads: £100,000

General administration, selling and distribution costs: £100,000

Requirement

Calculate the cost of production and net profit.

Solution

The **cost of production** should include an **appropriate share of production wages and production overheads**, but not **non-production expenses.** Exhibit 4. 6 shows the calculation.

Exhibit 4. 6

Calculate the cost of production		
	£	£
Sales (900 units×£600)		540,000
Cost of production (1,000 units)		
Opening inventory of raw materials (200×£100)	20,000	
Purchases of raw materials (1,050×£100)	105,000	
Less closing inventory of raw materials (250×£100)	(25,000)	
Cost of raw materials used	100,000	
Production wages	150,000	
Production overheads	100,000	
Cost of production (1,000 units cost £350,000/1,000 = £350 each)	350,000	
Less closing inventory of finished goods (100×£350)	(35,000)	
Cost of sales		(315,000)
Gross profit		225,000
Less General administration, selling and distribution costs		(100,000)
Net profit		125,000

The cost of production is spread over the units produced. Any unsold units are valued at a figure that reflects a share of these costs. When the inventory is eventually sold, the production overheads associated with its manufacture will be thereby properly matched with the revenues earned.

3. Different Valuations of Inventory

A business may be continually adding items to finished goods inventory or purchasing a particular component. As each batch of goods is received from suppliers, or each finished goods batch is added to inventory, they are stored in the appropriate place, where they will be mingled with items already there. These goods are considered interchangeable in that the storekeeper would not distinguish between items when they issue items to production or to despatch. They will simply pull out the nearest item to hand, which may have arrived in the latest batch, in an earlier batch or in several different /batches. There are several techniques which are used in practice to attribute a cost to interchangeable inventory items; remember that actual materials, components and finished goods items can be issued in any order irrespective of when each one entered inventory.

First in, first out method (FIFO)

This is usually referred to as FIFO, from the first letters of each word. This method says that the first items to be received are the first to be issued. Using this method, we are assuming the oldest items are issued first and inventory remaining is therefore the newer items and cost is measured as such.

Average cost method (AVCO)

As purchase prices change with each new batch of goods, the average price of goods held is constantly changed. Using the AVCO method, with each receipt of goods the average cost for each item is recalculated. Further issues of goods are then at that figure, until another receipt of goods means that another recalculation is needed.

Last in, first out method (LIFO)

This is usually referred to as LIFO. As each issue of items is made, they are assumed to be from the last batch received before that date. Where there is not enough left of the last batch, then the balance needed is assumed to come from the previous batch still unsold. Using this method, inventories are stated as the oldest receipts.

If you are preparing financial statements, you would normally expect to use FIFO or AVCO for the valuation of inventory. IAS 2 Inventories does not permit the use of LIFO. Furthermore, you should remember that terms such as FIFO and AVCO refer to pricing methods only. The actual components can be used in any order. To illustrate the different methods of FIFO and AVCO, the following transactions will be used in each case.

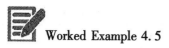

Worked Example 4. 5

Transactions during May 20×7 are shown in Exhibit 4. 7.

Exhibit 4. 7

Transactions during May 20×7				
Transactions Date	Quantity Units	Unit cost £	Total cost £	Market value per unit on date of transactions £
	100	2. 00	200	
Receipts 3 May	400	2. 10	840	2. 11
Issues 4 May	200			2. 11
Receipts 9 May	300	2. 12	636	2. 15
Issues 11 May	400			2. 20
Receipts 18 May	100	2. 40	240	2. 35
Issues 20 May	100			2. 35
Closing balance 31 May	200		——	2. 38
			1,916	

Receipts mean goods are received into store and issues represent the issue of goods from store.

The problem is to put a valuation on the following.

(1) The issues of materials.

(2) The closing inventory.

Requirement

How would issues and closing inventory be valued using FIFO and AVCO?

Solution

(1) FIFO assumes that goods are issued out of inventory in the order in which they were delivered into inventory, i.e. issues are priced at the cost of the earliest delivery remaining in inventory.

The cost of issues and closing inventory value in the example, using FIFO, would be as shown in Exhibit 4. 8.

Exhibit 4. 8

Using FIFO to value inventory			
Date of issue	Quantity Units	Value issued £	Cost of issues £
4 May	200	100 OI * at £2	200
		100 at £2. 10	210

Exhibit 4. 8(continued)

		200	410
11 May	400	300 at £2. 10	630
		100 at £2. 12	212
			842
20 May	100	100 at £2. 12	212
			1,464
Closing inventory value	200	100 at £2. 12	212
		100 at £2. 40	240
			452
			1,916

* OI = Opening Inventory

Note that the cost of materials issued plus the value of closing inventory equals the cost of purchases plus the value of opening inventory (£1,916).

(2) AVCO may be used in various ways in costing inventory issues. The most common is the cumulative weighted average pricing method illustrated below.

· A weighted average cost for all units in inventory is calculated. Issues are valued at this average cost, and the balance of inventory remaining has the same unit cost.

· A new weighted average cost is calculated whenever a new delivery of goods into store is received.

In our example, issue costs and closing inventory values would be as described in Exhibit 4. 9:

Exhibit 4. 9

				Using AVCO to value inventory		
Date	Received Units	Issued Units	Balance Units	Total inventory Value £	Unit cost £	Cost of Issue £
Opening inventory			100	200	2. 00	
3 May	400			840	2. 10	
			500	1,040	2. 08 *	
4 May		200		(416)	2. 08 **	416
			300	624	2. 08	
9 May	300			636	2. 12	
			600	1,260	2. 10 *	
11 May		400		(840)	2. 10 **	840
			200	420	2. 10	

Exhibit 4. 9(continued)

Using AVCO to value inventory						
Date	Received Units	Issued Units	Balance Units	Total inventory Value £	Unit cost £	Cost of Issue £
18 May	100			240	2. 40	
			300	660	2. 20*	
20 May		100		(220)	2. 20**	220
						1,476
Closing inventory			200	440	2. 20	440
						1,916

* A new unit cost is calculated whenever a new receipt of goods occurs.

* * Whenever goods are issued, the unit value of the items issued is the current weighted average cost per unit at the time of the issue.

For this method too, the cost of goods issued plus the cost of closing inventory equals the cost of purchases plus the cost of opening inventory (£1,916).

4. Inventory Valuation and the Calculation of Profits

FIFO and AVCO each produced different costs, both of closing inventories and also of materials issues. Since raw material costs affect the cost of production, and the cost of production works through eventually into the cost of sales (cost of goods sold), it follows that **different methods of inventory valuation will provide different profit figures.** Let's see the following example.

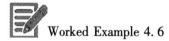 Worked Example 4. 6

On 1 November 20×2 a company held 300 units of finished goods in inventory. These cost £3,600. During November 20×2 three batches of finished goods were received into store from the production department. Please refer to Exhibit 4. 10:

Exhibit 4. 10

Good purchased during November 20×2		
Date	Units received	Production cost per unit £
10 November	400	12. 50
20 November	400	14
25 November	400	15

Finished goods sold during November were as shown in Exhibit 4. 11.

Exhibit 4. 11

Good sold during November 20×2		
Date	Units sold	Sale price per unit £
14 November	500	20
21 November	500	20
28 November	100	20

Requirement

Identify the profit from selling inventory in November 20×2, applying the principles of:

(1) FIFO.

(2) AVCO (using cumulative weighted average costing).

Ignore administration, sales and distribution costs.

Solution

(1) FIFO method calculation is shown in Exhibit 4. 12.

Exhibit 4. 12

Inventory valuation using FIFO method during November 20×2			
Date	Issue costs	Issue cost total £	Closing inventory £
14 November	(300 units×£12) + (200 units×£12. 50)	6,100	
21 November	(200 units×£12. 50) + (300 units×£14)	6,700	
28 November	(100 units×£14)	1,400	
Closing inventory	(400 units×£15)		6,000
		14,200	6,000

(2) AVCO (cumulative weighted average cost) method calculation is shown in Exhibit 4. 13.

Exhibit 4. 13

Inventory valuation using AVCO method during November 20×2					
Date	Unit	Unit cost	Balance in inventory	Total cost of issues	Closing inventory
		£	£	£	£
1 November (Opening inventory)	300	12. 000	3,600		
10 November	400	12. 500	5,000		
	700	12. 286	8,600		
14 November	(500)	12. 286	(6,143)	6,143	

Exhibit 4. 13(continued)

Inventory valuation using AVCO method during November 20×2					
Date	Unit	Unit cost	Balance in inventory	Total cost of issues	Closing inventory
		£	£	£	£
	200	12. 286	2,457		
20 November	400	14. 000	5,600		
	600	13. 428	8,057		
21 November	(500)	13. 428	(6,714)	6,714	
	100	13. 428	1,343		
25 November	400	15. 000	6,000		
	500	14. 686	7,343		
28 November	(100)	14. 686	(1,469)	1,469	
30 November	400	14. 686	5,874	14,326	5,874

Using different methods, Exhibit 4. 14 describes the calculation of November's profit.

Exhibit 4. 14

Statement of profit of loss for November 20×2		
	FIFO	AVCO
	£	£
Sales (1,100×£20)	22,000	22,000
Cost of sales		
Opening inventory	3,600	3,600
Add Cost of production (400×£12. 50) + (400×£14) + (400×£15)	16,600	16,600
Less Closing inventory	(6,000)	(5,874)
	14,200	14,326
Profit	7,800	7,674

Different inventory valuations produce different cost of sales and profits figures. Here opening inventory values are the same, therefore **the difference in the amount of profit under each method is the same as the difference in the valuations of closing inventory.**

The profit differences are only temporary. The opening inventory in December 20×2 will be £6,000 or £5,874, depending on the inventory valuation used. Different opening inventory values will affect the cost of sales and profits in December, so that in the long run inequalities in cost of sales each month will even themselves out.

4.4 Using Mark-up/Margin Percentages to Establish Cost

The purchase cost, gross profit and selling price of goods may be shown as:

> Cost Price + Gross Profit = Selling Price

When shown as a fraction or percentage of the cost price, the gross profit is known as the **mark-up.**

When shown as a fraction or percentage of the selling price, gross profit is known as the **margin.**

Margin and mark-up can help us to establish the cost of an item of inventory. It is also common to establish standard gross profit percentages in relation to cost to set the sales price, for example:

· Inventory that cost £120 may be sold at a margin of 40%, so the sales value is £120× 100/60 = £200, and the profit is £120×40/60 = £80.

· Inventory that cost £120 may be sold at a mark-up of 40% to reach a sales price of £168 (120×140/100).

These standard percentages can be set out as listed in Exhibit 4.15, using the above as an example:

Exhibit 4.15

	Margin on sales			Mark-up on cost		
	(sales is the 100% figure)			(cost is the 100% figure)		
	%	£	£	%	£	£
Sales	100	200	120×100/60	140	168	120×140/100
Cost	(60)	(120)		(100)	120	
Gross profit	40	80	120×40/60	40	48	120×40/100

Summary

· IAS 2 Inventories lays out the required accounting treatment for inventories under International Financial Reporting Standards.

· Inventories include assets held for sale (finished goods), assets in the production process for sale (work in process), and materials and supplies consumed in production (raw materials).

· The cost of goods sold is calculated as: opening inventory + purchases/ production −

closing inventory.

· The quantity of inventories held at the year end is established by means of a physical count of inventory in an annual counting exercise, or by a 'continuous' inventory count.

· The value of inventories is calculated at the lower of cost and net realisable value (NRV) for each separate item or group of items.

· Cost of inventory includes costs of purchase, costs of conversion and other costs incurred in bringing the inventories to their present location and condition.

· NRV is the expected selling price, less any costs still to be incurred in getting the inventory ready for sale.

· For items that are interchangeable, IAS 2 allows first in, first out (FIFO) or weighted average costing (AVCO) methods to value inventories.

· Margin and mark-up can help us to establish the cost of an item of inventory.

Exercise

4.1 Gross profit for 20×7 can be calculated from (   ).

    A.Purchases for 20×7, plus inventory at 31 December 20×7, less inventory at 1 January 20×7

    B.Purchases for 20×7, less inventory at 31 December 20×7, plus inventory at 1 January 20×7

    C.Cost of goods sold during 20×7, plus sales during 20×7

    D.Profit for the year for 20×7, plus expenses for 20×7

4.2 The inventory value for the financial statements of Global Inc for the year ended 30 June 20×3 was based on an inventory count on 7 July 20×3, which gave a total inventory value of £950,000. Between 30 June and 7 July 20×6, the following transactions took place.

	£
Purchase of goods	11,750
Sale of goods (mark up on cost at 15%)	14,950
Goods returned by Global Inc to supplier	1,500

What figure should be included in the financial statements for inventories at 30 June 20×3? (   )

    A.£952,750

    B.£949,750

    C.£926,750

    D.£958,950

4. 3 Which of the following costs may be included when arriving at the cost of finished goods inventory for inclusion in the financial statements of a manufacturing company? (   )

1 Carriage inwards

2 Carriage outwards

3 Depreciation of factory plant

4 Finished goods storage costs

5 Factory supervisors' wages

A.1 and 5 only

B.2, 4 and 5 only

C.1, 3 and 5 only

D.1, 2, 3 and 4 only

4. 4 In preparing its financial statements for the current year, a company's closing inventory was understated by £300,000. What will be the effect of this error if it remains uncorrected? (   )

A. The current year's profit will be overstated and next year's profit will be understated

B. The current year's profit will be understated but there will be no effect on next year's profit

C. The current year's profit will be understated and next year's profit will be overstated

D. The current year's profit will be overstated but there will be no effect on next year's profit

4. 5 Which one of the following statements about the use of a continuous inventory system is INCORRECT? (   )

A. In a retail organisation, a continuous inventory system can be used to keep track of the quantity of each stock item available in its distribution centers

B. Under continuous inventory, the cost of each receipt of inventory and the cost of each issue from inventory is recorded individually

C. A continuous inventory system removes the need for periodic physical inventory counts

D. Both the FIFO and average cost (AVCO) methods of pricing inventory may be used within a continuous inventory system

4. 6 You are preparing the final accounts for a business. The cost of the items in closing inventory is £41,875. This includes some items which cost £1,960 and which were damaged in transit. You have estimated that it will cost £360 to repair the items, and they can then be sold for £1,200. What is the correct inventory valuation for inclusion in the final accounts? (   )

A.£39,915

B.£40,755

C.£41,515

D.£42,995

4.7 Carlisle has the following inventory movements during May as listed in Exhibit 4.16.

Exhibit 4.16

Inventory movement during May		
	Units	£ per unit
Opening inventory	40	9
2 May Goods in	60	10
10 May Goods out	50	
15 May Goods in	70	11
18 May Goods out	45	
24 May Goods in	80	11

Assuming that the business values inventory on a FIFO basis, what will be the value of closing inventory at the end of the month? ( )

A.£1,615

B.£1,655

C.£1,700

D.£1,705

4.8 A trader used the LIFO method to value inventory at the end of July at £3,110. Sales and purchases in July were described in Exhibit 4.17:

Exhibit 4.17

Sales and purchases in July		
Date	Purchases (units)	Sales (units)
3 July	100 at £20/unit	
6 July		80
10 July		40
15 July	50 at £22/unit	
22 July		20
27 July	80 at £25/unit	

The opening inventory at 1 July was 50 units valued at £15 per unit. The trader needs to adopt the FIFO method. What is the effect of this change on the trader's profit? ( )

A.£190 decrease

B.£420 decrease

C.£420 increase

D.£190 increase

4.9 The inventory records for Simmons last month were as shown in Exhibit 4.18:

Exhibit 4.18

Simmons' inventory records in February		
Date	Purchases (units)	Sales (units)
2 February		500
13 February	800	
21 February		400
29 February		200

Opening inventory was 600 units valued at £12,000. Purchases in February were at £31.25 per unit. The total cost of sales in February, using the AVCO method, is (   ).(to the nearest £)

A.£37,000

B.£28,000

C.£17,625

D.£22,000

4.10 What would be the effect on a business's profit of discovering that inventory with a cost of £1,250 and a net realisable value of £1,000 had been omitted from the inventory count at the end of the reporting period? (   )

A.An increase of £1,250

B.An increase of £1,000

C.A decrease of £250

D.No effect

4.11 June Ltd has three lines of inventory at the end of its reporting period.

	X	Y	Z
Original purchase price (per unit)	£1.50	£6.50	£5.00
Estimated future selling price (per unit)	£4.25	£8.00	£3.50
Selling and distribution costs (per unit)	£0.75	£2.00	£0.50
Units in inventory	100	200	250

At what value should inventory appear in the financial statements at the end of the reporting period? (   )

A.£2,700

B.£2,325

C.£2,300

D.£2,100

4. 12 A company values its inventory using the first in, first out (FIFO) method. At 1 May 20×2 the company had 700 engines in inventory, valued at £190 each.

During the year ended 30 April 20×3 the following transactions took place:

20×2

1 July Purchased 500 engines at £220 each

1 November Sold 400 engines for £160,000

20×3

1 February Purchased 300 engines at £230 each

15 April Sold 250 engines for £125,000

What is the value of the company's closing inventory of engines at 30 April 20×3?

(   )

A.£188,500

B.£195,500

C.£166,000

D.None of these figures

4. 13 Which of the following statements about the valuation of inventory are correct, according to IAS 2 Inventories? (   )

1 Inventory items are normally to be valued at the higher of cost and net realisable value

2 The cost of goods manufactured by an entity will include materials and labour only. Overhead costs cannot be included

3 LIFO (last in, first out) cannot be used to value inventory

4 Selling price less estimated profit margin may be used to arrive at cost if this gives a reasonable approximation to actual cost

A.1, 3 and 4 only

B.1 and 2 only

C.3 and 4 only

D.None of the statements are correct

4. 14 The financial year of Mitex Co ended on 31 December 20×1. An inventory count on 4 January 20×2 gave a total inventory value of £527,300. The following transactions occurred between January 1 and January 4.

	£
Purchases of goods	7,900
Sales of goods (gross profit margin 40% on sales)	15,000
Goods returned to a supplier	800

What inventory value should be included in Mitex Cos financial statements at 31 December 20×1? (   )

    A.£525,400

    B.£527,600

    C.£529,200

    D.£535,200

4. 15 You are preparing the final accounts for a business. The cost of the items in closing inventory is £41,875. This includes some items which cost £1,960 and which were damaged in transit. You have estimated that it will cost £360 to repair the items, and they can then be sold for £1,200. What is the correct inventory valuation for inclusion in the final accounts? (   )

    A.£39,915

    B.£40,755

    C.£41,515

    D.£42,995

4. 16 * On 1 January 20×6, the Grand Union Food Stores had goods in inventory valued at £6,000. During 20×6 its proprietor purchased supplies costing £50,000. Sales for the year to 31 December 20×6 amounted to £80,000. The cost of goods in inventory at 31 December 20×6 was £12,500.

What is the gross profit for the year?

4. 17 * A business is established with capital of £2,000 and this amount is paid into a business bank account by the proprietor. During the first year's trading, the following transactions occurred.

	£
Purchases of goods for resale, on credit	4,300
Payments for trade accounts payable	3,600
Sales, all on credit	4,000
Payments from trade accounts receivable	3,200
Non-current assets purchased for cash	1,500
Other expenses, all paid in cash	900
The bank has provided an overdraft facility of up to	3,000

All 'other expenses' relate to the current year.

Closing inventory is valued at £1,800. (Because this is the first year of the business, there are no opening inventories.)

Requirement

Prepare the ledger accounts, a profit or loss account for the year and a statement of financial position as at the end of the year.

4.18 A firm has the following transactions with its product R.

Year 1

Opening inventory: nil

Buys 10 units at £300 per unit

Buys 12 units at £250 per unit

Sells 8 units at £400 per unit

Buys 6 units at £200 per unit

Sells 12 units at £400 per unit

Year 2

Buys 10 units at £200 per unit

Sells 5 units at £400 per unit

Buys 12 units at £150 per unit

Sells 25 units at £400 per unit

Requirement

Using FIFO, calculate the following on an item by item basis for both year 1 and year 2.

(1) The closing inventory.

(2) The sales.

(3) The cost of sales.

(4) The gross profit.

Reference

1. ACCA FA Financial Accounting/FIA FFA Interactive Text 2020, BPP Learning Media.

2. ACCA FA Financial Accounting/FIA FFA Practice & Revision Kit 2020, BPP Learning Media.

3. Accounting (Study Manual 2020), The Institute of Chartered Accountants in England and Wales.

4. Accounting (Question Bank 2020), The Institute of Chartered Accountants in England and Wales.

5. Alan Sangster, Frank Wood's Business Accounting Volume 1(2019), Pearson.

Chapter 5

Irrecoverable Debts and Allowance for Receivables

┌─────────■Learning Objectives ─────────────────────────────────┐
│ · Understand what irrecoverable debts are and how irrecoverable debts are written off. │
│ · Understand why allowance for receivables is made. │
│ · Make accounting entries for recording the allowance for receivables. │
│ · Make accounting entries for increasing or reducing the allowance for receivables. │
│ · Make all the entries in the statement of profit or loss and statement of financial po- │
│ sition for irrecoverable debts and allowances for doubtful debts. │
│ · Make accounting entries for irrecoverable debts recovered. │
└───┘

5. 1   Irrecoverable Debts

1. Introduction

With many businesses a large proportion, if not all, of the sales are on credit. Very few businesses expect to be paid immediately in cash, unless they are retail businesses on the high street. Most businesses buy and sell to one another on credit terms. This has the benefit of allowing businesses to keep trading without having to provide cash 'up front'. So a business will allow credit terms to customers and receive credit terms from its suppliers. Ideally a business wants to receive money from its customers as quickly as possible, but delay paying its suppliers for as long as possible. This can lead to problems that some of the customers may never pay for the goods sold to them on credit. This is a normal business risk that a business has to face.

Customers might fail to pay, perhaps out of various reason:

· Customers are dishonest and refuse to pay.

• Customers have gone bankrupt and cannot pay.

• There is a dispute between the parties about the amount payable.

• Customers in another country might be prevented from paying by the unexpected introduction of foreign exchange control restrictions by their country's government during the credit period.

Whatever the reason, a business might decide to give up expecting payment and to write the debt off. An **irrecoverable** (or 'bad') **debt** is a debt which is definitely not expected to be paid. Once a debt has been declared 'irrecoverable', the asset as shown by the debt in the trade receivables account is worthless. It must be eliminated from the account. Let's see how to record the irrecoverable debts in next section.

2. Writing off Irrecoverable Debts

To begin with, let's recap the ledger entries when a sale on credit is made to a customer.

		£	£
DEBIT	Trade receivables	X	
CREDIT	Sales		X

All being well, a few weeks later the customer will pay the debt and cash will be received, at which point the double entry is:

		£	£
DEBIT	Cash account	X	
CREDIT	Trade receivables		X

When a business decides that a particular debt will not be paid, the whole amount of the receivable in question is 'written off' as an expense in the statement of profit or loss:

		£	£
DEBIT	Irrecoverable debts expense (statement of profit or loss)	X	
CREDIT	Trade receivables (statement of financial position)		X

Irrecoverable debts written off are presented as follows.

• Revenue is recorded in the statement of profit or loss at the amount expected to be received from the customer, which in most cases is the invoice amount. The sale has been made, an expense has been incurred in making that sale and the gross profit should be recognised. The subsequent failure to collect the debt is a separate administrative matter.

• Irrecoverable debts expense is shown as an expense after gross profit in the statement of profit or loss.

• The receivable is removed from trade receivables.

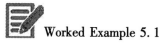 **Worked Example 5.1**

Design Co has a total balance for trade receivables of £25,000 at the year end. A review of the receivables balances highlights that one of its customers, Mann Co, has gone bankrupt.

Design Co is owed £4,000 by Mann Co for design work done during the year. This debt is now considered irrecoverable.

Requirement

(1) What is the balance for trade receivables to be shown in the statement of financial position at the year end?

(2) What is the irrecoverable debts expense to be shown in the statement of profit or loss at the year end?

Solution

Trade Receivables(SOFP)

	£		£
Balance b/d	25,000	Irrecoverable debts expense	4,000
		Balance c/d	21,000
	25,000		25,000
Balance b/d	21,000		

Trade receivables will be shown at £21,000 in the statement of financial position.

Irrecoverable Debts Expenses (SOPL)

	£		£
Trade receivables	4,000	P/L account	4,000

The irrecoverable debt expense in the statement of profit or loss is £4,000.

3. Irrecoverable Debts Written off and Subsequently Paid

An irrecoverable debt which has been written off might occasionally be unexpectedly paid. Because the debt has already been written off, it no longer exists in the statement of financial position and so the cash received cannot be offset against it in the usual way. Instead, the cash received is offset against the irrecoverable debts expense. **Regardless of when the payment is received,** the ledger entries are as follows.

		£	£
DEBIT	Cash account	X	
CREDIT	Irrecoverable debts expense		X

We do not need to credit trade receivables as this has already been done when the debt was initially written off.

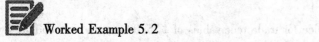

Worked Example 5.2

We have the following information in Exhibit 5.1 on Blacksmith's Forge for the year to 31

December 20×5.

Exhibit 5. 1

Transaction information of Blacksmith's Forge	
	£
Inventory, 1 January 20×5	6,000
Purchase of goods	122,000
Inventory, 31 December 20×5	8,000
Cash sales	100,000
Credit sales	70,000
Irrecoverable debts written off	9,000
Debts paid in 20×5 which were previously written off as irrecoverable in 20×4	2,000
Other expenses	31,800
Trade receivables	24,000

Requirement

Based on the above information, prepare the statement of profit or loss and the statement of financial position for Blacksmith's Forge?

Solution

We can prepare the statement of profit or loss as shown in Exhibit 5. 2:

Exhibit 5. 2

Blacksmith's Forge		
Statement of profit or loss for the year ended 31 December 20×5		
	£	£
Sales (100,000+70,000)		170,000
Cost of goods sold		
Opening inventory	6,000	
Purchases	122,000	
	128,000	
Less Closing inventory	(8,000)	
		(120,000)
Gross profit		50,000
Expenses		
Irrecoverable debts expense (9,000 − 2,000)	7,000	
Other expenses	31,800	(38,800)
Net profit		11,200

The extract of statement of financial position is shown in Exhibit 5.3:

Exhibit 5.3

Blacksmith's Forge	
Statement of financial position (Extract) as at 31 December 20×5	
	£
Current assets	
Inventory	8,000
Trade receivables (24,000 - 9,000)	15,000

5.2 Allowance for Receivables

1. Doubtful Debts

Irrecoverable debts are specific debts which are definitely not expected to be paid. However, there may be some debts which the business thinks might not be paid; these are known as doubtful debts.

A doubtful debt is a debt which is possibly irrecoverable. Doubtful debts may occur, for example, when an invoice is in dispute, or when a customer is in financial difficulty. In this situation, the debt is not written off, as it is not certain that the debt is irrecoverable. But because there is doubt over whether the debt will be paid, an allowance for receivables is made against the doubtful debt.

Allowance for receivables is an impairment amount in relation to receivables that reduces the receivables asset to its recoverable amount in the statement of financial position. It is offset against trade receivables, which are shown at the net amount.

An allowance for receivables accounts for potential irrecoverable debts, as a prudent precaution by the business. The business will therefore be more likely to avoid claiming profits which subsequently fail to materialise because some specific debts turn out to be irrecoverable.

2. Determining the Allowance for Receivables

A trade receivable is a type of financial asset, therefore the methods of determining the allowance for trade receivables fall under IAS 39/IFRS 9 as part of an impairment review of trade receivables, and can be quite complex.

Fortunately, these are beyond the scope of this textbook. In this chapter, the allowance for receivables is likely to be expressed simply as a percentage of trade receivables, e.g. 'an allowance equivalent to 2% of trade receivables'.

The allowance against the trade receivables balance is made after writing off any irrecoverable debts.

3. Allowance for Receivables: Ledger Accounting Entries

To record an allowance for receivables and show its movement, we need to consider the following journal entries:

When an allowance is first made, the amount of this initial allowance is charged as an expense in the statement of profit or loss for the period in which the allowance is created.

The double entry is:

		£	£
DEBIT	Irrecoverable debts expense	X	
CREDIT	Allowance for receivables		X

When preparing the statement of financial position, the credit balance on the allowance for receivables account is deducted from the balance on the trade receivables account.

In subsequent years, adjustments may be needed to the amount of the allowance. The procedure to be followed then is as follows:

(1) Calculate the new allowance required.

(2) Compare it with the existing balance on the allowance account (i.e. the balance b/f from the previous accounting period).

(3) Determine increase or decrease required.

· If the allowance has **increased**:

		£	£
DEBIT	Irrecoverable debts expense	X	
CREDIT	Allowance for receivables		X

with the amount of the increase.

· If the allowance has **decreased**:

		£	£
DEBIT	Allowance for receivables	X	
CREDIT	Irrecoverable debts expense		X

with the amount of the decrease.

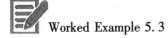 Worked Example 5. 3

Alexa has total trade receivables outstanding at 31 December 20×2 of £28,000. She expects that 1% of these balances may not be collected and wishes to make an appropriate allowance.

Before now, she has not made any allowance for receivables at all.

On 31 December 20×3 her trade receivables are £40,000. She believes an allowance of 5% needs to be made against trade receivables.

Requirement

What accounting entries should Alexa make on 31 December 20×2 and 31 December 20×3, and what figures for trade receivables will appear in the statement of financial position as at those dates?

Solution

At 31 December 20×2

Alexa will make the following entries:

		£	£
DEBIT	Irrecoverable debts expense (£28,000×1%)	280	
CREDIT	Allowance for receivables		280

In the statement of financial position trade receivables will be shown in Exhibit 5.4.

Exhibit 5.4

Alexa statement of financial position as at 31 December 20×2 (extract)	
	£
Current assets	
Trade receivables	28,000
Less allowance for receivables	(280)
	27,720
OR show trade receivables net of allowance for receivables	
Current assets	
Trade receivables (28,000 − 280)	27,720

At 31 December 20×3

Following the procedure described above, Alexa will calculate the new allowance required and compare it with the existing allowance to decide the movement of the receivables allowance.

	£
Allowance required now (5%× £40,000)	2,000
Existing allowance	(280)
Additional allowance required	1,720

So on calculating the irrecoverable debts expense, Alexa will make the following entries:

		£	£
DEBIT	Irrecoverable debts expense	1,720	
CREDIT	Allowance for receivables		1,720

The allowance account will by now appear as follows.

Allowance for receivables

20×2		£	20×2		£
31 Dec	Balance c/d	<u>280</u>	31 Dec	Irrecoverable debts	<u>280</u>
20×3			20×3		
31 Dec	Balance c/d	2,000	1 Jan	Balance b/d	280
		____	31 Dec	Irrecoverable debts	1,720
		<u>2,000</u>			<u>2,000</u>
			20×4		
			1 Jan	Balance b/d	2,000

In the statement of financial position trade receivables will be shown in Exhibit 5. 5.

Exhibit 5. 5

Alexa statement of financial position as at 31 December 20×3 (extract)	
	£
Current assets	
Trade receivables	40,000
Less allowance for receivables	(2,000)
	38,000
OR show trade receivables net of allowance for receivables	
Current assets	
Trade receivables (40,000 − 2,000)	38,000

4. Allowance for Receivables: Financial Statements

To recap, the accounting treatment for an allowance for receivables in financial statements is as follows.

· When an allowance is **first made,** the amount of this initial allowance is charged as an **expense** in the statement of profit or loss for the period in which the allowance is created.

· When an allowance already exists, but is subsequently increased in size, the amount of the **increase** in allowance is charged as an **expense** in the statement of profit or loss for the period in which the increased allowance is made.

· When an allowance already exists, but is subsequently reduced in size, the amount of the **decrease** in allowance is **credited back** to the statement of profit or loss for the period in which the reduction in allowance is made.

· Trade receivables in the statement of financial position are shown net of any receivables allowance.

Question

A business commences operations on 1 July 20×4, and in the twelve months to 30 June 20×5 makes credit sales of £300,000 and writes off irrecoverable debts of £6,000. Cash received from credit customers during the reporting period is £244,000. The above information is summarised in Exhibit 5.6.

Exhibit 5.6

Receivable information for the year ended 30 June 20×5	
	£
Credit sales during the reporting period	300,000
Add receivables at 1 July 20×4	0
Total debts owed to the business	300,000
Less cash received from credit customers	(244,000)
	56,000
Less irrecoverable debts written off	(6,000)
Trade receivables outstanding at 30 June 20×5	50,000

Of these outstanding trade receivables, an allowance of 10% is required to reflect the risk of non-payment of debts.

Requirement

What accounting entries should this business make on 30 June 20×5 and what figures for trade receivables will appear in the statement of financial position as at that date?

5.3 Example: Irrecoverable Debts Written off and Allowance for Receivables Combined

A business can have both irrecoverable debts written off and receivables allowance at the same time. For sole traders, it's better for them to present irrecoverable debts and the movement of receivables allowance separately in the statements of profit or loss. Later on, when you learn to prepare financial statements for listed companies in Chapter 12, you will see both irrecoverable debts written off and the changes in allowance for receivables are combined together as an administrative expense. In this chapter, let's consider the following example of sole trader Corin Flake.

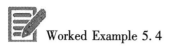 Worked Example 5. 4

Corin Flake owns and runs the Aerobic Health Foods Shop. He commenced trading on 1 January 20×1, selling health foods to customers, most of whom make use of a credit facility that Corin offers. (Customers are allowed to purchase up to £200 of goods on credit but must repay a certain proportion of their outstanding debt every month.)

This credit system initially gives rise to a large number of irrecoverable debts, but experience helps Corin to control them by the third year.

Corin Flake's results for his first three years of operations are shown in Exhibit 5. 7:

Exhibit 5. 7

Transactions of Corin Flake from 20×1 to 20×3	
Year to 31 December 20×1	£
Gross profit	27,000
Irrecoverable debts written off	8,000
Debts owed by customers as at 31 December 20×1	40,000
Allowance for receivables	1,000
Other expenses	20,000
Year to 31 December 20×2	
Gross profit	45,000
Irrecoverable debts written off	10,000
Debts owed by customers as at 31 December 20×2	50,000
Allowance for receivables	1,250
Other expenses	28,750
Year to 31 December 20×3	
Gross profit	60,000
Irrecoverable debts written off	7,000
Debts owed by customers as at 31 December 20×3	30,000
Allowance for receivables	800
Other expenses	32,850

Requirement

For each of these three reporting periods, calculate the net profit for the period, and state the value of trade receivables appearing in the statement of financial position as at 31 December.

Solution

Net profit calculation is shown in Exhibit 5. 8.

Exhibit 5. 8

Aerobic Health Foods Shop					
Statement of profit or loss for the years ended 31 December					
	20×1		20×2		20×3	
	£	£	£	£	£	£
Gross profit		27,000		45,000		60,000
Less Expenses						
Irrecoverable debts written off	8,000		10,000		7,000	
Increase/decrease in allowance for receivables *	1,000		250		(450)	
Other expenses	20,000		28,750		32,850	
		(29,000)		(39,000)		(39,400)
Net profit/(loss)		(2,000)		6,000		20,600

* We calculate the statement of profit or loss amount by:

· Preparing a T-account for the allowance for receivables.

· Carrying down the figure that we require at the end of each reporting period's statement of financial position.

· Treating the balancing figure in the reporting period as the charge or credit required in the statement of profit or loss for that reporting period.

Allowance for receivables

	£		£
31. 12. 20×1 Balance c/d	1,000	31. 12. 20×1 Irrecoverable debts	1,000
31. 12. 20×2 Balance c/d	1,250	1. 1. 20×2 Balance b/d	1,000
		31. 12. 20×2 Irrecoverable debts (bal. fig)	250
	1,250		1,250
31. 12. 20×3 Irrecoverable debts (bal. fig)	450	1. 1. 20×3 Balance b/d	1,250
31. 12. 20×3 Balance c/d	800		
	1,250		1,250
		1. 1. 20×4 Balance b/d	800

Trade receivables in statement of financial position is shown in Exhibit 5. 9.

Exhibit 5. 9

Trade receivables in the statement of financial position as at 31 December			
	20×1	20×2	20×3
Current assets	£	£	£
Trade receivables	40,000	50,000	30,000
Less allowance for receivables	(1,000)	(1,250)	(800)
	39,000	48,750	29,200

Summary

· Irrecoverable debts are specific debts owed to a business which it decides are never going to be paid. They are written off as an expense in the statement of profit or loss.

· Allowances for receivables are expected losses estimated based on trade receivables after irrecoverable debts have been written off.

· Trade receivables in the statement of financial position are shown net of any receivables allowance.

· When an allowance for receivables is first set up, the whole amount is debited to the statement of profit or loss.

· In subsequent years, only the movement on the receivables allowance is debited or credited to irrecoverable debts in the statement of profit or loss.

Exercise

5. 1 In which of the following situations does an irrecoverable debt arises? (   )

   A. A customer pays part of the account

   B. An invoice is in dispute

   C. The customer goes bankrupt

   D. A cheque received in settlement is dishonoured by the customer's bank

5. 2 Which of the following would a decrease in the allowance for receivables result in?
(   )

   A. An increase in liabilities

   B. A decrease in working capital

   C. An increase in net profit

   D. A decrease in net profit

5. 3 Irrecoverable debts are £5,000. Trade receivables at the year end are £120,000. If an allowance for receivables of 5% is required, what is the entry for irrecoverable debts and allowance for receivables in the statement of profit or loss? (   )

  A.£5,000

  B.£11,000

  C.£6,000

  D.£10,750

5. 4 An allowance for receivables of £4,000 is required at the end of a reporting period. The allowance for receivables brought forward from the previous period is £2,000. What change is required this reporting period? (   )

  A.Increase by £4,000

  B.Decrease by £4,000

  C.Increase by £2,000

  D.Decrease by £2,000

5. 5 On 1 January 20×5 Plodd had an allowance for receivables of £1,000. During 20×5 he wrote off debts of £600 and was paid £80 by the liquidator of a company whose debts had been written off completely in 20×4. At the end of 20×5 it was decided to adjust the allowance for receivables to £900.

What is the net expense for irrecoverable debts in the statement of profit or loss for 20×5? (   )

  A.£420

  B.£580

  C.£620

  D.£780

5. 6 Smith has receivables totalling £16,000 after writing off irrecoverable debts of £500, and he has an allowance for receivables brought forward of £2,000. He wishes to carry forward an allowance of £800.

What will be the effect on profit of adjusting the allowance? (   )

  A.£700 decrease

  B.£700 increase

  C.£1,200 decrease

  D.£1,200 increase

5. 7 At 31 December 20×9 Folland's receivables totalled £120,000. Folland wishes to have an allowance for receivables of £3,600, which is 25% higher than it was before. During the year irrecoverable debts of £3,200 were written off and irrecoverable debts (written off

three years previously) of £150 were recovered.

What is the net charge for irrecoverable debts for the 12-month reporting period ended 31 December 20×9? (   )

  A.£720

  B.£900

  C.£3,770

  D.£3,950

5.8 During the 12-month reporting period ended 31 December 20×8 Keele decreased its allowance for receivables by £600. An irrecoverable debt written off in the previous reporting period amounting to £300 was recovered in 20×8. If the profit for the reporting period after accounting for the above items is £5,000, what was it before accounting for them? (   )

  A.£4,100

  B.£4,700

  C.£5,300

  D.£5,900

5.9 At 30 September 20×4, Mathieson plc's allowance for receivables was £19,500. At 30 September 20×5 it was decided to write off irrecoverable debts totalling £6,000 and to decrease the allowance for the remaining receivables to £15,000.

The charge or credit to the statement of profit or loss in respect of irrecoverable debts for the year ended 30 September 20×5 is(   ).

  A.£1,500 credit

  B.£1,500 debit

  C.£21,000 debit

  D.£21,000 credit

5.10 At 30 June 20×1 Cameron plc has decided to write off two debts of £1,300 and £2,150 respectively and to make an allowance of £6,631 against the remaining trade receivables balance. The balance on this allowance at 1 July 20×0 was £8,540.

What is Cameron plc's net charge for irrecoverable debts expense for the year to 30 June 20×1? (   )

  A.£1,541

  B.£1,909

  C.£3,450

  D.£5,359

5.11 Enigma plc has reduced its allowance for receivables by £600. Indicate whether the following statements are true or false.

This will increase gross profit by £600. (　　)

    A.True

    B.False

This will increase net profit by £600. (　　)

    C.True

    D.False

5.12 Disaster plc's trial balance shows trade receivables of £50,000. However, no adjustment has been made for the following items.

1 £3,250 from J. Crisis & Sons who have gone into liquidation. The amount is considered irrecoverable.

2 An increase in the allowance for receivables of £2,000.

3 Cash received from P. Chaos of £2,500 which had previously been written off.

What is the revised trade receivables account balance after posting the above adjustments? (　　)

    A.£50,500

    B.£50,200

    C.£46,750

    D.£49,250

5.13 At 28 February 20×4, a company's allowance for receivables was £38,000. At 28 February 20×5 it was decided to write off £28,500 of receivables and to increase the allowance for the remaining receivables to £42,000.

The net irrecoverable debts expense in the statement of profit or loss for the year ended 28 February 20×5 is(　　).

    A.£42,000

    B.£28,500

    C.£70,500

    D.£32,500

5.14 During 20×5 Bow plc received £500 from a customer in respect of a balance that had previously been written off, and reduced its allowance for receivables to £100. The allowance brought down as at 1 January 20×5 was £1,000. At the year end the dishonour of a cheque received for £280 needs to be accounted for, and the debt related to it needs to be written off.

What is the irrecoverable debts debit or credit in the statement of profit or loss for the year ended 31 December 20×5? (　　)

    A.£880 debit

    B.£780 debit

C.£1,120 credit

D.£1,300 credit

5. 15 At 1 July 20×2 the receivables allowance of Quaint plc was £18,000. During the year ended 30 June 20×3 debts totaling £14,600 were written off. It was decided that the receivables allowance should be £16,000 as at 30 June 20×3.

What amount should appear in Quaint plc's statement of profit or loss for irrecoverable debts expense for the year ended 30 June 20×3? (   )

A.£12,600

B.£14,600

C.£16,600

D.£30,600

5. 16 If Poppy plc reduces its allowance for receivables by £300, which of the following statements is correct? (   )

A.Current assets decrease by £300

B.Current liabilities decrease by £300

C.Gross profit increases by £300

D.Net profit increases by £300

5. 17 Mario's trial balance includes the following items: non-current assets £50,000, inventory £15,000, payables £10,000, receivables £5,000, bank £110,000, allowance for receivables £1,000. What is the figure for current assets? (   )

A.£180,000

B.£170,000

C.£129,000

D.£134,000

5. 18 At 1 October 20×5 a business had total outstanding debts of £8,600. During the year to 30 September 20×6 the following transaction took place.

(a) Credit sales amounted to £44,000.

(b) Payments from various customers (accounts receivable) amounted to £49,000.

(c) Two debts, for £180 and £420, were declared irrecoverable and the customers are no longer purchasing goods from the company. These are to be written off.

Requirement

Prepare the trade receivables ledger account and the irrecoverable debts expense account for the year.

5. 19 Fatima's receivables at 31 May 20×7 were £723,800. The balance on the allowance

for receivables account at 1 June 20×6 was £15,250. Fatima has decided to change the allowance for receivables to 1.5% of receivables at 31 May 20×7.

On 14 May 20×7 Fatima received £540 in final settlement of an amount written off during the year ended 31 May 20×6.

Requirement

What total amount should be recognised for receivables in the statement of profit or loss for the year ended 31 May 20×7?

5.20* Shown below are the outstanding trade receivables and the probability of non-payment of those trade receivables at the end of each reporting period.

	£	£
	Balance on Trade receivables account	Probability of nonpayment
Y/e 28.2.20×6	15,200	2%
Y/e 28.2.20×7	17,100	2%
Y/e 28.2.20×8	21,400	1%

Requirement

For each of the three reporting periods:

(1) Calculate the amount of the allowance for receivables.

(2) Calculate the charge or credit required to the statement of profit or loss.

(3) Show how trade receivables should be presented in the statement of financial position.

Reference

1. ACCA FA Financial Accounting/FIA FFA Interactive Text 2020, BPP Learning Media.

2. ACCA FA Financial Accounting/FIA FFA Practice & Revision Kit 2020, BPP Learning Media.

3. Accounting (Study Manual 2020), The Institute of Chartered Accountants in England and Wales.

4. Accounting (Question Bank 2020), The Institute of Chartered Accountants in England and Wales.

5. Alan Sangster, Frank Wood's Business Accounting Volume 1(2019), Pearson.

Chapter 6

Depreciation: Calculations and Double Entry

---- ■Learning Objectives ---

· Explain why depreciation is provided.

· Define what is depreciation.

· Explain the causes of depreciation.

· Calculate depreciation using both the straight line and the reducing balance methods.

· Explain how to choose the method of depreciation.

· Specify the effects of changing residual values, useful lives and changing depreciation methods on amounts in the statement of profit or loss and statement of financial position.

· Explain ledger entries for depreciation.

6.1　What Is Depreciation?

1. Objective of Depreciation

Tangible non-current assets (i.e. long-term assets which can be touched, such as machinery, motor vehicles, fixtures and even buildings) do not last for ever. The need to depreciate tangible non-current assets arises from the accrual principle. If money is spent in purchasing an asset, then this amount must at some time be charged against profits. If the asset contributes to the generation of income over a number of reporting periods it would be inappropriate to charge any single period (e.g., the period in which the asset was acquired) with the whole of the expenditure. Therefore, some method must be found of spreading the cost of the asset over its useful life.

2. Definitions

Before you start to learn how to calculate and record deprecations, you shall understand the following key definitions related to depreciation.

Depreciation is part of the original cost of a non-current asset consumed during its period of use by the business. We can define **depreciation** as the systematic allocation of the cost of an asset, less its residual value, over its useful life. To calculate the depreciation charge for a reporting period, asset cost, useful life and residual value are all relevant.

Useful life of an asset is either the period over which a non-current asset is expected to be used by the enterprise; or the number of production or similar units expected to be obtained from the asset by the enterprise. The only tangible asset that is deemed to have an unlimited useful life is freehold land. All other tangible assets have a finite useful life and will be depreciated over that useful life.

Residual value of an asset is the net amount which the entity expects to obtain for an asset at the end of its useful life after deducting the expected costs of disposal. The cost of a non-current asset less its residual value represents the total amount to be depreciated (its **depreciable amount**) over its useful life. In this textbook, you can always assume the residual value is zero unless told otherwise.

The amount of depreciation deducted from the cost of a non-current asset to arrive at its **carrying amount** will build up (or 'accumulate') over time, as more depreciation is charged in each successive reporting period. This is called **accumulated depreciation.**

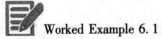 Worked Example 6.1

If a non-current asset costing £40,000 has a useful life of four years and an estimated residual value of nil, it might be depreciated by £10,000 per annum.

	Depreciation charge for the year	Accumulated depreciation at end of year	Cost of the asset	Carrying amount at end of year
	(A)	(B)	(C)	(C-B)
	£	£	£	£
At beginning of its life	–	–	40,000	40,000
Year 1	10,000	10,000	40,000	30,000
Year 2	10,000	20,000	40,000	20,000
Year 3	10,000	30,000	40,000	10,000
Year 4	10,000	40,000	40,000	0
	40,000			

At the end of Year 4, the full £40,000 of depreciation charges have been made over the four years. The carrying amount of the non-current asset is now nil.

6.2   Causes of Depreciation

Physical deterioration, economic factors, time and depletion all give rise to a reduction in the value of a tangible non-current asset. Let's look at these in more detail.

1. Physical Deterioration

Wear and tear —When a motor vehicle or machinery or fixtures and fittings are used they eventually wear out. Some last many years, others last only a few years. This is also true of buildings, although some may last for a long time.

Erosion, rust, rot and decay —Land may be eroded or wasted away by the action of wind, rain, sun or the other elements of nature. Similarly, the metals in motor vehicles or machinery will rust away. Wood will rot eventually. Decay is a process which will be present due to the elements of nature and a lack of proper attention.

2. Economic Factors

These may be said to be the reasons for an asset being put out of use even though it is in good physical condition. The two main factors are usually obsolescence and inadequacy.

Obsolescence. This is the process of becoming out of date. For instance, over the years there has been great progress in the development of synthesisers and electronic devices used by leading commercial musicians. The old equipment will therefore have become obsolete, and much of it will have been taken out of use by such musicians.

This does not mean that the equipment is worn out. Other people may well buy the old equipment and use it, possibly because they cannot afford to buy new up-to-date equipment.

Inadequacy. This arises when an asset is no longer used because of the growth and changes in the size of the business. For instance, a small ferryboat that is operated by a business at a coastal resort will become entirely inadequate when the resort becomes more popular. Then it will be found that it would be more efficient and economical to operate a large ferryboat, and so the smaller boat will be put out of use by the business.

In this case also it does not mean that the ferryboat is no longer in good working order, nor that it is obsolete. It may be sold to a business at a smaller resort.

3. Time

Obviously, time is needed for wear and tear, erosion, etc., and for obsolescence and inadequacy to take place. However, there are non-current assets to which the time factor is connected in a different way. These are assets which have a legal life fixed in terms of years.

For instance, you may agree to rent some buildings for 10 years. This is normally called a lease. When the years have passed, the lease is worth nothing to you, as it has finished. Whatever you paid for the lease is now of no value.

A similar case arises when you buy a patent so that only you are able to produce something. When the patent's time has finished it then has no value. The usual length of life of a patent is between 10 to 20 years.

Instead of using the term depreciation, the term amortisation is often used for these assets.

4. Depletion

Other assets are of wasting character, perhaps due to the extraction of raw materials from them. These materials are then either used by the business to make something else, or are sold in their raw state to other businesses. Natural resources such as mines, quarries and oil wells come under this heading.The consumption of an asset of a wasting character needs to be provided.

6. 3　Calculating Depreciation

In a computerised accounting system, depreciation can be calculated automatically provided standing data regarding the useful life and residual value of the asset is entered in the system. The accountant needs to understand how depreciation is calculated and accounted for by the system.

1. Methods of Depreciation

There are several different methods of depreciation.The two main methods in use for calculating deprecation charges are:
 · Straight line method.
 · Reducing balance method.

Although other methods may be used in certain cases, most accountants think that the straight line method is the one that is generally most suitable.

(1) Straight Line Method

Straight line method is the most commonly used method of all. The total depreciable amount (cost less residual value) is charged in equal amounts to each reporting period over the useful life of the asset. In this way, the carrying amount of the non-current asset declines at a steady rate, or in a 'straight line' over time.

The **annual** depreciation charge is:

$$\frac{\text{Cost of asset} - \text{residual value}}{\text{Useful life of the asset in years}}$$

The **monthly** depreciation charge is:

$$\frac{\text{Cost of asset} - \text{residual value}}{\text{Useful life in years} \times 12}$$

For instance, if a van was bought for £22,000 and we thought we would keep it for four years and then sell it for £2,000 the depreciation to be charged each year would be:

$$\frac{\text{Cost } (£22,000) - \text{Estimated disposal value } (£2,000)}{\text{Number of expected years of use } (4)} = \frac{£20,000}{4}$$

$$= £5,000 \text{ depreciation each year for four years.}$$

On the other hand, if we thought that after four years the van would have no disposal value, the charge for depreciation would be:

$$\frac{\text{Cost } (£22,000)}{\text{Number of expected years of use } (4)} = \frac{£22,000}{4}$$

$$= £5,500 \text{ depreciation each year for four years.}$$

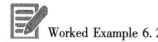 Worked Example 6.2

(1) A non-current asset costing £24,000 with a useful life of 10 years and no residual value would be depreciated at the rate of:

$$\frac{£24,000}{10 \times 12} = £200 \text{ per month, or } \frac{£24,000}{10} = £2,400 \text{ per annum}$$

(2) A non-current asset costing £60,000 has a useful life of five years and a residual value of £6,000. The monthly/yearly depreciation charge using the straight line method is:

$$\frac{£(60,000 - 6,000)}{5 \times 12} = £900 \text{ per month, or } £10,800 \text{ per annum}$$

The carrying amount of the non-current asset would be as follows:

	After 1 year	After 2 years	After 3 years	After 4 years	After 5 years
	£	£	£	£	£
Cost of the asset	60,000	60,000	60,000	60,000	60,000
Accumulated depreciation	(10,800)	(21,600)	(32,400)	(43,200)	(54,000)
Carrying amount	49,200	38,400	27,600	16,800	6,000 *

* i.e., its estimated residual value.

(2) Reducing Balance Method

Reducing balance depreciation calculates the annual depreciation charge as a fixed percentage of the brought forward carrying amount of the asset.

In this method, a fixed percentage for depreciation is deducted from the cost in the first year. In the second and later years the same percentage is taken of the reduced balance (i.e.

cost less depreciation already charged). This method is also known as the 'diminishing balance method' or 'the diminishing debit balance method'.

With reducing balance method, the formula used to find the percentage to apply is:

$$r = 1 - \sqrt[n]{s/c}$$

where n = the number of years

s = the net residual value (this must be a significant amount or the answers will be absurd, since the depreciation rate would amount to nearly one)

c = the cost of the asset

r = the rate of depreciation to be applied

However, when calculating reducing balance depreciation you will NOT be concerned with the asset's residual value nor how to calculate the percentage: just the carrying amount and the reducing balance percentage given to you. Let's see an example.

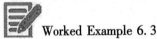 Worked Example 6. 3

A business purchases a non-current asset at a cost of £10,000 on 1 January 20×1, which it plans to keep for three years to 31 December 20×3. The business wishes to use the reducing balance method to depreciate the asset, and calculates that the rate of depreciation should be 40% of the reducing balance (carrying amount) of the asset.

The depreciation charge per annum and the carrying amount of the asset as at the end of each reporting period will be as described in Exhibit 6.1:

Exhibit 6. 1

Depreciation calculation from 20×1 to 20×3		
	£	Accumulated depreciation £
Asset at cost	10,000	
Depreciation in 20×1 (40%)	(4,000)	4,000
Carrying amount at end of 20×1	6,000	
Depreciation in 20×2 (40% of 6,000)	(2,400)	6,400(4,000 + 2,400)
Carrying amount at end of 20×2	3,600	
Depreciation in 20×3 (40% × 3,600)	(1,440)	7,840(6,400 + 1,440)
Carrying amount at end of 20×3	2,160	

The annual charge for reducing balance depreciation is higher in the earlier reporting periods of the asset's life, and lower in the later reporting periods (£4,000, £2,400 and £1,440 respectively).

In this example, 40% is calculated as ($1 - \sqrt[3]{2,160/10,000}$). Therefore, the estimated residual value of £2,160 was already taken into account when calculating the percentage. Just note that you will be given the percentage rate to apply in your exercise, and you will not have to calculate it.

2. Choice of Method

The purpose of depreciation is to spread the total cost of a non-current asset over the periods in which it is to be used. The method chosen should be that which allocates cost to each period in accordance with the proportion of the overall economic benefit from using the non-current asset that was expended during that period.

If, therefore, the main value is to be obtained from the asset in its earliest years, it may be appropriate to use the reducing balance method, which charges more in the early years. If, on the other hand, the benefits are to be gained evenly over the years, then the straight line method would be more appropriate.The advocates of the reducing balance method usually argue that it helps to even out the total amount charged as expenses for the use of the asset each year. Depreciation is not the only cost charged. There are also the running costs. The repairs and maintenance element of running costs usually increases with age. Therefore, in order to equate total usage costs for each year of use, the depreciation charge should fall over time, while the repairs and maintenance element increases.

The following example gives a comparison of the calculations using the two methods.

 Worked Example 6. 4

A business has just bought a machine for £8,000. It will be kept in use for four years, when it will be disposed of for an estimated amount of £500. The accountant has asked you to prepare a comparison of the amounts charged as depreciation using both methods.

For the straight line method, a figure of $(£8,000-£500) \div 4 = £7,500 \div 4 = £1,875$ per annum is to be used. For the reducing balance method, a percentage figure of 50 per cent will be used. Exhibit 6. 2 shows the calculation.

Exhibit 6. 2

Depreciation calculation using two methods			
Method 1 Straight Line		Method 2 Reducing Balance	
	£		£
Cost	8,000		8,000
Depreciation: Year 1	(1,875)	(50% of £8,000)	(4,000)
	6,125		4,000
Depreciation: Year 2	(1,875)	(50% of £4,000)	(2,000)

Exhibit 6. 2(continued)

	4,250		2,000
Depreciation: Year 3	(1,875)	(50% of £2,000)	(1,000)
	2,375		1,000
Depreciation: Year 4	(1,875)	(50% of £1,000)	(500)
Disposal value	500		500

This example illustrates the fact that using the reducing balance method has a much higher charge for depreciation in the early years, and lower charges in the later years.

3. Reviewing and Changing the Depreciation Method

The depreciation method used should be reviewed annually for appropriateness. If there are any changes in the expected pattern of use of the asset (and hence economic benefit), then the method used should be changed. The remaining carrying amount is depreciated under the new method, i.e., only current and future periods are affected. When the basis of depreciation is changed, the effect on current and future periods should be quantified and disclosed in the financial statements, and the reason for the change should be stated.

 Worked Example 6. 5

Jakob Co purchased an asset for £100,000 on 1 January 20×1. It had an estimated useful life of five years and it was depreciated using the reducing balance method at a rate of 40%. On 1 January 20×3 it was decided to change the depreciation method to straight line. There was no change to the useful life, and no residual value is anticipated.

Requirement

Show the depreciation charge for each year (to 31 December) of the asset's life.

Solution

Please refer to Exhibit 6. 3 for the depreciation calculation.

Exhibit 6. 3

Changing depreciation method			
Year		Depreciation charge	Accumulated depreciation
		£	£
20×1	£100,000×40%	40,000	40,000
20×2	£60,000×40%	24,000	64,000

Exhibit 6. 3(continued)

20×3		12,000	76,000
20×4	$\left.\begin{array}{l} \dfrac{£\,100,000-£\,64,000}{3 \text{ remaining years}} \end{array}\right\}$	12,000	88,000
20×5		12,000	100,000

4. Reviewing and Changing Useful Life or Residual Value

The depreciation charge on a non-current asset depends not only on the cost (or value) of the asset and its estimated residual value but also on its estimated useful life. The residual value and estimated useful life of a non-current asset should be reviewed and changed if they are no longer appropriate.

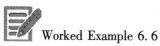 Worked Example 6. 6

A business purchased a non-current asset costing £ 12 ,000 with an estimated useful life of four years and no residual value. It was depreciated using the straight line method. However, after two years the business decides that the useful life of the asset has been underestimated, and it still has five more years in use to come, making its total useful life seven years.

Requirement

What's the annual depreciation charge for the final five years?

Solution

For the first two years, the asset would make an annual depreciation of £ 12 ,000/4 years = £ 3 ,000. The carrying amount of the asset after two years is £ (12 ,000−6 ,000) = £ 6 ,000. If the remaining useful life of the asset is now revised to five more years, the remaining amount to be depreciated (£ 6 ,000) is spread over the remaining useful life, giving an annual depreciation charge for the final five years of :

$$\frac{\text{Carrying amount at time of life readjustment} - \text{Estimated residual value}}{\text{New estimated of remaining useful life}} = \frac{£\,6,000}{5} = £\,1,200$$

Similar adjustments are made when there is a change in the expected residual value of the asset. For example, assume that the residual value was changed to £ 500 at the same time as the remaining useful life was revised. The new depreciation would then be £ (6 ,000 − 500)/5 = £ 1 ,100 per year.

6.4　Accounting for Depreciation

There are two basic aspects of accounting for depreciation to remember.

· A **depreciation charge** is made in the statement of profit or loss in each reporting period for every depreciable non-current asset. Nearly all non-current assets are depreciable, the most important exception being freehold land.

· The total **accumulated depreciation** on a non-current asset builds up as the asset gets older. The total accumulated depreciation is always getting larger, until the non-current asset is fully depreciated.

A business will set up an accumulated depreciation account for each separate category of non-current asset, for example plant and machinery, land and buildings, fixtures and fittings, motor vehicles. In a computerised system, the ledger code allocated to the accumulated depreciation will immediately follow the cost of the asset in order that the cost and accumulated depreciation for the same asset are presented consecutively when the initial trial balance is extracted.

The depreciation charge for an accounting period is a charge against profit. It is accounted for as follows.

		£	£
DEBIT	Depreciation expense (statement of profit or loss)	X	
CREDIT	Accumulated depreciation account (statement of financial position)		X

Please note:

· The balance on the accumulated depreciation account is the total accumulated depreciation. This is always a credit balance brought forward in the ledger account.

· The non-current asset cost accounts are unaffected by depreciation.

· In the statement of financial position, the balance on the accumulated depreciation account is set against the non-current asset cost accounts to derive the carrying amount of the non-current assets.

 **Worked Example 6.7**

Brian Box set up his own computer software business on 1 March 20×6. He purchased a computer system on credit from a manufacturer for £16,000. The system has a useful life of three years and a residual value of £2,500. Using the straight line method of depreciation, the non-current asset account, accumulated depreciation account and statement of profit or loss (extract) and statement of financial position (extract) would be as follows, for each of the next three reporting periods ending 28 February 20×7, 20×8 and 20×9.

Non-current asset: Computer equipment cost

		£			£
1 March 20×6	Trade payables	16,000	28 February 20×7	Balance c/d	16,000
1 March 20×7	Balance b/d	16,000	28 February 20×8	Balance c/d	16,000
1 March 20×8	Balance b/d	16,000	28 February 20×9	Balance c/d	16,000
1 March 20×9	Balance b/d	16,000			

The annual depreciation charge is $\dfrac{£\ (16,000 - 2,500)}{3\ \text{years}} = £4,500\ \text{pa}$

Accumulated depreciation

		£			£
28 February 20×7	Balance c/d	4,500	28 February 20×7	Depreciation expense	4,500
28 February 20×8	Balance c/d	9,000	1 March 20×7	Balance b/d	4,500
			28 February 20×8	Depreciation expense	4,500
		9,000			9,000
28 February 20×9	Balance c/d	13,500	1 March 20×8	Balance b/d	9,000
			28 February 20×9	Depreciation expense	4,500
		13,500			13,500
			1 March 20×9	Balance b/d	13,500

At the end of three reporting periods, the asset is fully depreciated down to its residual value (£16,000 − £13,500 = £2,500). If it continues to be used by Brian Box, it will not be depreciated any further (unless its estimated residual value is reduced).

The extract of statement of profit or loss is shown in Exhibit 6.4.

Exhibit 6.4

Statement of profit or loss (extract)	
Year ending:	£
28 Feb 20×7 Depreciation expense	4,500
28 Feb 20×8 Depreciation expense	4,500
28 Feb 20×9 Depreciation expense	4,500

The extract of statement of financial position is shown in Exhibit 6. 5.

Exhibit 6. 5

Statement of financial position (extract) as at 28 February			
	20×7	20×8	20×9
	£	£	£
Computer equipment at cost	16,000	16,000	16,000
Less accumulated depreciation	(4,500)	(9,000)	(13,500)
Carrying amount	11,500	7,000	2,500

In theory, the non-current asset is now at the end of its useful life. However, until it is sold off or scrapped, the asset will still appear in the statement of financial position at cost (less accumulated depreciation) and it should remain in the ledger accounts for computer equipment until disposal.

Summary

· Depreciation is charged on non-current assets in use during an accounting period.

· Non-current assets are defined as those assets of material value that are intended to be used in the business over a period of time and have not been bought with the intention of resale.

· The main causes of depreciation are physical deterioration, economic factors, the time factor and depletion.

· The straight line method is where an equal amount of depreciation is charged each year.

· The reducing balance method is where a fixed percentage for depreciation is taken from the cost of the asset in the first year in the second and later years, the same percentage is taken from the reduced balance (i.e. cost less depreciation already charged).

· Depreciation is an expense of the business and as such is charged to the profit and loss account.

· Accounting for depreciation is by debiting depreciation expense (statement of profit or loss), crediting accumulated depreciation account (statement of financial position).

Exercise

6. 1 Which one of the following statements correctly defines non-current assets? (   )

    A. Assets that are held for use in the production of goods or services and are expected to be used during more than one accounting period

    B. Assets which are intended to be used by the business on a continuing basis, including both tangible and intangible assets that do not meet the IASB definition of a current asset

C.Non-monetary assets without physical substance that are controlled by the entity and from which future benefits are expected to flow

D.Assets in the form of materials or supplies to be consumed in the production process

6. 2 Materials purchased and used by Pola & Co for repairs to office buildings have been included in the draft financial statements as purchases.

The necessary amendment will( ).

A.Increase gross profit with no effect on net profit

B.Increase gross profit and reduce net profit

C.Have no effect on either gross profit or net profit

D.Reduce gross profit and increase net profit

6. 3 Why is depreciation charged on non-current assets? ( )

A.To ensure that sufficient funds are available to replace the assets

B.To show the assets at replacement cost on the statement of financial position

C.To spread the cost of the assets over their useful lives

D.To show the fall in market value of the assets in the statement of profit or loss

6. 4 ABC, whose reporting period is the 12 months ended 31 December, has charged depreciation monthly at the rate of 10% per annum on cost on an item of plant bought on 1 September 20×0 costing £15,000. The depreciation method was changed from straight line to 10% reducing balance at the end of 20×3.

The depreciation charge on this asset for 20×5 was( ).

A.£1,500

B.£945

C.£900

D.£889

6. 5 A business buys a machine on 1 January 20×1 for £10,000 and depreciates it at 10% per annum straight line. At the end of 20×2 the machine's remaining useful life is reassessed at six years remaining and it is now believed that the machine has a residual value of £500.

What is the depreciation charge for the third year of the machine's use? ( )

A.£950

B.£1,250

C.£1,267

D.£1,350

6. 6 Vernon plc purchased some new equipment on 1 April 20×1 for £6,000. The scrap value of the new equipment in five years' time has been assessed as £300. Vernon charges de-

preciation monthly on the straight-line basis.

What is the journal entry to record the depreciation charge for the equipment in Vernon plc's reporting period of 12 months to 30 September 20×1? (   )

A.Debit Depreciation expense £570, Credit Accumulated depreciation £570

B.Debit Accumulated depreciation £570, Credit Depreciation expense £570

C.Debit Depreciation expense £600, Credit Accumulated depreciation £600

D.Debit Accumulated depreciation £600, Credit Depreciation expense £600

6.7 Which one of the following assets may be classified as a non-current asset in the accounts of a business? (   )

A.A tax refund due next year

B.A motor vehicle held for resale

C.A computer used in the office

D.Cleaning products used to clean the office floors

6.8 Beta purchased some plant and equipment on 1 July 20×1 for £40,000. The scrap value of the plant at the end of its 10-year useful life is £4,000. Beta plc's policy is to charge depreciation monthly on the straight-line basis.

The journal entry to record the depreciation charge on the plant in Beta's statement of profit or loss for the reporting period of 12 months ending 30 September 20×1 should be: (   )

A.Debit Depreciation expense £900; Credit Accumulated depreciation £900

B.Debit Accumulated depreciation £900; Credit Depreciation expense £900

C.Debit Depreciation expense £1,000; Credit Accumulated depreciation £1,000

D.Debit Accumulated depreciation £1,000; Credit Depreciation expense £1,000

6.9 Ben plc has a draft net profit for the year ended 31 December 20×8 of £56,780 before accounting for the depreciation on a new machine. Ben plc purchased the machine for £120,000 on 1 October 20×8. The useful life is four years with a residual value of £4,000. Ben plc uses the straight-line method for depreciation and charges depreciation on a monthly basis.

The net profit after charging depreciation on the machine for the year ended 31 December 20×8 is: (   )

A.£51,947

B.£49,530

C.£49,280

D.£27,780

6.10 Sam plc's statement of profit or loss for the year ended 31 December 20×4 showed a profit for the year of £83,600. It was later found that £18,000 paid for the purchase of a van on 1 January 20×4 had been debited to the motor expenses account. It is the company's policy to depreciate vans at 25% per year on the straight-line basis.

What is the profit for the year after adjusting for this error? (   )

    A.£106,100

    B.£70,100

    C.£97,100

    D.£101,600

6. 11 On 1 January 20×4 Joffa plc purchased a new machine at a cost of £96,720. Delivery costs were £3,660. At that time Joffa plc planned to replace the machine in five years, when it would have no value, and to depreciate the machine on a straight-line basis.

Joffa plc decides on 1 January 20×6 that the machine only has one remaining year of useful life. There is no change to the residual value at the end of its life.

How much depreciation will be charged in respect of this machine inJoffa plc's statement of profit or loss for the year ended 31 December 20×6? (   )

    A.£58,032

    B.£60,228

    C.£65,898

    D.£33,460

6. 12 On 1 June 20×3 Spam plc purchased some plant at a price of £43,000. It cost £1,500 to transport the plant to Spam plc's premises and set it up. The plant had a useful life of eight years and a residual value of £3,500. On 1 June 20×5 the directors of Spam plc decided to change the depreciation method to reducing balance, at 40%.

What is the carrying amount of Spam plc's machine in its statement of financial position at 31 May 20×6? (   )

    A.£20,025

    B.£20,280

    C.£20,550

    D.£20,955

6. 13 Yvette purchased some plant on 1 January 20×0 for £38,000. The payment for the plant was correctly entered in the cash at bank account but was incorrectly entered on the debit side of the plant repairs account.

Yvette charges depreciation monthly on the straight-line basis over five years and assumes no scrap value at the end of the life of the asset.

How will Yvette's profit for the year ended 31 March 20×0 be affected by the error? (   )

A. Understated by £30,400

B. Understated by £36,100

C. Understated by £38,000

D. Overstated by £1,900

6.14 A lorry bought for a business cost £17,000. It is expected to last for 5 years and then be sold for scrap for £2,000.

Requirement

Work out the depreciation to be charged each year under:

(1) The straight line method.

(2) The reducing balance method (using a rate of 35%).

6.15 Brian Box prospers in his computer software business, and before long he purchases two cars for business use. Relevant data are as follows:

	Date of purchase	Cost	Estimated life	Estimated residual value
A car	1 June 20×6	£20,000	3 years	£2,000
B car	1 June 20×7	£15,500	3 years	£2,000

The straight line method of depreciation is to be used.

Requirement

(1) Prepare the vehicles account and vehicles accumulated depreciation account for the reporting periods to 28 February 20×7 and 20×8.

(2) Calculate the carrying amount of the vehicles as at 28 February 20×8.

6.16* J. Chen runs a small joinery business and purchases a new machine for £6,000. It has an estimated life of four years and a scrap value of £1,000. Chen is not sure whether to use the straight line or reducing (diminishing) method of depreciation for the purpose of calculating depreciation on the machine.

You are required to calculate the depreciation on the machine using both methods, showing clearly the balance remaining in the machine account at the end of the four years for each method. Assume that 40% per annum is to be used for the reducing (diminishing) balance method.

6.17* A dumper is bought for £18,000. It will last for three years and will then be sold back to the supplier for £3,000. Show the depreciation calculations for each year using:

(1) Reducing (diminishing) balance method with a rate of 40%.

(2) Straight line method.

6.18* A company starts in business on 1 January 20×4, the financial year end being 31 December.

You are to show:

(1) The equipment account.

(2) The accumulated depreciation account.

(3) The statement of financial position extracts for each of the years 20×4, 20×5, 20×6, 20×7.

The equipment bought was:

20×4 1 January 1 machine costing £800

20×5 1 July 2 machines costing £1,200 each

　　　 1 October 1 machine costing £600

20×7 1 April 1 machine costing £1,400

Depreciation is over 10 years, using the straight line method, machines being depreciated for the proportion of the year that they are owned.

Reference

1. Alan Sangster, Frank Wood's Business Accounting Volume 1(2019), Pearson.

2. Accounting (Study Manual 2020), The Institute of Chartered Accountants in England and Wales.

3. Accounting (Question Bank 2020), The Institute of Chartered Accountants in England and Wales.

4. ACCA FA Financial Accounting/FIA FFA Interactive Text 2020, BPP Learning Media.

5. ACCA FA Financial Accounting/FIA FFA Practice & Revision Kit 2020, BPP Learning Media.

Chapter 7

Accruals and Prepayments

------ ■Learning Objectives ------------------------------

· Understand how accrual principle applies to accruals and prepayments.

· Identify and calculate the adjustments needed for accruals and prepayments in preparing financial statements.

· Illustrate the process of adjusting for accruals and prepayments in preparing financial statements.

· Prepare the journal entries and ledger entries for the creation of an accrual or prepayment.

· Understand and identify the impact on profit and net assets of accruals and prepayments.

7.1 Introduction

The statements of profit or loss you have looked at so far have taken the sales for a period and deducted all the expenses for that period, the result being a net profit or a net loss. Up to this part of the book it has always been assumed that the expenses incurred belong to the period of the statement of profit or loss when they took place.For example, if the statement of profit or loss for the year ending 31 December 20×2 was being prepared, then the rent paid as shown in the trial balance was all treated as relating to 20×2. There was no rent owing at the beginning of 20×2 nor any owing at the end of 20×2, nor had any rent been paid in advance relating to 20×3. This was done to make your first encounter with financial statements as straightforward as possible.

However, expenses may not actually be paid for during the period to which they relate.

For example, a business might pay £1,000 during the year and owe £200 rent at the end of the year, or pay £1,300 during the year, including £100 in advance for the next year. The accruals principles requires that expenses incurred are matched against revenue, regardless of whether they have yet been paid for. Therefore, in this example, a profit and loss account for the 12 months needs 12 months' rent as an expense, i.e. £1,200. This means that in either of two cases the double entry accounts will have to be adjusted.

You'll learn about adjustments needed in the following sections. In all the examples in this chapter, the trading and profit and loss accounts are for the period of year ended 31 December.

7.2 Accrued Expenses and Prepaid Expenses

1. Accrued Expenses

Accrued expenses or **accruals** are expenses which are charged against the profit for a particular period, even though they have not yet been paid for. They are shown in the statement of financial position as a **liability**.

Assume that rent of £1,000 per year is payable at the end of every three months. The rent was paid on time in March, but this is not always the case and please refer to Exhibit 7.1 for rest of the payments.

Exhibit 7.1

Rental payment records		
Amount	Rent due	Rent paid
£250	31 March 20×1	31 March 20×1
£250	30 June 20×1	2 July 20×1
£250	30 September 20×1	4 October 20×1
£250	31 December 20×1	5 January 20×2

The rent account is now shown:

Rent account

20×1		£	
Mar 31	Cash	250	
Jul 2	Cash	250	
Oct 4	Cash	250	

The rent for the last quarter was paid on 5 January 20×2 and so will appear in the books of the year 20×2 as the result of a double entry made on that date.

The expense for 20×1 is obviously £1,000 since that is the year's rent and is the amount needed to be transferred to the profit and loss account at the end of the period. But if £1,000 was put on the credit side of the rent account (the debit being in the profit and loss account), the account would not balance. We would have £1,000 on the credit side of the account and only £750 on the debit side.

To make the account balance, the £250 rent owing for 20×1 but paid in 20×2 must be carried down to 20×2 as a credit balance since it is a liability on 31 December 20×1. Instead of rent owing, it could be called rent accrued (or just simply an accrual). The completed account can now be shown, thus:

Rent account

20×1		£	20×1		£
Mar 31	Cash	250	Dec 31	Profit and loss	1,000
Jul 2	Cash	250			
Oct 4	Cash	250			
Dec 31	Accrued c/d	250			—
		1,000			1,000
			20×2		
			Jan 1	Accrued b/d	250
				(Accrual reversed)	

The balance c/d has been described as 'accrued c/d', rather than as a balance. This is to explain what the balance is for: it is for an accrued expense. As with this accrued expense, the double entry will be reversed in the following period by the 'accrued b/d', which will be paid soon.

Alternatively, you can open an accrual account and post any balances on expense account at the period end to the accrual account.

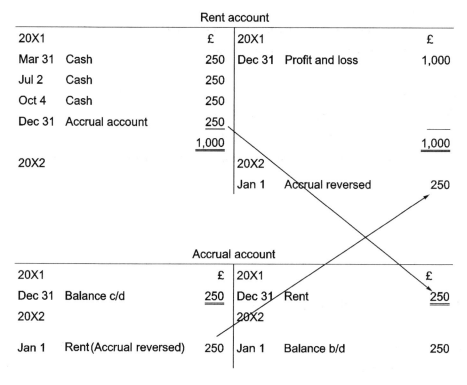

Rent account

20X1		£	20X1		£
Mar 31	Cash	250	Dec 31	Profit and loss	1,000
Jul 2	Cash	250			
Oct 4	Cash	250			
Dec 31	Accrual account	250			
		1,000			1,000
20X2			20X2		
			Jan 1	Accrual reversed	250

Accrual account

20X1		£	20X1		£
Dec 31	Balance c/d	250	Dec 31	Rent	250
20X2			20X2		
Jan 1	Rent(Accrual reversed)	250	Jan 1	Balance b/d	250

Under this method, there would be no balance in the expense account after the double entry to the accrual account. Instead, there will be a balance on accrual account which is then entered in the statement of financial position in exactly the same way as you did under the other method. At the start of the next period, you reverse the accrual by transferring the opening balance in the accrual account back to the expense account with the avoidance of charging the same expense twice.

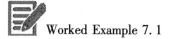 Worked Example 7. 1

Cleverley started in business as a paper plate and cup manufacturer on 1 January 20×2, preparing financial statements to 31 December 20×2. He is not registered for VAT. Electricity bills received in respect of charges for the previous quarter were as shown in Exhibit 7. 2:

Exhibit 7. 2

Electricity bills for year 20×2 & 20×3		
	20×2	20×3
	£	£
31 January	–	491. 52
30 April	279. 47	400. 93
31 July	663. 80	700. 94
31 October	117. 28	620. 00

Requirement

What is the electricity expense for the year ended 31 December 20×2? Prepare a journal entry to record the accrual as at 31 December 20×2.

Solution

The three invoices received during 20×2 totalled £1,060.55, but this is not the full charge for the reporting period: The November and December electricity charge was not invoiced until the end of January 20×3. To show the correct charge for the reporting period, we accrue the charge for November and December based on January's bill. The charge for 20×2 is:

	£
Paid in year	1,060.55
Accrual (2/3 x £491.52)	327.68
	1,388.23

The double entry for the accrual will be:

		£	£
DEBIT	Electricity account	327.68	
CREDIT	Accruals		327.68

2. Prepaid Expenses

Prepaid expenses or prepayments are payments which have been made in one accounting period, but should not be charged against profit until a later period, because they relate to that later period. They are shown in the statement of financial position as an **asset**.

Assume insurance for a business is at the rate of £840 a year, starting from 1 January 20×1. The business has agreed to pay this at the rate of £210 every three months. However, payments were not made at the correct times. The details are described in Exhibit 7.3:

Exhibit 7.3

Insurance payment records		
Amount	Insurance due	Insurance paid
£210	31 March 20×1	£210—28 February 20×1
£210	30 June 20×1	£420—31 August 20×1
£210	30 September 20×1	
£210	31 December 20×1	£420—18 November 20×1

The insurance account for the year ended 31 December 20×1 will be shown in the books as:

Insurance account

20×1		£			
Feb 28	Bank	210			
Aug 3	Bank	420			
Nov 18	Bank	420			

The last payment shown of £420 is not just for 20×1; it can be split as £210 for the three months to 31 December 20×1 and £210 for the three months ended 31 March 20×2. For a period of 12 months the cost of insurance is £840 and this is, therefore, the figure needing to be transferred to the profit and loss account.

If this figure of £840 is entered in the account then the amount needed to balance the account will be £210 and, at 31 December 20×1, there is a benefit of a further £210 paid for but not used up—an asset that needs carrying forward as such to 20×2, i.e. as a debit balance. It is a prepaid expense. The account can now be completed as follows:

Insurance account

20×1		£	20×1		£
Feb 28	Bank	210	Dec 31	Profit and loss	840
Aug 31	Bank	420	Dec 31	**Prepaid c/d**	210
Nov 18	Bank	420			
		1,050			1,050
20×2					
Jan 1	**Prepaid b/d**	210			
	(Prepayment reversed)				

The balance c/d has been described as 'prepaid c/d', rather than as a balance. This is to explain what the balance is for: it is for a prepaid expense. As with this prepaid expense, the double entry will be reversed in the following period by the 'prepaid b/d', which will be cleared soon.

Alternatively, you can also open a prepayment account and post any balances on expense account at the period end to the prepayment account.

Insurance account

20X1		£	20X1		£
Feb 28	Bank	210	Dec 31	Profit and loss	840
Aug 31	Bank	420	Dec 31	Prepayment account	210
Nov 18	Bank	420			
		1,050			1,050
20X2					
Jan 1	Prepayment reversed	210			

Prepayment account

20X1		£	20X1		£
Dec 31	Insurance	210	Dec 31	Balance c/d	210
20X2			20X2		
Jan 1	Balance b/d	210	Jan 1	Insurance	210
				(Prepayment reversed)	

Similar to the previous section, at the start of the next period, you reverse the prepayment by transferring the opening balance in the prepayment account back to the expense account with the avoidance of never charging the expense.

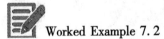

Worked Example 7. 2

A business opens on 1 January 20×4 in a shop where the rent is £20,000 per year, payable quarterly in advance at the beginning of each three-month period. Payments were made as follows:

	£
1 January 20×4	5,000
31 March 20×4	5,000
30 June 20×4	5,000
30 September 20×4	5,000
31 December 20×4	5,000

Requirement

What is the rental expense for the year ended 31 December 20×4?

Solution

The total amount paid in the year is £25,000. The yearly rental, however, is only £20,000. The last payment is a prepayment as it is a payment in advance for the first three months of 20×5. The charge for 20×4 is therefore:

		£
Paid in year		25,000
Prepayment		(5,000)
		20,000

The double entry for this prepayment is:

		£	£
DEBIT	Prepayments	5,000	
CREDIT	Rent		5,000

3. Accruals and Prepayments in Financial Statements

For accruals and prepayments, whilst one side of the double entry adjusts the expense account, the other side of the entry is taken to the statement of financial position: as an asset or a liability account that is needed only at the end of each reporting period.

· **Accruals** are included in **current liabilities** as they represent expenses which have been incurred but for which no invoice has yet been received. They nearly always clear soon after the end of the reporting period. The balance on the accruals account is brought down as a credit balance at the beginning of the next period.

· **Prepayments** are included in **current assets** in the statement of financial position as they represent money that has been paid out in advance of the expense being incurred. They usually clear within 12 months of the date of the statement of financial position. The balance on the prepayment ledger account is brought down as a debit balance at the beginning of the next period.

The above information is summarized in Exhibit 7.4.

Exhibit 7.4

Transaction	Statement of profit or loss	Statement of financial position	Description
Accrual	(Addition in) Expense	Current liability	Expense incurred in period, not paid/recorded
Prepayment	(Reduction in) Expense	Current asset	Expense paid/recorded in period, not incurred until next period

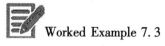 **Worked Example 7.3**

The Umbrella Shop has the following trial balance as at 30 September 20×8 (Exhibit 7.5):

Exhibit 7. 5

Umbrella Shop's Trial Balance as at 30 September 20×8		
	£	£
Sales		156,000
Purchases	65,000	
Non-current assets	200,000	
Inventory at 1. 10. 20×7	10,000	
Cash at bank	12,000	
Trade receivables	54,000	
Trade payables		40,000
Machinery rental	15,000	
Petty cash	2,000	
Insurance	10,000	
Finance costs	5,000	
Delivery inwards	1,000	
Delivery outwards	2,000	
Capital account at 1. 10. 20×7		180,000
	376,000	376,000

The following information is available:

(1) Closing inventory at 30 September 20×8 is £13,000, after writing off damaged goods of £2,000.

(2) Included in insurance is £1,500 has been paid in advance for next year.

(3) A late invoice for £3,000 covering machinery rental for the year ended 30 September 20×8 has not been included in the trial balance.

Requirement

Prepare a statement of profit or loss and statement of financial position for the year ended 30 September 20×8.

Solution

The statement of profit or loss is shown in Exhibit 7. 6.

Exhibit 7. 6

Umbrella Shop		
Statement of profit or loss for the year ended 30 September 20×8		
	£	£
Sales		156,000
Less Cost of sales (W1)		

Exhibit 7. 6(continued)

Opening inventory	10,000	
Purchases	65,000	
Delivery inwards	1,000	
Closing inventory	(13,000)	
		(63,000)
Gross profit		93,000
Less Expenses		
Machinery rental (W2)	18,000	
Insurance (W3)	8,500	
Delivery outwards	2,000	
Finance costs	5,000	
		(33,500)
Net profit		59,500

The statement of financial position is shown in Exhibit 7. 7.

Exhibit 7. 7

Umbrella Shop		
Statement of financial position as at 30 September 20×8		
Assets	£	£
Non-current assets		200,000
Current assets		
Inventory (W1)	13,000	
Trade receivables	54,000	
Prepayments (W3)	1,500	
Cash at bank	12,000	
Cash in hand	2,000	
		82,500
		282,500
Current liabilities		
Trade payables	40,000	
Accruals (W2)	3,000	
		(43,000)
Net assets		239,500
Owner's capital		

Exhibit 7.7(continued)

Balance brought forward		180,000
Net profit		59,500
		239,500

WORKINGS

(1) Closing inventory

As the figure of £13,000 is after writing off damaged goods, no further adjustments are necessary.

(2) Machinery rental expense = £15,000 + £3,000 = £18,000

		£	£
DEBIT	Machinery rental	3,000	
CREDIT	Accrual account		3,000

(3) Insurance expense = £10,000 - £1,500 = £8,500

		£	£
DEBIT	Prepayment account	1,500	
CREDIT	Insurance		1,500

7.3 Accrual Principle and Income

So far we have concentrated on accrued and prepaid expenses arising from the need to match expenses with the income to which they relate. It is also necessary sometimes to treat income in line with the accruals principle.

· Cash may be received in one period although the actual sale to which it relates occurs in the subsequent period. An example is a deposit (or advance payment, or payment on account) received from a customer on an item which will be delivered in the future. The deposit is banked but until the actual sale is recognised the cash should be treated as still being owing to the customer, not as income. This is known as **deferred income**, a **current liability** in the statement of financial position.

· Cash may be received in one period in relation to an event which arose in a previous period. An example is where a supplier makes a refund in relation to a purchase in a previous period. This is known as **accrued income**, a **current asset** on the statement of financial position.

The treatment is similar to accruals and prepayments of expenses:

· Calculate the amount of the deferred or accrued income.

· At the end of the reporting period, prepare a journal entry which updates the relevant profit or loss accounts, and which sets up the relevant asset and liability accounts.

· At the beginning of the next reporting period, reverse the journal entry.

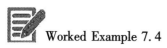

Worked Example 7. 4

Sunrise Carpets sells floor coverings to the public. At the end of its 12-month reporting period, 31 December 20×4, it has recorded as sales £1,200 received from customers as deposits on carpets which are not due to be invoiced until February 20×5. In January 20×5 it records a £500 refund from one of its main suppliers as a result of exceeding the agreed level of custom during 20×4.

Requirements

Recording these transactions in the ledger accounts for the reporting period ended 31 December 20×4.

Solution

On 31 Dec 20×4

		£	£
DEBIT	Sales	1,200	
CREDIT	Deferred income (liability)		1,200

Deposits from customers

On 31 Dec 20×4

		£	£
DEBIT	Accrued income (asset)	500	
CREDIT	Purchases		500

Refund from supplier

Summary

· The accrual principle applies to accruals and prepayments to match the expenses against revenue.

· Accrued expenses (accruals) are expenses which relate to an accounting period but have not yet been paid for. They are shown in the statement of financial position as a liability.

· Prepaid expenses (prepayments) are expenses which have already been paid but relate to a future accounting period. They are shown in the statement of financial position as an asset.

Exercise

7. 1 If a business has paid property tax of £1,000 for the year to 31 March 20×9, what is the prepayment in the financial statements for the 12-month reporting period ending on 31 December 20×8? (   )

 A.£0

 B.£250

 C.£750

D.£1,000

7.2 Rupa has the following balances in her ledger accounts.

	£
Purchases	75,000
Delivery outwards	800
Delivery inwards	1,000
Opening inventory	10,000
Closing inventory	12,000

What is Rupa's cost of sales? (　　)

    A.£72,000

    B.£73,000

    C.£74,000

    D.£74,800

7.3 On 5 May 20×8 Portals pays a rent bill of £1,800 for the 18 months ended 30 June 20×9. What is the charge in the statement of profit or loss and the entry for rent in the statement of financial position in respect of the 12-month reporting period ended 31 March 20×9? (　　)

    A.£1,200 with prepayment of £300

    B.£1,200 with accrual of £600

    C.£1,500 with accrual of £300

    D.£1,500 with prepayment of £300

7.4 A firm made the following rent payments.

    £9,000 for the six months ended 31 March 20×6

    £12,000 for the six months ended 30 September 20×6

    £11,196 for the 12 months ended 30 September 20×7

The charge to the statement of profit or loss for the 12-month reporting period ended 31 December 20×6 was(　　).

    A.£13,299

    B.£19,299

    C.£24,897

    D.£22,098

7.5 Elizabeth paid £2,500 for gas during the reporting period. At the beginning of the period, she owed £500; at the end she owed £1,000.

What charge should have appeared in her statement of profit or loss for that reporting period? (   )

    A.£2,000

    B.£2,500

    C.£3,000

    D.£3,500

7. 6 At the beginning of September Barney & Co were owed £200 in rent. At the end of September, they were owed £400. £800 cash for rent was received during September. What entry will be made in the statement of profit or loss for September for rent receivable? (   )

    A.Debit £600

    B.Debit £1,000

    C.Credit £600

    D.Credit £1,000

7. 7 A company pays rent quarterly in arrears on 1 January, 1 April, 1 July and 1 October each year. The rent was increased from £90,000 per year to £120,000 per year as from 1 October 20×2. What rent expense and accrual should be included in the company's financial statements for the year ended 31 January 20×3? (   )

	Rent expense	Accrual
	£	£
A.	100,000	20,000
B.	100,000	10,000
C.	97,500	10,000
D.	97,500	20,000

7. 8 The electricity account for the year ended 30 June 20×1 was as shown in Exhibit 7. 8.

Exhibit 7. 8

Electricity information	
	£
Opening balance for electricity accrued at 1 July 20×0	300
Payments made during the year	
1 August 20×0 for three months to 31 July 20×0	600
1 November 20×0 for three months to 31 October 20×0	720
1 February 20×1 for three months to 31 January 20×1	900
30 June 20×1 for three months to 30 April 20×1	840
1 August 20×1 for three months to 31 July 20×1	840

Which of the following is the appropriate entry for electricity? (　　)

	Accrued at 30 June 20×1	Charge to SOPL year ended 30 June 20×1
A.	£Nil	£3,060
B.	£460	£3,320
C.	£560	£3,320
D.	£560	£3,420

7.9 The following Exhibit 7.9 are balances on the accounts of Luigi, a sole trader, as at the end of the current financial year and after all entries have been processed and the profit for the year has been calculated.

Exhibit 7.9

Balances of Luigi as at the year end of...	
	£
Non-current assets	85,000
Trade receivables	7,000
Trade payables	3,000
Bank loan	15,000
Accumulated depreciation, non-current assets	15,000
Inventory	4,000
Accruals	1,000
Prepayments	2,000
Bank overdraft	2,000

What is the balance on Luigi's capital account? (　　)

A.£59,000

B.£66,000

C.£62,000

D.£64,000

7.10 A business compiling its accounts for the year to 31 January each year pays rent quarterly in advance on 1 January, 1 April, 1 July and 1 October each year. After remaining unchanged for some years, the rent was increased from £24,000 per year to £30,000 per year as from 1 July 20×0.

Which of the following figures is the rent expense which should appear in the statement of profit or loss for year ended 31 January 20×1? (　　)

A.£27,500

B.£29,500

C.£28,000

D.£29,000

7.11 Which three of the following sets of items all appear on the same side of the trial balance? （   ）

1 Sales, interest received and accruals

2 Receivables, drawings and discount received

3 Non-current assets, cost of sales and carriage outwards

4 Capital, trade payables and other operating expenses

5 Sundry expenses, prepayments and purchases

 A.1, 4 and 5

 B.1, 3 and 5

 C.1, 2 and 3

 D.3, 4 and 5

7.12 The trainee accountant at Judd Co has forgotten to make an accrual for rent for December in the financial statements for the year ended 31 December 20×2. Rent is charged in arrears at the end of February, May, August and November each year. The bill payable in February is expected to be £30,000. Judd Co.'s draft statement of profit or loss shows a profit of £25,000 and draft statement of financial position shows net assets of £275,000.

What is the profit or loss for the year and what is the net asset position after the accrual has been included in the financial statements? （   ）

	Profit for the year	Net asset position
A.	£15,000	£265,000
B.	£15,000	£285,000
C.	£35,000	£265,000
D.	£35,000	£285,000

7.13 Buster's draft accounts for the year to 31 October 20×5 report a loss of £1,486. When he prepared the accounts, Buster did not include an accrual of £1,625 and a prepayment of £834.

What is Buster's profit or loss for the year to 31 October 20×5 following the inclusion of the accrual and prepayment? （   ）

 A.A loss of £695

 B.A loss of £2,277

 C.A loss of £3,945

 D.A profit of £1,807

7.14 Bookz Co pays royalties to writers annually, in February, the payment covering the previous calendar year.

As at the end of December 20×2, Bookz Co had accrued £100,000 in royalties due to writers. However, a check of the royalty calculation performed in January 20×3 established that the actual figure due to be paid by Bookz Co to writers was £150,000.

Before this under-accrual was discovered, Bookz Co's draft statement of profit or loss for the accounting year ended 31 December 20×2 showed a profit of £125,000 and their draft statement of financial position showed net assets of £375,000.

What will Bookz Co's profit and net asset position be after an entry to correct the under-accrual has been processed? (   )

	Profit for the year	Net asset position
A.	£175,000	£425,000
B.	£125,000	£375,000
C.	£75,000	£325,000
D.	£25,000	£225,000

7.15 A business preparing its financial statements for the year to 31 October each year pays rent quarterly in advance on 1 January, 1 April, 1 July and 1 October each year. The annual rent was increased from £48,000 to £60,000 per year from 1 March 20×4.

What figure should appear for rent in the statement of profit or loss for the year ended 31 October 20×4 and in the statement of financial position at that date? (   )

	Statement of profit or loss	Statement of financial position
A.	£56,000	£10,000
B.	£52,000	£5,000
C.	£56,000	£5,000
D.	£55,000	£10,000

7.16 During 20×4, Bibi paid a total of £60,000 for rent, covering the period from 1 October 20×3 to 31 March 20×5.

What figures should appear in the financial statements for the year ended 31 December 20×4? (   )

	Statement of profit or loss	Statement of financial position
A.	£40,000	£10,000 Prepayment
B.	£40,000	£15,000 Prepayment
C.	£50,000	£10,000 Accrual
D.	£50,000	£15,000 Accrual

7.17 Horace Goodrunning ends his motor spares business's reporting period on 28 February each year. His telephone was installed on 1 April 20×1 and he receives his telephone bill quarterly at the end of each quarter. Telephone expense for the three months ended:

	£
30 June 20×1	23. 50
30 September 20×1	27. 20
31 December 20×1	33. 40
31 March 20×2	36. 00

All the bills were paid on the final day of each three-month period.

Requirement

Calculate the telephone expense to be charged to the statement of profit or loss for the year ended 28 February 20×2.

7. 18 J. Wright, a sole trader, extracted the following trial balance from his books at the close of business on 31 March 20×6 (Exhibit 7. 10):

Exhibit 7. 10

J. Wright Trial Balance as at 31 March 20×6		
	Dr	Cr
	£	£
Purchases and sales	61,420	127,245
Inventory 1 April 20×5	7,940	
Capital 1 April 20×5		25,200
Bank overdraft		2,490
Cash	140	
Discounts	2,480	62
Returns inwards	3,486	
Returns outwards		1,356
Carriage outwards	3,210	
Rent and insurance	8,870	
Allowance for doubtful debts		630
Fixtures and fittings	1,900	
Van	5,600	
Trade receivables and payables	12,418	11,400
Drawings	21,400	
Wages and salaries	39,200	
General office expenses	319	—
	168,383	168,383

Notes:

(1) Inventory 31 March 20×6: £6,805.

(2) Wages and salaries accrued at 31 March 20 × 6: £3, 500; Office expenses owing: £16.

(3) Rent prepaid 31 March 20×6: £600.

(4) Increase the allowance for receivables by £110 to £740.

(5) Provide for depreciation as follows: Fixtures and fittings £190; Van £1,400.

Requirement

Prepare the statement of profit or loss for the year ending 31 March 20×6 together with a statement of financial position as at that date.

7. 19* The Batley Print Shop, which is not registered for VAT, rents a photocopying machine. It makes a quarterly payment as follows:

(1) Three months' rental in advance.

(2) A charge of 2 pence per copy made during the quarter just ended.

The rental agreement began on 1 August 20×4. The first six quarterly bills were as listed in Exhibit 7. 11:

Exhibit 7. 11

Rental bills			
Bills dated	Rental	Cost of copies taken	Total
	£	£	£
1 August 20×4	2,100	0	2,100
1 November 20×4	2,100	1,500	3,600
1 February 20×5	2,100	1,400	3,500
1 May 20×5	2,100	1,800	3,900
1 August 20×5	2,700	1,650	4,350
1 November 20×5	2,700	1,950	4,650

The bills are paid promptly, as soon as they are received.

Requirement

(1) Calculate the charge for photocopying expenses for the year to 31 August 20×4 and the amount of prepayments and/or accrued charges as at that date.

(2) Calculate the charge for photocopying expenses for the following year to 31 August 20×5, and the amount of prepayments and/or accrued charges as at that date.

7. 20 * Please refer to Exhibit 7. 12 for Lee's trial balance as at 28 Feb 20×7.

Exhibit 7. 12

Lee's trial balance as at 28 Feb 20×7		
	Dr	Cr
	£	£
Owner's capital at 1 March 20×6		228,164
Advertising	18,563	
Irrecoverable debts	5,835	
Bank overdraft		4,852
Bank interest paid	100	
Cash in hand	650	
Trade payables		24,510
Trade receivables	16,540	
Accumulated depreciation on motor cars, at 1 Mar 20×6		126,800
Accumulated depreciation on fixtures and fittings, at 1 Mar 20×6		16,503
Drawings	62,005	
Fixtures and fittings (cost)	124,210	
Loan		10,000
Insurance	2,640	
Light and heat	6,420	
Motor cars (cost)	165,920	
Purchases	678,000	
Rent and rates	5,900	
Salaries and wages	107,400	
Sales		922,994
Inventory	114,700	
Sundry expenses	13,700	
Telephone	11,240	
	1,333,823	1,333,823

Notes:

(1) Inventory at 28 Feb 20×7 was £112,600.

(2) The allowance for receivables is to be created of £1,500.

(3) Fixtures and fittings are to be depreciated at 10%, straight line method; motor cars by 25%, reducing balance method.

(4) There was an accrual for telephone of £2,500 and insurance had been prepaid

by £600.

Requirement

Prepare the statement of profit or loss account for the year ended 28 Feb 20×7, and a statement of financial position as at that date. Show all workings.

7.21* From the following Rachel's trial balance (Exhibit 7.13) and notes, prepare a statement of profit or loss and a statement of financial position for the year ended at 31 March 20×7.

Exhibit 7.13

Rachel's trial balance as at 31 March 20×7		
	Dr	Cr
	£	£
Bank	12,600	
Cash	450	
Shop fittings—cost	12,000	
Shop fittings—Depreciation to 1 April 20×6		2,500
Motor car	16,200	
Motor car—Depreciation to 1 April 20×6		4,860
Sales		196,540
Purchases	87,520	
Inventory	8,680	
Allowance for receivables		200
Rent	4,700	
Electricity	2,400	
Telephone	2,100	
Trade receivables	1,890	
Trade payables		2,450
Wages and salaries	36,300	
Owner's drawings	28,000	
Capital		6,290
	212,840	212,840

Notes:

(1) Closing inventory is £9,420.

(2) Telephone charges of £220 are to be accrued at the year end.

(3) Rent of £800 has been prepaid at the year end.

(4) Depreciation on the shop fittings is calculated over 4 years on the straight line method, assuming a residual value of £2,000.

(5) Depreciation on the car is calculated at 30% using the reducing balance method.

(6) The allowance for receivables is to be increased by £300.

7. 22* The trial balance for Sharmar for the period ended 31. March 20×3 before making year-end adjustments is as shown in Exhibit 7. 14:

Exhibit 7. 14

Sharmar's trial balance as at 31 March 20×3		
	Dr	Cr
	£	£
Capital 1. 04. 20×2		49,630
Drawings	6,300	
Trade receivables and payables	12,750	9,830
Sales		121,340
Purchases	85,670	
Inventory	17,110	
Rent and rates	6,700	
Heat and lighting	1,900	
Wages and salaries	12,450	
Irrecoverable debts	1,100	
Allowance for receivables		490
General expenses	710	
Building	55,500	21,300
Fixtures	12,300	4,700
Vehicles	33,000	8,200
Loan		26,000
Bank		4,270
Cash	270	—
	245,760	245,760

The following matters have not been taken into account when preparing the above trial balance:

(1) Closing inventory is valued at £15,990.

(2) Heat and lighting due at 31 March 20×3 is £230.

(3) Rent paid in advance on 31 March 20×3 is £1,500.

(4) Depreciation is to be provided as follows:

Premises 3% on cost

Fixtures and fittings 12.5% on cost

Vehicles 20% reducing balance

(5) Allowance for receivables is to be 4% of accounts receivables.

Requirement

Please prepare a statement of profit or loss for the year ending 31 March 20×3 and a statement of financial position as at that date.

7.23* G. Lea, a sole trader, extracted the following trial balance from his books for the year ended 31 March 20×6 (Exhibit 7.15).

Exhibit 7.15

G. Lea's trial balance as at 31 March 20×6	Dr	Cr
	£	£
Purchases and sales	224,000	419,700
Inventory 1 April 20×5	51,600	
Capital 1 April 20×5		72,000
Bank overdraft		43,500
Cash	900	
Carriage inwards	4,600	
Discounts	14,400	9,300
Return inwards	8,100	
Return outwards		5,700
Carriage outwards	21,600	
Rent and insurance	17,400	
Allowance for receivables		6,600
Office equipment	20,000	
Delivery vans	27,000	
Trade receivables and payables	119,100	61,200
Drawings	28,800	
Irrecoverable debts written off	400	
Wages and salaries	89,000	
General office expenses	4,500	
Accumulated depreciation		
Office equipment		8,000
Delivery vans		5,400
	631,400	631,400

Notes:

(1) Inventory 31 March 20×6 was values at £42,900.

(2) Wages and salaries accrued £2,100 and office expenses owing £200 at 31 March 20×6.

(3) Rent prepaid 31 March 20×6 was £1,800.

(4) Increase the allowance for receivables to £8,100.

(5) Provide for depreciation on the office equipment at 20 per cent per annum using the straight line method.

(6) Provide for depreciation on the delivery vans at 20 per cent annum using the reducing balance method.

Requirement

Prepare a statement of profit or loss for the year ended 31 March 20×6 and statement of financial position as at that date.

7. 24* The following trial balance (Exhibit 7. 16) was extracted from the records of L. Robinson, a trader, as at 31 December 20×6.

Exhibit 7. 16

L. Robinson's trial balance as at 31 December 20×6		
	Dr	Cr
	£	£
Discounts allowed	410	
Discounts received		506
Carriage inwards	309	
Carriage outwards	218	
Returns inwards	1,384	
Returns outwards		810
Sales		120,320
Purchases	84,290	
Inventory at 31 December 20×5	30,816	
Motor expenses	4,917	
Repairs to premises	1,383	
Salaries and wages	16,184	
Sundry expenses	807	
Rates and insurance	2,896	
Premises at cost	40,000	

Exhibit 7. 16(continued)

Motor vehicles at cost	11,160	
Accumulated depreciation—motors		3,860
Trade receivables and payables	31,640	24,320
Cash at bank	4,956	
Cash in hand	48	
Drawings	8,736	
Capital		50,994
Loan from P.Hall (repayable 20×9)		40,000
Irrecoverable debts	1,314	
Allowance for receivables	——	658
	241,468	241,468

The following matters are to be taken into account at 31 December 20×6:

(1) Inventory at £36,420.

(2) Expenses owing: sundry expenses £62; motor expenses £33.

(3) Prepayment: rates £166.

(4) Allowance for receivables to be reduced to £580.

(5) Depreciation for motor vehicles to be £2,100 for the year.

(6) Part of the premises were let to a tenant, who owed £250 at 31 December 20×6.

(7) Loan interest owing to P.Hall £4,000.

Requirement

Draw upa statement of profit or loss for the year ended 31 December 20×6 and a statement of financial position as at that day.

7. 25 * Freddy Tuilagi is baker. His trial balance as at 30 September is as shown in Exhibit 7. 17:

Exhibit 7. 17

Freddy Tuilagi's trial balance as at 30 September 20×6		
	Dr	Cr
	£	£
Motor van (at cost)	7,000	
Discount received		230
Bank		50
Opening inventory	850	
General expenses	610	

Exhibit 7. 17(continued)

Accumulated depreciation: Equipment		2,000
Drawings	1,400	
Sales		30,490
Cash	30	
Trade payables		845
Purchases	13,725	
Wages	3,880	
Advertising	420	
Telephone	160	
Equipment (at cost)	17,000	
Capital		11,460
	45,075	45,075

The following additional information is available at 30 September.

(1) Inventory at cost amounted to £960.

(2) Over the year Freddy Tuilagi took purchases for his own use, at cost £320.

(3) The advertising was prepaid by £46.

(4) Depreciation is to be provided for as follows:

Equipment 30 per cent reducing (diminishing) balance method.

Motor van 15 per cent straight line (on cost) method.

(5) Discounts received of £80 have not yet been entered in the books.

Requirement

Prepare Freddie Tuigali's statement of profit or loss for the year ended 30 September and statement of financial position as at 30 September.

Reference

1. Alan Sangster, Frank Wood's Business Accounting Volume 1(2019), Pearson.

2. Accounting (Study Manual 2020), The Institute of Chartered Accountants in England and Wales.

3. Accounting (Question Bank 2020), The Institute of Chartered Accountants in England and Wales.

4. ACCA FA Financial Accounting/FIA FFA Interactive Text 2020, BPP Learning Media.

5. ACCA FA Financial Accounting/FIA FFA Practice & Revision Kit 2020, BPP Learning Media.

Chapter 8

Provisions and Contingencies

- - - ■Learning Objectives -

· Understand the definition of 'provision', 'contingent liability' and 'contingent asset'.

· Distinguish between and classify items as provisions, contingent liabilities or contingent assets.

· Identify and illustrate the different methods of accounting for provisions, contingent liabilities and contingent assets.

· Calculate provisions and changes in provisions.

· Account for the movement in provisions.

· Report provisions in the final accounts.

8. 1 Provisions

In order for financial statements to show a true and fair view, it is essential that reporting entities recognise all the liabilities that satisfy the Conceptual Framework criteria. Given that the recognition of a liability often involves a charge against profits, and the derecognition of a liability sometimes involves a credit to profits, there is the possibility that, unless this area of financial reporting is appropriately regulated, there is scope for manipulation of reporting profits when liabilities are recognised or derecognised inappropriately. IAS 37 Provisions, Contingent Liabilities and Contingent Assets deals with the recognition, measurement and disclosure of these liabilities or potential liabilities.

1. Definition

A **liability** is an obligation of an entity to transfer economic benefits as a result of past transactions or events.

A **provision** is a liability of uncertain timing or amount.

Note that while the definition in IAS 37 means that provisions are viewed as a sub-class of liabilities, IAS 37 distinguishes provisions from other liabilities such as trade payables and accruals, say, gas supplies, where it is known that there will be one gas bill, to be paid X weeks after the end of the reporting period for roughly £ Y. However, a provision is where there is **uncertainty** about the timing or amount of the future expenditure.

Provisions are a common feature of financial statements and can arise from many transactions. IAS 37 states that a provision should be recognised as a liability in the financial statements when all three of the following conditions are met:

· When an entity has incurred a **present obligation** (legal or constructive) to incur the expenditure.

· When it is **probable** (i.e. more than 50% likely) that a transfer of economics benefits will be required to settle it.

· When a reliable estimate can be made of the amount involved.

What do we mean by a legal or constructive obligation? An **obligation** means in simple terms that the business owes something to someone else. A **legal obligation** usually arises from a contract and might, for example, include warranties sold with products to make good any repairs required within a certain time frame. A **constructive obligation** arises through past behaviour and actions where the entity has raised a valid expectation that it will carry out a particular action. For example, a constructive obligation would arise if a business which doesn't offer warranties on its products has a history of usually carrying out free small repairs on its products, so that customers have come to expect this benefit when they make a purchase.

2. Accounting for Provisions

Provisions are accounted for in the following stages.

Stage 1: Create provision

At the point at which a provision is created, an expense is recorded in the statement of profit or loss and a corresponding liability is recorded in the statement of financial position. The journal entry to record this is:

| DEBIT | Expense (statement of profit or loss) | X | |
| CREDIT | Provisions (statement of financial position) | | X |

Stage 2: Incur expenditure

In subsequent years, adjustments may be needed to the amount of the provision. The procedure to be followed then is as follows.

(1) Calculate the new provision required.

(2) Compare it with the existing balance on the provision account (i.e. the balance b/d from the previous accounting period).

(3) Calculate increase or decrease required.

· If a higher provision is required now:

| DEBIT | Expenses (statement of profit or loss) | X | |
| CREDIT | Provisions (statement of financial position) | | X |

with the amount of the increase.

· If a lower provision is needed now than before:

| DEBIT | Provisions (statement of financial position) | X | |
| CREDIT | Expenses (statement of profit or loss) | | X |

with the amount of the decrease.

Consider the following example.

 Worked Example 8.1

A company sells a product with a standard two-year warranty. The company estimates that 5% of warranties will be invoked * , at a cost of £15,000.

The journal entries would be as follows:

		£	£
DEBIT	Expense (statement of profit or loss)	15,000	
CREDIT	Warranty provision (statement of financial position)		15,000

The following year, due to a change in material used, the company estimated that only 3% of warranties would be invoked, at a cost of £9,000. There have been no claims against the warranty provision in the year.

As the estimated amount of the warranty claims has decreased, some of the warranty provision should be released:

The journal entry required is as follows:

		£	£
DEBIT	Warranty provision (statement of financial position)	6,000	
CREDIT	Expense (statement of profit or loss)		6,000

* You can assume that this means it is probable that this expenditure will be incurred.

 Question

A business has been told by its lawyers that it is likely to have to pay £10,000 damages for a product that failed. The business duly set up a provision at 31 December 20×7. However, the following year, the lawyers found that damages were more likely to be £50,000.

Requirement

How is the provision treated in the accounts at 31 December 20×7 and 31 December 20 ×8?

3. Measuring the Amount of Provisions

IAS 37 states that the amount recognised as a provision should be the best estimate of the expenditure required to settle the present obligation at the period-end date. 'Best estimate' is defined as the amount that a company would rationally pay to settle the obligation or to transfer it to a third party. The estimates of outcome and financial effect are determined by the judgement of management supplemented by experience of similar transactions and reports from independent experts.

If the provision relates to just one item, the best estimate of the expenditure will be the most likely outcome.

When a provision is needed that involves a lot of items (for example, a warranty provision, where each item sold has a warranty attached to it), then the provision is calculated using the expected value approach. The expected value approach takes each possible outcome (i. e. the amount of money that will need to be paid under each circumstance) and weights it according to the probability of that outcome happening. This is illustrated in the following example.

For example, a company had been using unlicensed parts in the manufacture of its products and, at the year end, no decision had been reached by the court. The plaintiff was seeking damages of £10 million.

The possible outcome that will need to be paid to the plaintiff under each circumstance is estimated as below:

% of circumstances	Payable to plaintiff
	£
25	nil
20	10 million
55	7 million

The company should provide on the basis of the expected value of all possible outcome.

The expected payable is calculated as $(25\% \times £\,nil) + (20\% \times £10\ m) + (55\% \times £7\ m)$ = £5. 85 m.

A provision of £5. 85 million should be included in the financial statements.

8. 2   Contingent Liabilities and Contingent Assets

1. Contingent Liabilities

IAS 37 defines a contingent liability as:

· A possible obligation depending on whether some uncertain future event occurs, or

· A present obligation but payment is not probable or the amount cannot be measured reliably

IAS 37 distinguishes between provisions and contingent liabilities in that:

· Provisions are a present obligation requiring a probable transfer of economic benefits that can be reliably estimated—a provision can therefore be recognised as a liability.

· Contingent liabilities fail to satisfy these criteria, e.g. lack of a reliable estimate of the amount; not probable that there will be a transfer of economic benefits; yet to be confirmed that there is actually an obligation. A contingent liability cannot therefore be recognised in the accounts but may be **disclosed by way of note** to the accounts or not disclosed if an outflow of economic benefits is remote.

As a general rule, probable means more than 50% likely.**If an obligation is probable, it is not a contingent liability** —instead, a **provision** is needed. If the obligation is **remote**, it does not need to be disclosed in the accounts.

2. Contingent Assets

IAS 37 defines a contingent asset as:

A possible asset that arises from past events and whose existence will be confirmed by the occurrence of one or more uncertain future events not wholly within the enterprise's control.

Recognition as an asset is only allowed if the asset is **virtually certain**, and therefore by definition no longer contingent.

Disclosure by way of note is required if an inflow of economic benefits is **probable.** The disclosure would include a brief description of the contingent assets, an estimate of their likely financial effect and uncertainties and, where material, the time value of money.

No disclosure is required where the chance of occurrence is anything less than probable.

3. Decision Tree of IAS 37

The IAS 37 sets out a useful decision tree, shown in Exhibit 8. 1, for determining whether an event requires the creation of a provision, the disclosure of a contingent liability or no action.

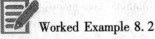 **Worked Example 8. 2**

During 20×9 Smack Co gives a guarantee of £500,000 borrowings of Pony Co, whose financial condition at that time is sound. During 20Y0, the financial condition of Pony Co deteriorates and at 30 June 20Y0 Pony Co files for protection from its creditors.

Requirement

What accounting treatment is required for Smack Co at 31 December 20×9 and 31 December 20Y0?

Solution

(1) At 31 December 20×9

There is a present obligation as a result of a past obligating event. The obligating event is the giving of the guarantee, which gives rise to a legal obligation. However, at 31 December 20×9 no transfer of economic benefits is probable in settlement of the obligation. No provision is recognised. The guarantee is disclosed as a contingent liability unless the probability of any transfer is regarded as remote.

An appropriate note to the accounts would be as follows:

"Contingent liability

The company has given a guarantee in respect of the bank borrowings (currently £500,000) of Pony Co. At the reporting date, Pony Co was sound and it is unlikely that the company will be required to fulfill its guarantee."

(2) At 31 December 20Y0

As above, there is a present obligation as a result of a past obligating event, namely the giving of the guarantee.

At 31 December 20Y0 it is probable that a transfer of economic benefits will be required to settle the obligation. A provision is therefore recognised for the best estimate of the obligation.

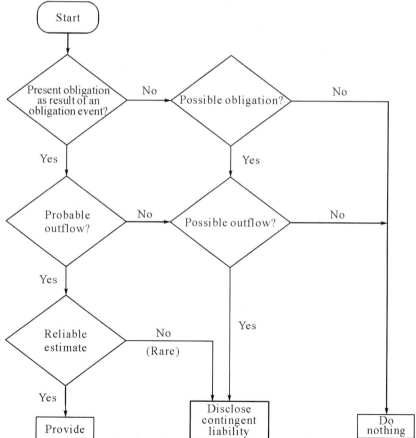

Exhibit 8.1

8.3　Disclosure in Financial Statements

IAS 37 requires certain items for provisions and contingent assets and liabilities to be disclosed in the financial statements.

Disclosures required in the financial statements for each class of **provision**:

· Details of the change in carrying amount of a provision from the beginning to the end of the year, including additional provisions made, amounts used and other movements.

· A brief description of the nature of the provision and the expected timing of any resulting outflows.

· An indication of the uncertainties about the amount or timing, and the major assumptions.

· The amount of any expected reimbursement, if any.

Where the likelihood of a **contingent liability** is possible but not probable and not remote, disclosure should be made of:

· A brief description of the nature of the contingent liability.

· An estimate of its financial effect.

· An indication of the uncertainties that exist.

· The possibility of any reimbursement.

Where an inflow of **economic benefits is probable**, an entity should disclose:

· A brief description of its nature, and where practicable.

· An estimate of the financial effect.

Summary

· IAS 37, Provisions, Contingent Liabilities and Contingent Assets provides guidance on when provisions and contingencies should be recognised and if so, at what amount.

· A provision should be recognised:

—When an entity has a present obligation

—When it is probable that a transfer of economic benefits will be required to settle it

—When a reliable estimate can be made of its amount

· A contingent liability must not be recognised as a liability in the financial statements. Instead, it should be disclosed in the notes to the accounts, unless the possibility of an outflow of economic benefits is remote.

· A contingent asset must not be recognised as an asset in the financial statements. Instead, it should be disclosed in the notes to the accounts if it is probable that the economic benefits associated with the asset will flow to the entity.

· IAS 37 requires certain items for provisions and contingent assets and liabilities to be disclosed in the financial statements.

Exercise

8. 1 A company is being sued for £10,000 by a customer. The company's lawyers reckon that it is likely that the claim will be upheld. Legal fees are currently £5,000. Given this fact, how much of a provision should be made if further legal fees of £2,000 are likely to be incurred? (   )

      A.£10,000

      B.£5,000

      C.£15,000

      D.£12,000

8. 2 A company has a provision for warranty claims b/f of £50,000. It does a review and decides that the provision needed in future should be £45,000. What is the effect on the financial statements? (   )

Statement of profit or loss	Statement of financial position
A. Increase expenses by £5,000	Provision £50,000
B. Increase expenses by £5,000	Provision £45,000
C. Decrease expenses by £5,000	Provision £50,000
D. Decrease expenses by £5,000	Provision £45,000

8. 3 A contingent liability is always disclosed on the face of the statement of financial position. (   )

      A.True

      B.False

8. 4 How does a company account for a contingent asset that is not probable? (   )

      A.By way of note

      B.As an asset in the statement of financial position

      C.It does nothing

      D.Offset against any associated liability

8. 5 How should a contingent liability be included in a company's financial statements if the likelihood of a transfer of economic benefits to settle it is remote? (   )

      A.Disclosed by note with no provision being made

      B.No disclosure or provision is required

8. 6 The following conditions exist.

· An event has occurred which means Booker Co has incurred a present obligation.

· It is probable that Booker Co will have to pay out cash in order to settle the obligation.

· A reliable estimate of the amount involved cannot be determined.

What is the effect of the above on the financial statements of Booker Co? (   )

    A.A provision should be created

    B.A contingent liability should be disclosed

    C.A contingent asset should be disclosed

    D.No effect

8. 7 Raider Co has to include the following items in its financial statements.

1 Raider Co has been sued by Space Co for breach of trademark. Raider Co strongly disputes the claim and Raider Co's lawyers advise that the likelihood of having to pay any money to Space Co for the claim is remote.

2 Raider Co gives warranties on its products. Data from previous years show that about 15% of sales give rise to a warranty claim.

How should the items be reflected in the financial statements of Raider Co? (   )

Item 1	Item 2
A.create a provision	disclose by note only
B.disclose by note only	create a provision
C.disclose by note only	disclose by note only
D.no provision or disclosure required	create a provision

8. 8 Punt Co sells vacuum cleaners with a warranty. Customers are covered for the cost of repairs of any manufacturing defect that becomes apparent within the first year of purchase. The company's past experience and future expectations indicate the following pattern of likely repairs.

% of goods sold	Defects	Cost of repairs
		£000
80	None	–
12	Minor	545
8	Major	800

The warranty provision brought forward is £99,750.

What amounts should be recognised in the financial statements of Punt Co relating to the warranty provision for the year to 20×3? (   )

	Statement of profit or loss	Statement of financial position
A.	£99,750 Cr	nil
B.	£99,750 Dr	nil
C.	£29,650 Dr	£129,400 Cr
D.	£29,650 Cr	£129,400 Cr

8. 9 Which of the following statements about provisions and contingencies is/are correct? (　)

1 A company should disclose details of the change in carrying value of a provision from the beginning to the end of the year.

2 Contingent assets must be recognised in the financial statements in accordance with the prudence concept.

3 Contingent liabilities must be treated as actual liabilities and provided for if it is probable that they will arise.

A.3 only

B.2 and 3 only

C.1 and 3 only

D.All three statements are correct

8. 10 Munch Co is a fast food retailer. One of its customers has started a legal claim for damages after contracting food poisoning at a Munch Co restaurant. Munch Co's lawyers believe that there is a 70% chance that the claim will be successful and they estimate that the award to the customer will be £90,000.

Which of the following statements is correct? (　)

A.Munch Co should not create a provision because payment of damages is not certain.

B.Munch Co should create a provision for 70% of the expected award of £90,000.

C.Munch Co should create a provision for the full amount of the expected award of £90,000.

D.Munch Co should create a provision for £90,000 plus an additional amount in case other claimants launch similar legal claims.

8. 11 Which of the following statements about contingent assets and contingent liabilities are correct? (　)

1 A contingent asset should be disclosed by note if an inflow of economic benefits is probable.

2 A contingent liability should be disclosed by note if it is probable that a transfer of economic benefits to settle it will be required, with no provision being made.

3 No disclosure is required for a contingent liability if it is not probable that a transfer of economic benefits to settle it will be required.

4 No disclosure is required for either a contingent liability or a contingent asset if the likelihood of a payment or receipt is remote.

A.1 and 4 only

B.2 and 3 only

C.2, 3 and 4

D.1, 2 and 4

8. 12 An ex-director of X company has commenced an action against the company claiming substantial damages for wrongful dismissal. The company's solicitors have advised that the ex-director is unlikely to succeed with his claim, although the chance of X paying any monies to the ex-director is not remote. The solicitors' estimates of the company's potential liabilities are:

	£
Legal costs (to be incurred whether the claim is successful or not)	50,000
Settlement of claim if successful	500,000
	550,000

According to IAS 37 Provisions, contingent liabilities and continent assets, how should this claim be treated in the financial statements? (　　)

A.Provision of £550,000

B.Disclose a contingent liability of £550,000

C.Provision of £50,000 and a contingent liability of £500,000

D.Provision for £500,000 and a contingent liability of £50,000

8. 13 Wanda Co allows customers to return faulty goods within 14 days of purchase. At 30 November 20×5 a provision of £6,548 was made for sales returns. At 30 November 20×6, the provision was re-calculated and should now be £7,634.

What should be reported in Wanda Co's statement of profit or loss for the year to 31 October 20×6 in respect of the provision? (　　)

A.A charge of £7,634

B.A credit of £7,634

C.A charge of £1,086

D.A credit of £1,086

8. 14 Which of the following items does the statement below describe? (　　)

"A possible obligation that arises from past events and whose existence will be confirmed only by the occurrence or non-occurrence of one or more uncertain future events not wholly within the entity's control"

A.A provision

B.A current liability

C.A contingent liability

D.A contingent asset

8. 15 When a provision is needed that involves a number of outcomes, the provision is calculated using the expected value of expenditure. The expected value of expenditure is the total expenditure of (   ).

    A.Each possible outcome

    B.Each possible outcome weighted according to the probability of each outcome happening

    C.Each possible outcome divided by the number of outcomes

    D.Each possible outcome multiplied by the number of outcomes

Reference

1. ACCA FA Financial Accounting/FIA FFA Interactive Text 2020, BPP Learning Media.

2. ACCA FA Financial Accounting/FIA FFA Practice & Revision Kit 2020, BPP Learning Media.

3. Accounting (Study Manual 2020), The Institute of Chartered Accountants in England and Wales.

4. Accounting (Question Bank 2020), The Institute of Chartered Accountants in England and Wales.

Chapter 9

Tangible Non-current Assets

---- ■Learning Objectives ---
· Explain the difference between capital and revenue items.

· Classify expenditure as capital or revenue expenditure.

· Determine the initial cost and subsequent cost of non-current assets.

· Prepare ledger entries to record the acquisition and disposal of non-current assets.

· Calculate and record profits or losses on disposal of non- current assets in the statement of profit or loss, including part-exchange transactions.

· Record the revaluation of a non-current asset in ledger accounts, the statement of profit or loss and other comprehensive income and in the statement of financial position.

· Illustrate how non-current asset balances and movements are disclosed in financial statements.

9.1 Capital vs Revenue Expenditure

Assets are non-current assets when they are expected to be used over more than one reporting period. Non-current assets may be tangible, which means they have physical substance such as property, machinery, delivery vehicle (referred to as property, plant and equipment) or intangible which means they do not have physical substance, such as a patent. Tangible and intangible assets are presented separately on the statement of financial position.

Before you start to learn the subject of non-current assets, you need to be familiar with an important distinction, the distinction between capital and revenue expenditure.

1. The Distinction Between Capital and Revenue Expenditure

Before you start this topic, you need to be aware that 'capital expenditure' has nothing to do with the Owner's Capital account.

Capital expenditure is expenditure which results in the acquisition of non-current assets, or an improvement or enhancement to existing non-current assets.

Capital expenditure is not charged as an expense in the statement of profit or loss, although a depreciation or amortisation charge will usually be made to write off the capital expenditure gradually over time. Depreciation and amortisation charges are expenses in the statement of profit or loss.

Capital expenditure on non-current assets results in the recognition of a non-current asset in the statement of financial position of the business.

Revenue expenditure is expenditure which is incurred for either of the following reasons.

· For trade purpose of the business. This includes purchases of raw materials or items for resale, expenditure classified as selling and distribution expenses, administration expenses and finance charges.

· To maintain the existing earning capacity of non-current assets.

Revenue expenditure is charged to the statement of profit or loss of a period, provided that it relates to the trading activity and sales of that particular period.

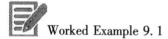 Worked Example 9. 1

A business purchases a building for £30,000. It then adds an extension to the building at a cost of £10,000. The building needs to have a few broken windows mended, its floors polished and some missing roof tiles replaced. These cleaning and maintenance jobs cost £900.

Requirement

Can you identify the capital expenditure and revenue expenditure in this example? And give your explanations.

Solution

In this example, the original purchase (£30,000) and the cost of the extension (£10,000) are capital expenditure, because they are incurred to acquire and then improve a non-current asset and so can be capitalised as part of it.

The other costs of £900 are revenue expenditure, because these merely maintain the building and thus the 'earning capacity' of the building.

 Question

State the type of expenditure, capital or revenue, incurred in the transactions listed in Exhibit 9. 1:

Exhibit 9. 1

Distinction between capital and revenue expenditure	
Expenditure	Type of expenditure
1. Buying van	
2. Petrol costs for van	
3. Repairs to van	
4. Putting extra headlights on van	
5. Buying machinery	
6. Electricity costs of using machinery	
7. We spent £1,500 on machinery: £1,000 was for an item (improvement) added to the machine; and £500 was for repairs	
8. Painting outside of new building	
9. Three years later—repainting outside of the building in (8)	

2. Capital Income and Revenue Income

Capital income is the proceeds from the sale of non-trading assets (i.e. proceeds from the sale of non-current assets, including long-term investments). The profits (or losses) from the sale of non-current assets are included in the statement of profit or loss of a business, for the accounting period in which the sale takes place. For instance, the business may sell vehicles or machinery which it no longer needs—the proceeds will be capital income.

Revenue income is income derived from the following sources.

· The sale of trading assets, such as goods held in inventory.

· The provision of services.

· Interest and dividends received from investments held by the business.

9. 2   IAS 16 Property, Plant and Equipment

The accounting treatment of tangible non-current assets is covered by IAS 16 Property, plant and equipment. This standard deals with the recognition of assets, the determination of their carrying amounts and the depreciation charges relating to them (covered in Chapter 6).

1. Definition of Property, Plant and Equipment

IAS 16 defined **property, plant and equipment** as 'tangible assets' that:

· Are held by an entity for use in the production or supply of goods or services, for rental to others, or for administrative purposes.

· Are expected to be used during more than one period.

This definition covers the majority of the tangible non-current assets that might normally be held by a business entity.

Carrying amount is the amount at which an asset is recognised after deducting any accumulated depreciation and impairment losses.

2. Measurement of Property, Plant and Equipment ├──────────

(1) Initial Measurement

IAS 16 requires that items of property, plant and equipment should be measured at cost on initial recognition. The entries to record an acquisition of a non-current asset are:

DEBIT	Non-current asset—cost	X
CREDIT	Cash (or payable, if a credit transaction)	X

The **cost of PPE** includes all amounts incurred to acquire the asset and any amounts that can be directly attributable to bringing the asset to the location and working condition for its intended use.

Directly attributable costs include:

· Import duties.

· The cost of site preparation, e.g. levelling the floor of the factory so the machine can be installed.

· Initial delivery and handling costs.

· Installation and assembly costs.

· Professional fees (lawyers, architects, engineers).

· Costs of testing whether the asset is working properly, after deducting the net proceeds from selling samples produced when testing equipment.

· Staff costs arising directly from the construction or acquisition of the asset.

Please note that the costs of training staff to use a new asset cannot be capitalised because it is not probable that economic benefits will be generated from training the staff, as we can't guarantee that those staff will stay and use the asset. The costs of training staff should be expensed.

(2) Subsequent Measurement

The cost of subsequent capital expenditure on a non-current asset will be added to the cost of the asset, provided this expenditure enhances the benefits of the non-current asset or restores any benefits consumed.

This means that costs of major improvements or a major overhaul may be capitalised. However, the costs of repairs that are carried out simply to maintain existing performance may not be capitalised: they will be treated as expenses of the reporting period in which the work is done and charged in full as an expense in that period.

(3) Part Exchange

A business might purchase a new item of PPE for cash or on credit, or it may hand over an old asset in part-exchange. This is common, for example, with motor vehicles. The supplier of the new asset agrees to take the old asset and gives the buyer a reduction in the purchase price of the new asset. This reduction is the part-exchange value of the old asset.

For example, a business purchases a new delivery van, trading in an old van in part exchange. The cost of the new van is £ 25,000 and the part exchange value of the old van is £ 10,000, so the business will pay the van dealer £ 15,000. As we will see in section 9. 4 below, profit or loss on the disposal of the old van must also be calculated and recorded.

9.3　Revaluation of Non-current Assets

IAS 16 allows entities to revalue non-current assets to fair value. Largely because of inflation, it is now quite common for the market value of certain non-current assets to go up, in spite of getting older. The most obvious example of rising market values is land and buildings.

IAS 16 allows entities to choose between keeping an asset recorded at cost or revaluing it to fair value. An entity may decide that in order to give a fairer view of the position of the business, some non-current assets should be revalued, otherwise the total value of the assets of the business might seem unrealistically low.

IAS 16 requires that when an item of property, plant and equipment is revalued, the whole class of assets to which it belongs should be revalued. A 'class' of assets is simply a group of assets of similar nature and use—e.g. land and buildings, machinery, motor vehicles, fixtures and fittings. All the items within a class should be revalued at the same time to prevent selective revaluation of certain assets and to avoid disclosing a mixture of costs and values from different dates in the financial statements.

1. Accounting Treatment for Revaluation Gain and Losses

(1) Revaluation Gain

If the carrying amount of an asset is increased as a result of a revaluation, the accounting treatment for the revaluation involves:

①Adjust cost account to revalued amount.

②Remove accumulated depreciation charged on the asset to date.

③Put the balance to the revaluation reserve.

A revaluation upward is recorded as follows:

DEBIT　　Non-current asset (revalued amount less original cost)　　　X

DEBIT　　Accumulated depreciation (total depreciation to date)　　　X

CREDIT　Revaluation surplus/reserve (revalued amount less CV)　　　　　X

Revaluation surplus /revaluation reserve is part of the capital section in statement of financial position. The gain can't be recorded in the profit and loss because it is not realised in the form of cash.

Please note that revaluation gain is shown as 'other comprehensive income' in the 'statement of profit or loss and other comprehensive income' ('statement of comprehensive income'). This will be discussed in detail in Chapter 12.

(2) Revaluation Loss

If the carrying amount of an asset is decreased as a result of a revaluation, the decrease is normally recognised as an expense in profit or loss.

If the asset has been previously revalued, a revaluation loss may be taken to the revaluation surplus first. If the revaluation surplus is not sufficient to cover the loss, loss is charged in profit or loss.

2. A Worked Example

We now will work through an example to show the accounting treatment for revaluation gain and losses. Remember when non-current assets are revalued, depreciation should be charged on the revalued amount.

 Worked Example 9. 2

When Ira Vann commenced trading as a car hire dealer on 1 January 20×1, he purchased business premises at a cost of £50,000.

For the purpose of accounting for depreciation, he decided the following.

· The land part of the business premises was worth £20,000; this would not be depreciated.

· The building part of the business premises was worth the remaining £30,000. This would be depreciated by the straight-line method to a nil residual value over 30 years.

After five years of trading, on 1 January 20×6 Ira decides that his business premises are now worth £150,000, divided into:

	£
Land	75,000
Building	75,000
	150,000

He estimates that the building still has a further 25 years of useful life remaining.

Requirement

(1) Calculate the annual charge for depreciation for the first five years of the building's life and the statement of financial position value of the land and building as at 31 December 20×5.

(2) Demonstrate the impact the revaluation will have on the depreciation charge and the statement of financial position value of the land and building as at 31 December 20×6.

(3) Five years after the revaluation to £75,000, the market value of building has fallen to £40,000 on 31 December 20Y0. Demonstrate the impact the revaluation will have on the depreciation charge and the statement of financial position value of the land and building as at 31 December 20Y0.

Solution

(1) **Before the revaluation:**

Annual depreciation = £30,000/30 years = £1,000

Accumulated depreciation after the first five years = £5,000

So the statement of financial position value of the land and building as at 31 December 20×5 is: £50,000 − £5,000 = £45,000

(2) **When the revaluation takes place,** the accounting treatment for the revaluation above will be:

		£	£
DEBIT	Building—cost (£75,000 − £30,000)	45,000	
DEBIT	Building—accumulated depreciation	5,000	
DEBIT	Land—cost (£75,000 − £20,000)	55,000	
CREDIT	Revaluation surplus		105,000

After the upward revaluation:

Depreciation will be charged on the building at a new rate of:

Annual depreciation of the building = Revalued amount/Remaining useful life

$$= £75,000/25 = £3,000$$

The effect of these entries is as follows.

Land—Cost

20×6		£	20×6		£
1 Jan	Balance b/d	20,000	31 Dec	Balance c/d	75,000
	Revaluation surplus	55,000			
		75,000			75,000

Building—Cost or Valuation

20×6		£	20×6		£
1 Jan	Balance b/d	30,000	31 Dec	Balance c/d	75,000
	Revaluation surplus	45,000			
		75,000			75,000

·158·

Introduction to
Financial Reporting
财务报告导论

Building—Accumulated depreciation

20×6		£	20×6		£
1. Jan	Revaluation surplus	5,000	1 Jan	Balance b/d (£1,000× 5)	5,000
31 Dec	Balance c/d	3,000	31 Dec	Depreciation	3,000
		8,000			8,000

Revaluation surplus

20×6		£	20×6		£
31 Dec	Balance c/d	105,000	1 Jan	Land—cost	55,000
				Building—cost	45,000
				Building—accu depreciation	5,000
		105,000			105,000

Building—Depreciation

20×6		£	20×6		£
31 Dec	Building—accu depreciation	3,000	31 Dec	Profit and loss	3,000

After the upward revaluation,

the carrying amount of the land as at 31 December 20×6 is £75,000.

the carrying amount of the building as at 31 December 20×6 is: £75,000 − £3,000 = £72,000

(3) **After the downward revaluation:**

The accounting treatment for the downward revaluation is:

		£	£
DEBIT	Revaluation surplus	20,000	
	Building—accumulated depreciation	15,000	
CREDIT	Buildings—Cost (£75,000 − £40,000)		35,000

The effect of these entries is as follows:

Land—Cost

20Y0		£	20Y0		£
1 Jan	Balance b/d	75,000	31 Dec	Balance c/d	75,000

Building—Cost or Valuation

20Y0		£	20Y0		£
1 Jan	Balance b/d	75,000	31 Dec	Revaluation surplus	35,000
			31 Dec	Balance c/d	40,000
		75,000			75,000

Building—Accumulated depreciation

20Y0		£	20Y0		£
31 Dec	Revaluation surplus	15,000	31 Dec	Balance b/d (£3,000×5)	15,000

Revaluation surplus

20Y0		£	20Y0		£
31 Dec	Building—cost	35,000	1 Jan	Balance b/d	105,000
31 Dec	Balance c/d	85,000	31 Dec	Building—accu depreciation	15,000
		120,000			120,000

The carrying amount of the land as at 31 December 20Y0 is £75,000.

The carrying amount of the building as at 31 December 20Y0 is: £40,000.

Note: From 1 Jan 20Y1, depreciation will be charged on the building at a new rate of:

Annual depreciation of the building = Revalued amount/Remaining useful life

$$= £40,000/20 = £2,000$$

Question

Company X prepares financial statements to 31 May each year. On 31 May 20×5, the company acquired land for £400,000. This land was revalued at £450,000 on 31 May 20×6 and at £375,000 on 31 May 20×7.

Explain how the revaluations should be dealt with in the financial statements.

9.4   Non-current Assets Disposals

1. The Principles Behind Calculating the Profit or Loss on Disposal

Non-current assets are not purchased by a business with the intention of reselling them in the normal course of trade. However, they might be sold off at some stage during their life, either when their useful life is over or before then. A business might decide to sell off a non-current asset long before its useful life has ended.

Whenever a business sells something, it will make a profit or a loss. When non-current assets are disposed of, there will be a profit or loss on disposal. As it is a capital item being sold, the profit or loss will be capital income or a capital expense. These gains or losses are reported in the income and expenses part of the statement of profit or loss of the business, after gross profit. They are commonly referred to as 'profit (or loss) on disposal of non-current assets'.

The profit or loss on the disposal of a non-current asset is the difference between:

· The carrying amount of the asset at the time of its sale.

· Its net disposal proceeds, which is the amount received less any costs of making the sale.

A profit is made when the net disposal proceeds exceed the carrying amount, and a loss is made when the net disposal proceeds are less than the carrying amount.

2. Accounting Treatment for Asset Disposals

Upon the sale of a non-current asset, we will want to remove it from our ledger accounts. This means:

(1) The cost of that asset needs to be taken out of the asset account.

(2) The accumulated depreciation on the asset which has been sold will have to be taken out of the accumulated provision.

(3) Finally, the profit and loss on sale, if any, will have to be calculated and posted to the profit and loss account.

Accounting entries needed

On the sale of a non-current asset, the following entries are needed:

Step 1: Transfer the cost price of the asset sold to the asset disposal account

DEBIT	Asset disposal account	X	
CREDIT	Asset—cost account		X

Step 2: Transfer the accumulated depreciation of the asset sold to the asset disposal account:

DEBIT	Asset—accumulated depreciation	X	
CREDIT	Asset disposal account		X

Step 3: For the amount received on disposal

DEBIT	Cash/Bank/Receivable account	X	
CREDIT	Asset disposal account		X

Step 4: Transfer the difference (i.e. the amount needed to balance the asset disposal account) to the profit and loss account.

· If a difference on the debit side, there is a profit on the sale:

DEBIT	Asset disposal account	X	
CREDIT	Profit and loss account		X

· If a difference on the credit side, there is a loss on sale:

DEBIT	Profit and loss account	X	
CREDIT	Asset disposal account		X

 **Worked Example 9. 3**

A business purchased a non-current asset on 1 January 20×1 for £25,000. It had an estimated life of six years and an estimated residual value of £7,000 and is depreciated on the straight line basis. The asset was sold after three years on 1 January 20×4 to another trader who paid £17,500 for it.

Requirement

What was the profit or loss on disposal?

Solution

Annual depreciation = £(25,000 − 7,000)/6 = £3,000

Asset—Cost

20×4		£	20×4		£
1 Jan	Balance b/d	25,000	1 Jan	Asset disposal	25,000

Asset—Accumulated depreciation

20×4		£	20×4		£
1 Jan	Asset disposal	9,000	1 Jan	Balance b/d (£3,000×3)	9,000

Asset disposal account

20×4		£	20×4		£
1 Jan	Cost	25,000	1 Jan	Accu depreciation	9,000
1 Jan	Profit and loss	1,500	1 Jan	Proceeds	17,500
		26,500			26,500

Check

	£	£
Disposal proceeds		17,500
Carrying amount at time of sale		
Asset at cost	25,000	
Accumulated depreciation at time of sale	(9,000)	(16,000)
Profit on disposal		1,500

This profit will be shown in the statement of profit or loss as an item of other income, added to the gross profit to arrive at net profit.

 Question

A business has £110,000 worth of machinery at cost. Its policy is to depreciate at 20% per annum straight line. The total accumulated depreciation now stands at £70,000. The business sells for £19,000 a machine which it purchased exactly two years ago for £30,000.

Requirement

Show the relevant ledger entries.

3. Accounting for Disposals of Non-current Assets Given in Part Exchange

Quite often a business does not receive cash for the asset, but instead get a 'part-exchange' or 'trade-in value' for it against the cost of a new asset. Instead of disposal proceeds being received in the form of cash or promised in the form of a receivable, use the part exchange value given to the asset by the other party as its disposal value.

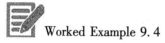 Worked Example 9.4

A business trades in a machine that cost £30,000 two years ago for a new machine that costs £60,000. A cheque for £41,000 was also handed over in full settlement. Machines are depreciated on the straight line basis over five years.

Requirement

What are the relevant ledger account entries?

Solution

Annual depreciation of the old machine = £30,000/5 = £6,000

The part exchange value given to the old machines = £60,000 − £41,000 = £19,000. So £19,000 will be used as the disposal value of the old machine.

The ledger accounts are as follow:

Machine—cost

	£		£
Balance b/d	30,000	Machine disposal	30,000
Cash at bank	41,000		
Machine disposal (part exchange value)	19,000	Balance c/d	60,000
	90,000		90,000

The new asset is recorded in the non-current asset—machine account at cost (£41,000 + £19,000) = £60,000.

Machine—Accumulated depreciation

	£		£
Machine disposal	12,000	Bal. b/d (£6,000×2)	12,000

Machine disposal account

	£		£
Cost	30,000	Accu depreciation	12,000
Profit and loss	1,000	Part exchange value	19,000
	31,000		31,000

	£	£
Disposal value		19,000
Carrying amount at time of sale		
Machine at cost	30,000	
Accumulated depreciation at time of disposal	(12,000)	(18,000)
Profit on disposal		1,000

9.5   Disclosure in Financial Statements

The disclosure requirements in IAS 16 are extensive and include both numerical and narrative disclosures. The financial statements should show a reconciliation of the carrying amount of non-current assets at the beginning and end of the period. The reconciliation should show the movement on the non-current asset balance and include the following.

· Additions.

· Disposals.

· Increases/decreases from revaluations.

· Reductions in carrying amount.

· Depreciation.

· Any other movements.

An illustration is given as Exhibit 9.2.

Exhibit 9.2

Property, Plant and Equipment Note			
	Land and buildings	Plant and equipment	Total
	£	£	£
Cost			
At 1 January 20×4	40,000	10,000	50,000
Revaluation surplus	12,000	–	12,000
Additions	–	4,000	4,000
Disposals		(1,000)	(1,000)
At 31 December 20×4	52,000	13,000	65,000
Accumulated depreciation			
At 1 January 20×4	10,000	6,000	16,000
Charge for year	1,000	3,000	4,000

Exhibit 9. 2(continued)

Disposals	_____	(500)	(500)
At 31 December 20×4	11,000	8,500	19,500
Carrying amount			
At 31 December 20×4	41,000	4,500	45,500
At 1 January 20×4	30,000	4,000	34,000

As well as the reconciliation above, the financial statements should disclose the following.

· An accounting policy note should disclose the measurement bases used for determining the amounts at which depreciable assets are stated, along with the other accounting policies.

· For each class of property, plant and equipment:

—Depreciation methods used

—Useful lives or the depreciation rates used

—Total depreciation allocated for the period

—Gross amount of depreciable assets and the related accumulated depreciation at the beginning and end of the period

For revalued assets:

· Basis used to revalue the assets.

· Effective date of the revaluation.

· Whether an independent valuer was involved.

· Carrying amount of each class of property, plant and equipment that would have been included in the financial statements had the assets been carried at cost less depreciation.

· Revaluation surplus, indicating the movement for the period and any restrictions on the distribution of the balance to shareholders.

Summary

· Tangible non-current assets are those with physical form.

· Capital expenditure is expenditure which forms part of the cost of non-current assets.

· Revenue expenditure is expenditure incurred for the purpose of the trade or to maintain non-current assets.

· The accounting treatment of tangible non-current assets is covered by IAS 16 Property, plant and equipment.

· The cost of an item of PPE includes: purchase price; delivery costs; taxes and duties; installation and assembly costs; professional fees; testing costs.

· Subsequent capital expenditure may be added to the cost of an item of PPE provided the expenditure enhances or restores any benefits consumed.

· Part of the purchase price of an item of PPE may be settled by trading in an old asset in part-exchange.

· IAS 16 allows entities to revalue non-current assets to fair value. When a non-current asset is revalued, depreciation is charged on the revalued amount.

· A disposal account is used to calculate the profit or loss on disposal of an asset, which is the amount by which the sales proceeds of the asset differs from its carrying amount at the date of disposal.

· When an old asset has been given in part-exchange for a new one, the part-exchange value is accounted for as the old asset's disposal proceeds.

· IAS 16 requires a reconciliation of the opening and closing carrying amounts of non-current assets to be given in the financial statements.

Exercise

9. 1 Materials purchased and used by Pola & Co for repairs to office buildings have been included in the draft financial statements as purchases. The necessary amendment will(   ).

A.Increase gross profit with no effect on net profit

B.Increase gross profit and reduce net profit

C.Have no effect on either gross profit or net profit

D.Reduce gross profit and increase net profit

9. 2 Marcellus acquired new premises at a cost of £250,000 on 1 January 20 × 1. Marcellus paid the following further costs during the year ended 31 December 20×1.

	£
Costs of initial adaptation	13,900
Legal costs relating to purchase	1,200
Monthly cleaning contract	9,600
Office furniture	6,500

What amount should appear as the cost of premises in the company's statement of financial position at 31 December 20×1? (   )

A.£250,000

B.£263,900

C.£265,100

D.£271,600

9. 3 In the year to 31 December 20 × 9, Jason recorded some capital expenditure as revenue expenditure. What is the effect on his profit for the year to 31 December 20×9 and his net assets at that date? (   )

	Profit	Net assets
A.	Overstated	Overstated
B.	Overstated	Understated
C.	Understated	Overstated
D.	Understated	Understated

9. 4 Which of the following are capital, as opposed to revenue, expenses? (   )

1 The repair of a machine currently used in the production process that has broken down

2 The cost of an extension to a factory building, which doubles the size of the production area

3 The cost of installing a new machine in a factory

    A.2 only

    B.1 and 2 only

    C.2 and 3 only

    D.1, 2 and 3

9. 5 A business with a reporting period of the 12 months ended 30 June buys a non-current asset on 1 July 20×3 for £200,000. Depreciation is charged at 15% per annum on the reducing balance basis. On 30 June 20×5 the asset was sold for £54,800.

What was the loss on sale of the asset? (   )

    A.£89,700

    B.£85,200

    C.£68,025

    D.£55,200

9. 6 A business purchased a motor car on 1 July 20×3 for £20,000. It is to be depreciated at 20 per cent per year on the straight line basis, assuming a residual value at the end of five years of £4,000, with a proportionate depreciation charge in the years of purchase and disposal. The £20,000 cost was correctly entered in the cash book but posted to the debit of the motor vehicles repairs account.

How will the business profit for the year ended 31 December 20×3 be affected by the error? (   )

    A.Understated by £18,400

    B.Understated by £16,800

    C.Overstated by £18,400

    D.Overstated by £16,800

9. 7 At 31 December 20×4 Q, a limited liability company, owned a building that it had purchased 10 years ago for £800,000. It was being depreciated at 2% per year on the straight-

line basis. On 1 January 20×5 a revaluation to £1,000,000 was recognised. At this date the building had a remaining useful life of 40 years.

What is the depreciation charge for the year ended 31 December 20×5 and the revaluation surplus balance as at 1 January 20×5? (　　)

	Depreciation charge for year ended 31 December 20×5	Revaluation surplus as at 1 January 20×5
	£	£
A.	25,000	200,000
B.	25,000	360,000
C.	20,000	200,000
D.	20,000	360,000

9. 8 Which of the following should be disclosed for tangible non-current assets according to IAS 16 Property, plant and equipment? (　　)

1 Depreciation methods used and the total depreciation allocated for the period

2 A reconciliation of the carrying amount of non-current assets at the beginning and end of the period

3 For revalued assets, whether an independent valuer was involved in the valuation

4 For revalued assets, the effective date of the revaluation

A.1, 2 and 4 only

B.1 and 2 only

C.1, 2, 3 and 4

D.1, 3 and 4 only

9. 9 Which of the following should be included in the reconciliation of the carrying amount of tangible non-current assets at the beginning and end of the accounting period? (　　)

1 Additions

2 Disposals

3 Depreciation

4 Increases/decreases from revaluations

A.1 and 3 only

B.1, 2, and 3 only

C.1, 3 and 4

D.1, 2, 3 and 4

9. 10 Banter Co purchased an office building on 1 January 20×1. The building cost was £1,600,000 and this was depreciated by the straight-line method at 2% per year, assuming a 50-year life and nil residual value. The building was revalued to £2,250,000 on 1 January 20× 6. The useful life was not revised. The company's financial year ends on 31 December. What is

the balance on the revaluation surplus at 1 January 20×6? (   )

      A.£650,000

      B.£792,000

      C.£797,000

      D.£810,000

9. 11 Your firm bought a machine for £5,000 on 1 January 20×1, when it had a useful life of four years and a residual value of £1,000. Straight-line depreciation is to be applied on a monthly basis. On 31 December 20×3, the machine was sold for £1,600.

The amount to be entered in the 20×3 statement of profit or loss for profit or loss on disposal is(   ).

      A.profit of £600

      B.loss of £600

      C.profit of £350

      D.loss of £400

9. 12 Alpha sells machine B for £50,000 cash on 30 April 20×4. Machine B cost £100,000 when it was purchased and has a carrying value of £65,000 at the date of disposal. What are the journal entries to record the disposal of machine B? (   )

A.Dr Accumulated depreciation	£35,000	
Dr Loss on disposal	£15,000	
Dr Cash	£50,000	
Cr Non-current assets—cost		£100,000
B.Dr Accumulated depreciation	£65,000	
Dr Loss on disposal	£35,000	
Cr Non-current assets—cost		£100,000
C.Dr Accumulated depreciation	£35,000	
Dr Cash	£50,000	
Cr Non-current assets		£65,000
Cr Profit on disposal		£20,000
D.Dr Non-current assets	£65,000	
Dr Accumulated depreciation	£35,000	
Cr Cash		£50,000
Cr Profit on disposal		£50,000

9. 13 In the year ended 31 December 20×7 Bobby traded in for £6,860 a vehicle costing £12,000 on 1 November 20×5 against the cost (£9,600) of a new vehicle. The balance due for the new vehicle has been paid in cash and debited to the cost of vehicles account and credited to cash at bank.

What net adjustment is required to the company's cost of vehicles account as a result of this transaction? (　　)

A.£9,600 DR

B.£12,000 CR

C.£6,800 DR

D.£5,140 CR

9.14 A non-current asset (cost £10,000, depreciation £7,500) is given in part exchange for a new asset costing £20,500. The agreed trade-in value was £3,500. Which of the following will the statement of profit or loss include? (　　)

A.A loss on disposal £1,000

B.A profit on disposal £1,000

C.A loss on purchase of a new asset £3,500

D.A profit on disposal £3,500

9.15 A company purchased a car for £18,000 on 1 January 20×0. The car was traded in on 1 January 20×2. The new car has a list price of £30,000 and the garage offered a part-exchange allowance of £5,000. Company provides depreciation on cars using the reducing balance method at a rate of 25% per annum.

What loss on disposal will be recognised in the statement of profit or loss for the year ended 31 December 20×2? (　　)

A.£5,125

B.£8,500

C.£10,125

D.£11,175

9.16 A car was purchased by a newsagent business in May 20×0 for £10,000. The business adopts a date of 31 December as its year end. The car was traded in for a replacement vehicle in August 20×3 at an agreed value of £5,000. It has been depreciated at 25% per annum on the reducing balance method, charging a full year's depreciation in the year of purchase and none in the year of sale.

What was the profit or loss on disposal of the vehicle during the year ended December 20×3? (　　)

A.Profit: £718

B.Profit: £781

C.Profit: £1,788

D.Profit: £1,836

9.17 A business acquired a car on 1 October 20×5 for £117,000 and has depreciated it on a reducing balance basis at 20% per annum. On 30 September 20×7 the car was sold for £58,000.

What is the loss on disposal of the car in the financial statements for the 12-month reporting period to 30 September 20×7? (　　)

    A.£14,560

    B.£14,800

    C.£16,880

    D.£29,360

9.18 The following information relates to the disposal of two machines by Paddock.

	Machine 1	Machine 2
	£	£
Cost	120,000	140,000
Disposal proceeds	90,000	80,000
Profit/(loss) on disposal	30,000	(40,000)

What was the total carrying amount of both machines sold at the date of disposal? (　　)

    A.£100,000

    B.£160,000

    C.£180,000

    D.£240,000

9.19 Cataract plc purchases a machine for which the supplier's list price is £28,000. Cataract plc pays £23,000 in cash and trades in an old machine, which has a carrying amount of £8,000. It is the company's policy to depreciate machines at the rate of 10% per annum on cost.

What is the carrying amount of the machine after one year? (　　)

    A.£18,000

    B.£25,200

    C.£20,700

    D.£22,200

9.20 Demolition plc purchases a machine for £15,000 on 1 January 20×1. After incurring transportation costs of £1,300 and spending £2,500 on installing the machine it breaks down and costs £600 to repair. Depreciation is charged at 10% per annum.

At what carrying amount will the machine be shown in Demolition plc's statement of financial position at 31 December 20×1? (　　)

    A.£13,500

B.£14,670

C.£16,920

D.£18,800

9.21 Derek plc purchased a van on 1 October 20×0 for a total cost of £22,000 by paying £17,500 cash and trading in an old van. The old van had cost £20,000 and the related accumulated depreciation was £14,200.

The loss on disposal of the old van in Derek plc's statement of profit or loss for the year ended 31 December 20×0 is( ).

A.£1,300

B.£2,000

C.£2,500

D.£5,800

9.22 A company's plant and machinery ledger account for the year ended 30 September 20×2 was as follows:

Plant and machinery

	£		£
20×1		20×2	
1 Oct Balance b/d	381,200	1 Jun Disposal account	36,000
1 Dec Cash—addition at cost	18,000	30 Sep Balance	363,200
	399,200		399,200

The company's policy is to charge depreciation at 20% per year on the straight-line basis, with a proportionate charge in the years of acquisition and disposal.

What is the journal entry to record the depreciation charge in the statement of profit or loss for the year ended 30 September 20×2? ( )

A.Debit Accumulated depreciation £84,040, Credit Depreciation expense £84,040

B.Debit Depreciation expense £84,040, Credit Accumulated depreciation £84,040

C.Debit Accumulated depreciation £76,840, Credit Depreciation expense £76,840

D.Debit Depreciation expense £76,840, Credit Accumulated depreciation £76,840

9.23 A business purchased two machines on 1 January 20×5 at a cost of £15,000 each. Each had an estimated life of five years and a nil residual value. The straight-line method of depreciation is used, with a proportionate charge in the years of acquisition and disposal.

Owing to an unforeseen slump in market demand for its end product, the business decided to reduce its output, and switch to making other products instead. On 31 March 20×7, one machine was sold (on credit) to a buyer for £8,000. Later in the reporting period, however, it was decided to abandon production altogether, and the second machine was sold on 1 December 20×7 for £2,500 cash.

Requirement

Prepare the machinery account, accumulated depreciation of machinery account and disposal account for the 12-month reporting period to 31 December 20×7 to determine the profit or loss on disposal of each machine.

9.24 * The following balances appear in the ledger of Rogers and Co at 1 March 20×8.

Vans—cost £13,100

Accumulated depreciation—vans £8,975

The policy of the company is to provide a full year's depreciation in the year of purchase and none in the year of sales. Vans are depreciated at 25% per annum using the straight-line method.

A new van was purchased on 1 December 20×8 at a cost of £14,800. On the same date, a van that had originally been purchased in June 20×5 for £8,600 was sold for £3,650.

Prepare the vans account, accumulated depreciation of vans account and vans disposal account for the year ended 28 February 20×9.

9.25 * The accounting records of Riffon, a limited liability company included the following balance at 30 June 20×2:

	£000
Office buildings—cost	1,600
Office buildings—accumulated depreciation	320

(The estimated life of building is 50 years; it has been used for 10 years already)

	£000
Plant and machinery—cost (all purchased in 20×1 or later)	840
Plant and machinery—accumulated depreciation	306

(straight line basis at 25% per year)

20×2

1 Jul   It was decided to revalue the office building to £2,000,000, with no change to the estimate of its remaining useful life.

1 Oct   New plant costing £200,000 was purchased.

20×3

1 Apr   Plant which had cost £240,000 and with accumulated depreciation at 30 June 20×2 of £180,000 was sold for £70,000.

It is the company's policy to charge a full year's depreciation on plant in the year of acquisition and none in the year of sale.

Requirement

Draw up the following ledger accounts to record the above balances and events for the year ended 30 June 20×3:

    (1) Office buildings—cost

        Office buildings—accumulated depreciation

    (2) Plant and machinery—cost

        Plant and machinery—accumulated depreciation

    (3) Disposal account

    (4) Revaluation surplus

9. 26 A machine costs £75,000 and will be kept for four years when it will be traded in at an estimated value of £30,720. Show the calculations of the figures for depreciation for each of the four years using the:

    (1) Straight line method.

    (2) Reducing (diminishing) balance method, using a depreciation rate of 20%.

Reference

1. ACCA FA Financial Accounting/FIA FFA Interactive Text 2020, BPP Learning Media.

2. ACCA FA Financial Accounting/FIA FFA Practice & Revision Kit 2020, BPP Learning Media.

3. Accounting (Study Manual 2020), The Institute of Chartered Accountants in England and Wales.

4. Accounting (Question Bank 2020), The Institute of Chartered Accountants in England and Wales.

Chapter 10

Intangible Non-current Assets

■Learning Objectives

· Recognise the difference between tangible and intangible non- current assets.

· Identify types of intangible assets.

· Calculate amounts to be capitalised as development expenditure or to be expensed from given information.

· Calculate and account for the charge for amortisation.

· Identify the definition and treatment of 'research costs' and 'development costs' in accordance with IFRSs.

10.1　Intangible Assets

In the latter part of the twentieth and in the twenty-first centuries more of the economic growth of companies is being driven by investments not in physical assets such as property plant and equipment, but in non-physical or intangible items, such as intellectual capital, organisational and institutional assets and reputation. The dot.com boom of the 1990s saw enormous growth in Internet and telecommunications companies, which has continued the twenty-first century with large technology companies, such as Microsoft, Google, Apple and Huawei, playing an increasingly important role in the world's economy. Today's products are increasingly intangible, and the assets used to produce them are increasingly intangible. Even traditional companies are more reliant now on knowledge-based assets as a source of competitive advantage and to generate their wealth. The ability to identify, measure, and account for these intangible assets and, ultimately provide sound information about them is of great importance to users of financial reports.

1. Intangible Assets Defined

Intangible assets are identifiable non-monetary assets that cannot be seen, touched or physically measured but are identifiable as a separate asset. Examples include patents, trademarks, licences, brands, intellectual property rights, customer relationships, and computer software. Businesses expend vast resources on intangible assets, and this chapter explains and illustrates when such asset should be recogised, and how they should be valued in the business's financial statements.

Tangible and intangible assets are presented separately on the statement of financial position. Examples of intangible assets that should be recognised and reported in the statement of financial position are set out in IAS 38. They include:

• **Marketing-related** intangible assets which are used primarily in the marketing or promotion of products or services such as trademarks, newspaper mastheads, Internet domain names and non-compete agreements.

• **Technology-related** intangible assets which arise from contractual rights to use technology (patented and unpatented), databases, formulae, designs, software, processes and recipes.

• **Customer-or supplier-related** intangible assets which arise from relationships with or knowledge of customers or suppliers such as licensing, royalty and standstill agreements, servicing contracts and use rights such as airport landing slots and customer list.

• **Artistic-related** intangible assets which arise from the right to benefits such as royalties from artistic works such as plays, books, films and music, and from non-contractual copyright protection.

2. Accounting Treatment

In accordance with IAS 38, intangible assets are capitalised in the accounts and amortised (another word for depreciation but referring specifically to intangible assets). Amortisation is intended to write off the asset over its useful life (under the accruals concept).

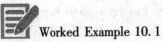 **Worked Example 10.1**

A business buys a patent for £8,000. It expects to use the patent for the next five years, after which it will be valueless. Amortisation is calculated in the same way as for tangible assets:

$$\frac{\text{Cost} - \text{residual value}}{\text{Estimated useful life}}$$

In this case, amortisation will be £1,600 per annum (£8,000/5).

The double entry treatment is similar to that for depreciation. The entries for the amortisation calculated above will be:

		£	£
DEBIT	Amortisation account (statement of profit or loss)	1,600	
CREDIT	Accumulated amortisation account (statement of financial position)		1,600

10. 2　Research and Development

1.　Definition of Research and Development

Large companies may spend significant amounts of money on research and development (R&D) activities. Obviously, any amounts so expended must be credited to cash and debited to an account for research and development expenditure. The accounting problem is how to treat the debit balance on the R&D account at the reporting date.

There are two possibilities.

· The debit balance may be classified as an expense and transferred to the statement of profit or loss. This is referred to as 'writing off' the expenditure.

· The debit balance may be classified as an asset and included in the statement of financial position. This is referred to as 'capitalising' or 'carrying forward' the expenditure. If R&D activity eventually leads to new or improved products which generate revenue, the costs should be carried forward to be matched against that revenue in future accounting periods.

So the main question surrounding research and development (R&D) costs is whether they should be treated as an expense or capitalised as an asset. This question is dealt with in IAS 38 Intangible Assets.

Research is original and planned investigation undertaken with the prospect of gaining new scientific or technical knowledge and understanding.

Development is the application of research findings or other knowledge to a plan or design for the production of new or substantially improved materials, devices, products, processes, systems or services prior to the commencement of commercial production or use.

2.　Recognition of Research and Development

Under IAS 38 Intangible Assets, research expenditure must be expensed whereas development expenditure must be capitalised provided a strict set of criteria is met.

IAS 38 takes a view that, a business undertaking research activity cannot demonstrate that any intangible asset which may result will generate probable future economic benefits and so all such expenditure is recognised as an expense when it is incurred. Whilst expenditure on development is recognised as an asset if the entity can demonstrate that the expenditure will generate probable future economic benefits.

Development expenditure must be recognised as an intangible asset if, and only if, the business can demonstrate **all** of the criteria in IAS 38 have been met. The recognition criteria are as follows:

(a) the technical feasibility of completing the intangible asset so that it will be available for use or sale.

(b) the intention to complete the intangible asset and use or sell it.

(c) its ability to use or sell the intangible asset.

(d) how the intangible asset will generate probable future economic benefits.

(e) the availability of adequate technical, financial and other resources to complete the development and to use or sell the intangible asset.

(f) its ability to measure reliably the expenditure attributable to the intangible asset during its development.

It is important to note that if the answers to all the conditions (a) to (f) above are 'Yes' then the entity must capitalise the development expenditure.

3. Accounting Treatment of Research and Development

When development expenditure is to be recognised as an asset, the accounting entries are:

		£	£
DEBIT	Intangible non-current assets	X	
CREDIT	Cash/payables		X

Once capitalised as an asset, development costs must be amortised and recognised as an expense to match the costs with the related revenue or cost savings. The amortisation will begin when the asset is available for use.

Amortisation must be done on a systematic basis to reflect the pattern in which the related economic benefits are recognised. If the pattern cannot be determined reliably, the straight-line method should be used. If the intangible asset is considered to have an indefinite useful life, it should not be amortised but should be subjected to an annual impairment review (which falls outside the scope of this textbook).

10. 3   Disclosure in Financial Statements

The disclosure requirements in IAS 38 are extensive and include both numerical and narrative disclosures.

The financial statements should show a reconciliation of the carrying amount of intangible assets at the beginning and at the end of the period. The reconciliation should show the movement on intangible assets, including:

· Additions.

· Disposals.

· Reductions in carrying amount.

- Amortisation.

- Any other movements.

An illustration is given as Exhibit 10. 1.

Exhibit 10. 1

Intangible Asset Note			
	Development costs	Patents	Total
	£	£	£
Cost			
At 1 January 20×4	30,000	10,000	40,000
Additions	15,000	4,000	19,000
Disposals	_____	(1,000)	(1,000)
At 31 December 20×4	45,000	13,000	58,000
Amortisation			
At 1 January 20×4	5,000	6,000	11,000
Charge for year	1,000	3,000	4,000
Disposals	_____	(500)	(500)
At 31 December 20×4	6,000	8,500	14,500
Carrying amount			
At 31 December 20×4	39,000	4,500	43,500
At 1 January 20×4	25,000	4,000	29,000

Summary

- Intangible assets are non-current assets with no physical substance.

- Expenditure on research must always be written off in the period in which it is incurred.

- If the criteria laid down by IAS 38 are satisfied, development expenditure must be capitalised as an intangible asset. If it has a finite useful life, it should then be amortised over that life. If the criteria in IAS 38 are not satisfied, development expenditure must be written off in the period in which it is incurred.

- IAS 38 requires both numerical and narrative disclosures for intangible assets.

Exercise

10. 1 The required accounting treatment for expenditure on research is to capitalise it and carry it forward as an asset.(   )

A.True

B.False

10. 2 Which of the following items is an intangible asset? （　　　）

A. Land

B. Patents

C. Buildings

D. Van

The following information is relevant for questions 10. 3 and 10. 4.

10. 3 XY Co has development expenditure of £500,000. Its policy is to amortise development expenditure at 2% per annum. Accumulated amortisation brought forward is £20,000.

What is the charge in the statement of profit or loss for the year's amortisation? （　　　）

A. £10,000

B. £400

C. £20,000

D. £9,600

10. 4 What is the amount shown in the statement of financial position for development expenditure? （　　　）

A. £500,000

B. £480,000

C. £470,000

D. £490,000

10. 5 According to IAS 38 Intangible assets, which of the following statements about research and development expenditure are correct? （　　　）

1 Research expenditure, other than capital expenditure on research facilities, should be recognised as an expense as incurred.

2 In deciding whether development expenditure qualifies to be recognised as an asset, it is necessary to consider whether there will be adequate finance available to complete the project.

3 Development expenditure recognised as an asset must be amortised over a period not exceeding five years.

A. 1, 2 and 3

B. 1 and 2 only

C. 1 and 3 only

D. 2 and 3 only

10. 6 According to IAS 38 Intangible assets, which of the following statements about research and development expenditure are correct? （　　　）

1 If certain conditions are met, an entity may decide to capitalise development expenditure.

2 Research expenditure, other than capital expenditure on research facilities, must be written off as incurred.

3 Capitalised development expenditure must be amortised over a period not exceeding 5 years.

4 Capitalised development expenditure must be disclosed in the statement of financial position under intangible non-current assets.

    A.1, 2 and 4 only

    B.1 and 3 only

    C.2 and 4 only

    D.3 and 4 only

10. 7 According to IAS 38 Intangible assets, which of the following statements is/are correct? (　　)

1 If all the conditions specified in IAS 38 are met, development expenditure may be capitalised if the directors decide to do so.

2 Capitalised development costs are shown in the statement of financial position under the heading of non-current assets.

3 Amortisation of capitalised development expenditure will appear as an item in a company's statement of changes in equity.

    A.2 only

    B.1 and 2

    C.1 and 3

    D.2 and 3

10. 8 According to IAS 38 Intangible assets, which of the following are intangible non-current assets in the accounts of Iota Co? (　　)

1 A patent for a new glue purchased for £20,000 by Iota Co

2 Development costs capitalised in accordance with IAS 38

3 A licence to broadcast a television series, purchased by Iota Co for £150,000

4 A state of the art factory purchased by Iota Co for £1. 5million

    A.1 and 3 only

    B.1, 2 and 3 only

    C.2 and 4 only

    D.2, 3 and 4 only

10. 9 According to IAS 38 Intangible assets, which of the following statements about intangible assets are correct? (　　)

1 If certain criteria are met, research expenditure must be recognised as an intangible asset.

2 If certain criteria are met, development expenditure must be capitalised.

3 Intangible assets must be amortised if they have a definite useful life.

A.2 and 3 only

B.1 and 3 only

C.1 and 2 only

D.All three statements are correct

10. 10 Theta Co purchased a patent on 31 December 20×3 for £250,000. Theta Co expects to use the patent for ten years, after which it will be valueless. According to IAS 38 Intangible assets, what amount will be amortised in Theta Co's statement of profit or loss and other comprehensive income for the year ended 31 December 20×4? (   )

A.£250,000

B.£125,000

C.£25,000

D.£50,000

10. 11 What is the purpose of amortisation? (   )

A.To allocate the cost of an intangible non-current asset over its useful life

B.To ensure that funds are available for the eventual purchase of a replacement non-current asset

C.To reduce the cost of an intangible non-current asset in the statement of financial position to its estimated market value

D.To account for the risk associated with intangible assets

10. 12 PF purchased a quota for carbon dioxide emissions for £15,000 on 30 April 20×6 and capitalised it as an intangible asset in its statement of financial position. PF estimates that the quota will have a useful life of 3 years. What is the journal entry required to record the amortisation of the quota in the accounts for the year ended 30 April 20×9? (   )

A.Dr Expenses   £15,000

  Cr Accumulated amortisation   £15,000

B.Dr Expenses   £5,000

  Cr Accumulated amortisation   £5,000

C.Dr Intangible assets   £5,000

  Cr Accumulated amortisation   £5,000

D.Dr Accumulated amortisation   £15,000

  Cr Intangible assets   £15,000

10. 13 Bluebottle Co has incurred development expenditure of £500,000 and research expenditure of £400,000 in the year ended 31 December 20×1. The development expenditure

has been capitalised in accordance with IAS 38. Bluebottle Co's policy is to amortise capitalised development expenditure over 25 years.

What balances relating to research and development would appear in the financial statements of Bluebottle for the year ended 31 December 20×1? (   )

	Statement of financial position	Statement of profit or loss
A.	£900,000	£nil
B.	£500,000	£400,000
C.	£864,000	£36,000
D.	£480,000	£420,000

10. 14 Dodger Co's financial statements show a carrying value of £950,000 for capitalised development expenditure. Its policy is to amortise development expenditure on a straight-line basis at 5% per annum. Accumulated amortisation brought forward is £50,000.

What is the charge in the statement of profit or loss for the year's amortisation? (   )

A.£43,500

B.£47,500

C.£45,000

D.£50,000

10. 15 Which of the following items (that all generate future economic benefits, and whose costs can be measured reliably), are NOT intangible non-current assets? (   )

1 Computer hardware owned by a business

2 Operating software that operates the computer hardware in (1)

3 A patent bought by a business

4 An extension to an office building owned by a business

A.All four items

B.1, 2 and 4 only

C.1 and 2 only

D.1 and 4 only

Reference

1. ACCA FA Financial Accounting/FIA FFA Interactive Text 2020, BPP Learning Media.

2. ACCA FA Financial Accounting/FIA FFA Practice & Revision Kit 2020, BPP Learning Media.

3. Jennifer Maynard. Financial Accounting, Reporting and Analysis (2017). Oxford University Press.

4. Barry Elliott and Jamie Elliott. Financial Accounting and Reporting (2019). Pearson

Chapter 11 | Introduction to Company Accounting

╭─────■Learning Objectives──────────────────────────────────────╮

　　· Understand the capital structure of a limited liability company, including ordinary shares, preference shares and loan stock.

　　· Record movements in the share capital and share premium accounts.

　　· Identify and record the other reserves which may appear in the company statement of financial position.

　　· Record dividends in ledger accounts and the financial statements.

　　· Record and account for bonus (capitalisation) issues and rights issues.

　　· Calculate and record income tax and finance costs in ledger accounts and the financial statements.

╰──╯

11.1　The Nature of a Limited Company

There are several different legal forms of organisation. These can be grouped into two categories, known as unincorporated bodies and corporate bodies. Unincorporated bodies consist of sole traders and partnerships. All other forms of organisation are corporate bodies. A key feature of corporate bodies, or incorporated bodies, is that they are recognised by law as being a legal entity separate from their members.

1. Separate Legal Entity and Limited Liabilities ├──────────────

A company is defined as a legal entity that is formed by registration under the company law. It has a **separate legal existence,** independent of its owner(s). It can enter contracts in its own name, it can sue or be sued, and it is liable to the tax authorities for tax on the profits that it earns. Because a company has this legal identity, separate from its owners, the way it raises capital from its owners is more formalised than for sole traders or partnerships.

The liabilities of sole traders and partnerships are unlimited. It means that if the business runs up debts that it is unable to pay, the proprietors will become personally liable for the unpaid debts and would be required, if necessary, to sell their private possessions to repay them. For example, if a sole trader has some capital in their business, but the business now owes £40,000 which it cannot repay, the trader might have to sell their house to raise the money to pay off their business debts.

Limited liability companies offer limited liability to their owners. **Limited liability** means that the maximum amount that an owner stands to lose, in the event that the company becomes insolvent and cannot pay off its debts, is their share of the capital in the business.

2. The Classes of Limited Companies

Companies are either public or private companies.

A **public company** has 'plc' in its name. A public company may offer its securities (shares and loan stock such as bonds) for sale to persons who are unrelated to the company ('the public') but is subject to stricter regulation than private companies. In particular, a public company must have issued capital of at least £50,000 (under UK's Companies Act 2006). Before it can trade, at least £12,500 plus the whole of any premium on issue must have been received as cash. Effectively this means that a public limited company must have net assets (assets less liabilities) of at least £12,500. Note that all companies whose shares are traded on a stock market must be 'plcs', but not all plcs have their shares traded on a stock market. The principal reason for forming a public limited company is to gain access to greater amounts of capital from investment institutions and members of the public. The shares of many, but not all, public companies in the UK are quoted on the London Stock Exchange. The shares of public companies in China are quoted on the Shanghai Stock Exchange, Shenzhen Stock Exchange or Hongkong Stock Exchange.

A **private company** ends its name with 'Limited' or 'Ltd'. A private company is any company that is not a public company. Private companies cannot offer their securities for sale to the public at large and thus do not have a stock exchange quotation. There is no minimum level of net assets. One of the main reasons for forming a private rather than a public company is that it enables its owners to keep control of the business, for example, within a family.

3. The Capital of Limited Liability Companies

A company's **initial capital** is divided into units of equal size, known as shares, issued to individuals or companies, called **shareholders.** The total capital raised is referred to as equity share capital.

Ownership of a share entitles the shareholder to receive payment of a share of profit, or **dividend.**

By law, shares must have a **par value** (UK's Companies Act 2006 calls this the 'nominal value'), which can be any amount, for example 1p, 5p, 10p, 25p, 50p, £1 and so on. For example, £100,000 par value of share capital might be represented by 100,000 shares of £1 each, or 200,000 shares of 50p each, or 1,000,000 shares of 10p each, and so on.

A company will often issue shares at above ('at a premium to') par value. For example, a company might issue 100,000 £1 shares at a price of £1.20 each. Subscribers will then pay a total of £120,000. The issued share capital of the company would be shown in its accounts at par value, £100,000. The excess of £20,000 is described not as share capital, but as **share premium** or capital paid-up in excess of par value.

The **issued share capital** of a company (also known as its allotted share capital) is the par value of the shares that have actually been issued to shareholders.

If a company issues shares but 'calls up' the issue amounts in instalments, instead of raising cash immediately, it then has **called-up share capital** that is less than its issued share capital.

When capital is called up, some shareholders might delay their payment (or even default on payment). **Paid-up capital** is the amount of called-up capital that has been paid.

 Worked Example 11.1

If a company issues 400,000 ordinary shares of £1 each, calls up 75 pence per share, and receives payments of £290,000, we would have:

	£
Issued capital	400,000
Called-up capital	300,000
Paid-up capital	290,000
Capital not yet paid-up	10,000

11.2   Equity: Share Capital

At this stage we need to distinguish between the two types of shares most often encountered: ordinary shares and preference shares.

1. Ordinary Shares and Preference Shares

(1) Ordinary Shares

Ordinary shares are by far the most common type of share, which are referred to as 'equity share capital' because each share represents an equal interest in the ownership of the company. Possession of an ordinary voting share represents part ownership of a company and it entitles the holder to one vote in general meetings of the company's ordinary shareholders. This gives shareholders the power to appoint and dismiss a company's directors. The holder of an ordinary share is also entitled to a share of the company's annual profit in the form of a dividend. The amount of the dividend per share is decided each year by the company's directors and varies according to the amount of profit. In years when the company earns high profits, the ordinary shareholders are more likely to receive a large dividend. However, ordinary shareholders run two risks. First, when profits are low they may receive little or no dividend. Second, should the company go bankrupt ('into liquidation' is the correct legal term) the ordinary shareholders are not entitled to be repaid the value of their shares until all the other debts have been paid. Often, where a company has made substantial losses, there is little or nothing left for ordinary shareholders after the company has paid its other debts.

It should also be noted that a company does not normally repay its ordinary shareholders the money they have invested except in the event of liquidation (or by court order). If an ordinary shareholder wishes to sell his or her shares, a buyer must be found. Shareholders in public limited companies can dispose of their shares in the stock market. Similarly, a prospective buyer may acquire 'second-hand' shares through the stock market.

(2) Preference Shares

A company might also issue **preference shares.** Unlike ordinary shares, preference shares carry no voting rights. Preference shareholders are entitled to a fixed rate of dividend each year based on the nominal value of the shares. For example, 8% preference shares with a nominal value of £1 each carry an annual dividend of 8 pence per share. Preference shareholders are entitled to their dividend after all the company's expenses, tax and debt commitments have been paid. Therefore, they rank behind normal company creditors and lenders in yearly terms when it comes to receiving their dividend, but rank in front of ordinary shareholders and will receive their dividend before ordinary shareholders can get any distribution (dividend).

In the event of a company going into liquidation, the preference shareholders are normally entitled to be repaid the nominal value of their shares before the ordinary shareholders. However, if no money is left after paying the other debts they would receive nothing.

As in the case of ordinary shares, companies do not normally repay preference shareholders the money they have invested except in the event of liquidation. Should a preference shareholder wish to dispose of shares, he or she must find a buyer or sell them in the stock market, if the company has a quotation for the preference shares.

Preference shares may be classified in one of two ways.

· Redeemable.

· Irredeemable.

Redeemable preference shares mean that the company will redeem (repay) the nominal value of those shares at a later date. For example, 'redeemable 5% £1 preference shares 20× 9' means that the company will pay these shareholders £1 for every share they hold on a certain date in 20×9. The shares will then be cancelled and no further dividends paid. Redeemable preference shares are treated like loans and are included as non-current liabilities in the statement of financial position. Remember to reclassify them as current liabilities if the redemption is due within 12 months. Dividends paid on redeemable preference shares are treated like interest paid on loans and are included in financial costs in the statement of profit or loss.

Irredeemable preference shares are treated just like other shares. They form part of equity and their dividends are treated as appropriations of profit.

Once the preference dividend has been paid, the remaining profit 'belongs' to the ordinary shareholders. However, the directors will usually decide to retain some profits (**retained earnings**) within the company, and the ordinary dividend will be an amount declared by the directors as being appropriate and affordable.

2. Accounting for Share Capital

In this section, you'll learn about how to record the issue of shares at par value and at a price greater than their nominal value and the share capital not fully paid up.

(1) Shares Issued at Par

When shares are issued at their **par value** and they are **fully paid**:

DEBIT	Cash	X
CREDIT	Share capital (par value)	X

 Worked Example 11. 2

One million ordinary shares with a nominal value of 10p each are issued. Money is received for exactly 1 million shares.

		£	£
DEBIT	Cash	100,000	
CREDIT	Ordinary shares (10p×1,000,000)		100,000

(2) Shares Issued at Premium

When shares are issued at a **premium to their par value**, and the full amount is paid:

DEBIT	Cash	X
CREDIT	Share capital (par value)	X
	Share premium (excess over par value)	X

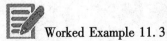 Worked Example 11. 3

One million ordinary shares with a nominal value of 10p each are issued for 25p each. Thus a premium of 15p per share has been charged. Money is received for exactly 1 million shares.

		£	£
DEBIT	Cash	250,000	
CREDIT	Ordinary shares(10p×1,000,000)		100,000
	Share premium(15p×1,000,000)		150,000

(3) Partly Paid-up Share Capital

When shares are issued and called-up at their par value but an amount remains unpaid:

		£	£
DEBIT	Cash	X	
	Other receivables (unpaid capital)	X	
CREDIT	Share capital (par value)		X

 Worked Example 11.4

A company issues 1 million shares of £1 at par, and asks for payment in full on issue, but it is still owed £5,000 by shareholders who have yet to pay what they owe.

		£	£
DEBIT	Cash	995,000	
	Other receivables(unpaid capital)	5,000	
CREDIT	Ordinary shares		1,000,000

11.3   Equity: Retained Earnings and Other Reserves

Share capital is shown in the statement of financial position at its called-up value. The share capital itself might consist of both ordinary shares and preference shares. All reserves, however, are owned by the ordinary shareholders, who own the 'equity' in the company. We've looked at share capital in section 11.2 above. Any other amounts attributable to owners (ordinary shareholders) are shown separately as reserves.

A company might have a number of different reserves, each set up for a different purpose, including the following:

- Retained earnings.
- Share premium.
- Other reserves.

1. Retained Earnings

Retained earnings is a reserve used to accumulate the company's profit earned. Retained earnings comprise the income (profits and gains less losses) that the company retains within the business, i.e., income that has not been paid out as dividends or transferred to any other reserve.

The retained earnings ledger account would look like this (note that if there was a loss this would be debited to the ledger account):

Retained Earnings

	£		£
Dividends for the period	X	Balance b/d	X
Transfers to other reserve	X		
Balance c/d	X	Profit for the reporting period	X
	X		X

We shall look at the transfer to general reserve shortly.

The balance carried down on the retained earnings ledger account represents the company's accumulated profits and losses over time out of which it may, if it wishes, pay dividends to its shareholders in the future. Even if a loss is made in one particular year, a dividend can be paid from previous years' retained earnings.

2. Share Premium

'Premium' means the difference between the issue price of the share and its par value. The account is sometimes called 'capital paid-up in excess of par value'. When a company is first incorporated (set up) the issue price of its shares will probably be the same as their par value and so there would be no share premium. If the company does well, the market value of its shares will increase, but not the par value. The price of any new shares issued will be approximately their market value.

The difference between cash received by the company and the par value of the new shares issued is transferred to the share premium account (see worked example 11.3).

A share premium account only comes into being when a company issues shares at a price in excess of their par value. The market price of the shares, once they have been issued, has no bearing at all on the company's accounts, and so if their market price goes up or down, the share premium account would remain unaltered.

There are tight legal restrictions on the use of the share premium reserve. **Dividends** cannot be paid out from it, but it may be reclassified as share capital via a **bonus issue**, as we shall see shortly.

3. Other Reserves

A company might have other reserves in its financial statements. The result of an upward revaluation of a non-current asset is a '**revaluation surplus**'. This reserve is non-distributable, as it represents unrealised profits on the revalued assets.

Company managers may choose to set up reserves for a specific purpose, e.g., a plant and machinery replacement reserve or a foreign exchange reserve or without any purpose, a general reserve. The creation of these reserves usually indicates a general intention not to distribute the profits involved at any future date, although legally any such reserves remain available for the payment of dividends.

Profits are transferred to these reserves by making an appropriation out of profits.

DEBIT	Retained earnings	X	
CREDIT	Other reserves		X

4. Dividends

As discussed in section 11.2 already, dividends are appropriations of profit after tax. You'll see the terminologies on dividends and how to record the dividends in this section.

(1) Ordinary Dividend

The dividend to be paid to the shareholders is decided by the board of directors. The dividend rate can be expressed in a number of different ways.

Many companies pay dividends in two stages during the course of their accounting year.

· In mid-year, after the half-year financial results are known, the company might pay an **interim dividend.**

· At the end of the year, the company might propose a further **final dividend.**

The total dividend to be included in the financial statements for the year is the sum of the dividends actually paid in the year. (Not all companies by any means pay an interim dividend. Interim dividends are, however, commonly paid out by larger limited liability companies.)

The terminology of dividend payments can be confusing, since they may be expressed either in the form, of 'X p per share' or of 'Y%'. In the latter case, the meaning is always 'Y% of the par value of the shares in issue'.

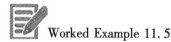 Worked Example 11. 5

Suppose a company's issued share capital consists of 100,000 50p ordinary shares. If the managers wish to pay a dividend of £5,000, they may propose either of the following:

· A dividend of 5p per share (100,000× 5p = £5,000).

· A dividend of 10% (10%× £50,000 = £5,000).

(2) Preference Dividends

A company may also issue preference shares, which entitle the holders to a dividend out of profits (preference dividend) before the ordinary shareholders are entitled to any ordinary dividend.

Preference shares are often expressed as follows:

	DR	CR
	£	£
7% £1 irredeemable preference shares		100,000

This means that the preference dividend to be paid will be £7,000 (£100,000× 7%).

(3) Accounting for Dividends

The total dividends paid are not shown in the statement of profit or loss. The dividends actually paid during the year are reported as deductions from equity (deductions from retained earnings) in another financial statement, the statement of changes in equity. If dividends are proposed or declared after the reporting period but before the financial statements are authorised for issue, the dividends are not recognised as a liability at the end of the reporting period because no obligation exists at that time. Such dividends are disclosed in the notes to the financial statements.

A separate account is usually kept for the dividends for each different class of shares. When dividends are paid, the following entries are made (dividend paid will be transferred to retained earnings):

DEBIT   Dividends paid account   X

CREDIT   Cash   X

Dividends could also be paid out of retained earnings directly, as follows

DEBIT   Retained earnings   X

CREDIT   Bank account   X

 Worked Example 11. 6

The retained earnings of a company at 1 January 20×9 were £800,000. The retained earnings at 31 December 20×9 are £1,140,000. The profit for the year is £370,000.

Requirement

What was the total dividend paid during the year?

Solution

The total dividend paid during the year is £30,000.

WORKING

Retained Earnings

	£		£
Dividends (balancing figure)	30,000	Balance b/d	800,000
Balance c/d	1,140,000	Profit for the year	370,000
	1,170,000		1,170,000

11. 4　Bonus and Rights Issue

Sometimes companies need to alter their issued share capital. Bonus issue and rights issues are the different ways in which a limited company can increase its share capital. You'll learn about the difference between bonus issues and rights issues and how to record the appropriate ledger account entries.

1. Bonus Issue

Bonus issue (or **capitalisation issue** or **scrip issue**) : An issue of fully paid shares to existing owners, free of charge, in proportion to their existing shareholdings. A bonus issue does not involve any cash inflow for the company. This is used when a company wishes to increase its share capital without needing to raise additional finance by issuing new shares or when a company has a reserve larger than the capital. This is actually a reclassify between reserve and share capital, and purely a paper exercise which raises no funds. Any reserves may be utilised for the purpose including share premium account.

Advantages of bonus issue include following:

· Increases capital without diluting current shareholders' holdings.

· Capitalises reserves, so they cannot be paid as dividends.

· Larger proportion of permanent capital gives creditors more protection.

· Reduce market value of each share when share prices are too high.

Disadvantages of bonus issue are:

· Does not raise any cash.

· Could jeopardise payment of future dividends if profits fall.

The company converts some of its reserves (share premium or retained earnings or both) into new fully-paid share capital issued at its par value. The double entry for the par value of the bonus shares issued is:

DEBIT	Share premium OR retained earnings (OR both)	X
CREDIT	Share capital	X

The balance on share premium cannot (by law) be paid to owners as dividends. There are only a few transactions that can ever reduce share premium. One of these is a **bonus issue** of shares.

In our exercise you should assume that a company uses the share premium account as fully as it can before using retained earnings, unless told otherwise.

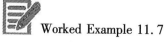 Worked Example 11.7

Bubble Company's statement of financial position before bonus issue is given as Exhibit 11.1.

Exhibit 11.1

Bubbles Co.
Statement of financial position (before bonus issue)

Exhibit 11. 1(continued)

	£000
ASSETS	<u>5,800</u>
EQUITY AND LIABILITIES	
Equity	
Share capital: £1 ordinary shares (fully paid)	1,000
Share premium	500
Retained earnings	<u>2,000</u>
Total equity	3,500
Total liabilities	<u>2,300</u>
Total equity and liabilities	<u>5,800</u>

Requirement

Bubbles Co. decided to make a "3 for 2" bonus issue (i.e. 3 new shares for every 2 already held). What is the double entry to record the issue of shares and what is the adjusted financial position after the issue?

Solution

The company is issuing (1,000,000/2× 3) = 1,500,000 new shares of £1 each to its owners, in proportion to their existing shareholdings. It will:

	£000	£000
DEBIT Share premium (total balance of the share premium reserve)	500	
Retained earnings (remainder)	1,000	
CREDIT Share capital		1,500

The statement of financial position after the issue shows no change in assets or liabilities, but equity has changed, as Exhibit 11. 2:

Exhibit 11. 2

Bubbles Co.	
Statement of financial position (after bonus issue)	
	£000
ASSETS	<u>5,800</u>
EQUITY AND LIABILITIES	
Equity	
Share capital: £1 ordinary shares (1,000,000+1,500,000)	2,500
Share premium (500−500)	0
Retained earnings (2,000−1,000)	<u>1,000</u>
Total equity	3,500

Exhibit 11. 2(continued)

Bubbles Co.	
Total liabilities	2,300
Total equity and liabilities	5,800

2. Rights Issue

Rights issue: New shares are offered to existing owners in proportion to their existing share-holding, usually at a discount to the current market price, so a rights issue (unlike a bonus issue) is an issue of shares for cash. The 'rights' are offered to existing shareholders, who can ignore the offer, or take the offer, or sell the rights on the stock market if they wish. Rights issues are a popular way of raising cash by issuing shares and they are cheap to administer. In addition, shareholders retain control of the business, as their holding is not diluted.

Advantages of rights issue include following:

· A cheap way to raise further finance by issuing shares.

· Easier to persuade current shareholders to buy.

· Keeps reserves available for future dividends.

Disadvantage of rights issue is:

· Dilutes shareholder' holdings if they do not take up rights issue.

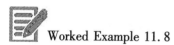 Worked Example 11. 8

Following Example 11. 7, Bubbles Co. decides to make a rights issue, shortly after the bonus issue (share capital: £2,500,000). The terms are '1 for 5 @ £1.20' (i.e. 1 new share for every 5 already held, at a price of £1.20), assuming that all shareholders take up their rights (which they are not obliged to).

Requirement

What is the double entry to record the issue of shares and what is the adjusted financial position after the issue?

Solution

The company is issuing (2,500,000/5× 1) = 500,000 new shares of £1.2 each to its owners, in proportion to their existing shareholdings. It will:

		£000	£000
DEBIT	Cash (500×£1.2)	600	
CREDIT	Share capital(500×£1)		500
	Share premium (500×£0.2)		100

The statement of financial position after the issue (Exhibit 11.3) shows an increase in assets and equity, as follows:

Exhibit 11. 3

Bubbles Co.	
Statement of financial position (after rights issue)	
	£ 000
ASSETS (5,800,000 + 600,000)	6,400
EQUITY AND LIABILITIES	
Equity	
Share capital: £1 ordinary shares (2,500,000+500,000)	3,000
Share premium (0+100,000)	100
Retained earnings	1,000
Total equity	4,100
Total liabilities	2,300
Total equity and liabilities	6,400

 Question

X Co has the following capital structure.

EQUITY	£
400,000 ordinary shares of 50p	200,000
Share premium	70,000
Retained earnings	230,000
Total equity	500,000

Show its capital structure following:

(1) A '1 for 2' bonus issue.

(2) A rights issue of '1 for 3' at 75p following the bonus issue, assuming all rights taken up.

11. 5 Ledger Accounts of a Limited Liability Company

Limited companies keep ledger accounts. The only difference between the ledger accounts of companies and sole traders is the nature of some of the transactions, assets and liabilities for which accounts need to be kept.

For example, there will be an account for each of the following items.

1. Taxation

A company as a separate legal entity is liable to pay tax on its profits to government. Tax is therefore treated as a deduction from profit. Any outstanding liability for unpaid tax is shown as a liability on the statement of financial position (tax payable), either current or non-current depending on the circumstances.

When a tax liability arises and is identified, the double entry to record it is:

DEBIT	Tax expense (statement of profit or loss)	X	
CREDIT	Tax payable account (statement of financial position)		X

When a tax payment is made:

DEBIT	Tax payable account	X	
CREDIT	Cash at bank		X

At the end of the reporting period, any balance on the tax payable account is carried down. Usually this is a credit balance and is shown as 'Tax payable' under current liabilities on the statement of financial position.

Since a company's statement of profit or loss is usually prepared before the tax due is finally agreed with tax authority, the expense in the statement of profit or loss is an estimate. It nearly always proves to be too high (**over-provision**) or too low (**under-provision**). Instead of going back to the financial statements for the reporting period and changing them:

· Any over-provision from the previous reporting period reduces the tax expense for the subsequent reporting period.

· Any under-provision from the previous reporting period increases the tax expense for the subsequent reporting period.

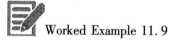 Worked Example 11.9

A company has a tax liability brought forward of £15,000. The liability is finally agreed at £17,500 and this is paid during the year. The company estimates that the tax liability based on the current year's profits will be £20,000. Prepare the tax liability account for the year.

Solution

Tax payables

	£		£
Cash paid	17,500	Balance b/d	15,000
Balance c/d	20,000	Profit or loss account	22,500
	37,500		37,500

Notice that the statement of profit or loss charge consists of the following.

		£
Underprovision for prior year (17,500 − 15,000)		2,500
Provision for current year		20,000
		22,500

Notice also that the balance carried forward consists solely of the provision for the current year.

2. Loan Stock

So far we have looked at the issue of shares. A company may also issue loan stock, debentures or bonds. These securities are normally issued as certificates, each with a par value, in return for cash (the loan principal). The certificate's owner is legally entitled to interest on its par value, and is entitled to repayment of the principal 'at maturity', i.e., when the loan period reaches its end at a specifiable future date. Loan stocks are different from share capital in the following ways.

· Shareholders are members of a company, while providers of loan stocks are creditors.

· Shareholders receive dividends whereas the holders of loan stocks are entitled to a fixed rate of interest.

· Loan stock holders can take legal action against a company if their interest is not paid when due, whereas shareholders cannot enforce the payment of dividends.

· Loan stock is often secured on company assets, whereas shares are not.

Loan stock being a long-term liability will be shown as a credit balance in a loan stock account. Unless they are due to reach maturity within 12 months, they are included in non-current liabilities in the statement of financial position. Any amount due for redemption within 12 months is shown under current liabilities.

On issue of debt:

DEBIT	Cash	X	
CREDIT	Non-current liabilities		X

On repayment of debt:

DEBIT	Non-current liabilities	X	
CREDIT	Cash		X

Remember that: Any redeemable preference shares in issue will also be treated as liabilities (either current or non-current) rather than equity. Any debt that is due for repayment in less than 12 months after the statement of financial position date is reclassified from non-current to current liabilities.

3. Finance Costs

Finance costs mean interest paid. The company has a contractual obligation to pay interest on loan stocks. Interest due for the period will be included as a finance cost within the statement of profit or loss and any unpaid interest at the year end must be included in the statement of financial position within accruals and other payables.

DEBIT   Interest account (an expense, chargeable against profits)   X

CREDIT   Interest payable (a current liability until eventually paid)   X

Summary

· Companies are legally separate from their owners, so the presentation of owners' capital is particularly important.

· In preparing a statement of financial position you must be able to deal with:

—Ordinary and preference share capital

—Reserves

—Loan stock

· Share capital can be split into:

—Ordinary shares

—Irredeemable preference shares

· Share premium is set up with premium over par value of issued share capital. The account may be reduced by a bonus issue.

· Other reserves can be created as a requirement of IFRS for certain transactions.

· An ordinary share entitles its holder to dividends which vary in amount depending on the performance and policy of the company.

· A preference share entitles the holder to a fixed dividend, whose payment takes priority over that of ordinary share dividends.

· Share capital and reserves are ' owned ' by the shareholders. They are known collectively as "shareholders' equity".

· A company can increase its share capital by means of a bonus issue or a rights issue. A rights issue of shares is made to existing owners in proportion to their shareholdings.

Exercise

11. 1 A company's share capital consists of 20,000 25p ordinary shares all of which were issued at a premium of 20%. The market value of the shares is currently 70p each.

What is the balance on the company's ordinary share capital account? (   )

A.£5,000

B.£6,000

C.£14,000

D.£24,000

11. 2 Which of the following may appear as current liabilities in a company's statement of financial position? (   )

1 Loan due for repayment within one year

2 Taxation

3 Warranty provision

  A.1, 2 and 3

  B.1 and 2 only

  C.1 and 3 only

  D.2 and 3 only

11. 3 Should dividends paid appear on the face of a company's statement of profit or loss? (   )

  A.Yes

  B.No

11. 4 Which of the following should appear in a company's equity? (   )

1 Profit for the financial year

2 Dividends proposed during the year

3 Surplus on revaluation of non-current assets

  A.All three items

  B.2 and 3 only

  C.1 and 3 only

  D.1 and 2 only

11. 5 Lorel Co, a limited liability company, has the following capital structure.

	£
Share capital:50p ordinary shares	45,000
Share premium	60,000
	105,000

The company made a bonus issue of two shares for every three shares held, using the share premium account for the purpose.

What was the company's capital structure after the bonus issue? (   )

	Ordinary share capital	Share premium account
	£	£
A.	60,000	45,000
B.	75,000	30,000
C.	105,000	Nil

D.   112,500   (7,500)

11.6 A company has a balance on share premium account of £50,000 and on retained earnings of £75,000. Issued share capital is 400,000 25p shares. The company decides to make a bonus issue of 1 for 1. What are the closing balances on share premium and retained earnings? (   )

	Share premium	Retained earnings
A.	£25,000	Nil
B.	£10,000	£15,000
C.	Nil	£25,000
D.	Nil	£(275,000)

11.7 Sanders plc issued 50,000 ordinary shares of 25p each at a premium of 50p per share. The cash received was correctly recorded but the full amount was credited to the share capital account.

Which of the following journals corrects this error? (   )

A. Debit Share premium £25,000, Credit Share capital £25,000

B. Debit Share capital £25,000, Credit Share premium £25,000

C. Debit Share capital £37,500, Credit Share premium £37,500

D. Debit Share capital £25,000, Credit Cash at bank £25,000

11.8 Which of the following journals correctly records a bonus issue of shares? (   )

A. Debit Cash at bank, Credit Share capital

B. Debit Share capital, Credit Share premium

C. Debit Share premium, Credit Share capital

D. Debit Investments, Credit Cash at bank

11.9 At 31 December 20×1 the capital structure of a company was as follows:

	£
100,000 ordinary shares of 50p each	50,000
Share premium	180,000

During 20×2 the company made a 1 for 2 bonus issue, using the share premium for the purpose, and later issued for cash another 60,000 shares at 80p per share.

What is the company's capital structure at 31 December 20×2? (   )

	Ordinary share capital	Share premium
A.	£130,000	£173,000
B.	£105,000	£173,000
C.	£130,000	£137,000
D.	£105,000	£137,000

11.10 In the year to 31 March 20×2 Kable had the following capital structure:

	£
200,000 ordinary shares of 25p each	50,000
Share premium	70,000

On 15 March Kable paid an ordinary dividend of 15p per share. What is the total dividend paid? (   )

    A.£7,500

    B.£30,000

    C.£50,000

    D.£72,000

11.11 The retained earnings of Posti plc at 1 July 20×5 were £900,000. The retained earnings at 30 June 20×6 are £1,080,000. The profit for the year is £455,000.

What was the total dividend paid during the year? (   )

    A.£180,000

    B.£275,000

    C.£445,000

    D.£635,000

11.12 Touch plc is finalising certain figures that will appear in its financial statements as at 30 April 20×7. Relevant initial trial balance figures are as follows:

	£
Trade and other payables (excluding interest payable)	246,800
6% debentures as at 1 May 20×6	400,000

Touch plc issued 6% debentures of £120,000 at par on 1 February 20×7, repayable at par in 10 years' time. No interest was outstanding at 1 May 20×6, and the company paid interest in respect of debentures of £24,000 in the period to 30 April 20×7.

The trade and other payables figure (including interest payable) that will appear in Touch plc's statement of financial position as at 30 April 20×7 is (   ).

    A.£222,800

    B.£246,800

    C.£248,600

    D.£272,600

11.13 Which one of the following items does not appear under the heading 'equity and reserves' on a company statement of financial position? (   )

    A.Share premium account

    B.Retained earnings

C.Revaluation surplus

D.Loan stock

11. 14 Which two of the following transactions could affect a company's retained earnings for the reporting period? (　　)

A.Rights issue of shares

B.Transfer to other reserves

C.Purchase of land

D.Repayment of debentures at their par value

E.Increase in income tax due to tax authority

11. 15 At 30 June 20×2 a company had £1 million 8% loan notes in issue, interest being paid half-yearly on 30 June and 31 December.

On 30 September 20×2 the company redeemed £250,000 of these loan notes at par, paying interest due to that date.

On 1 April 20×3 the company issued £500,000 7% loan notes at par, interest payable half-yearly on 31 March and 30 September.

What figure should appear in the company's statement of profit or loss for finance costs in the year ended 30 June 20×3? (　　)

A.£88,750

B.£82,500

C.£65,000

D.£73,750

11. 16 Grease plc is a large company with a share capital of 3 million 20p ordinary shares. To raise funds it has made a 1 for 4 rights issue of its ordinary shares at £3. 60 per share. The rights issue was fully taken up but only £1. 9 million had been paid up at the year end, 30 September 20×2. Grease plc correctly debited cash at bank with £1. 9 million and recorded the other side of the transaction in the suspense account.

Which adjustment should Grease plc make to correctly record the rights issue? (　　)

A.Debit Other receivables £2,700,000, Credit Share capital £150,000, Credit Share premium £2,550,000

B. Debit Suspense £1,900,000, Debit Other receivables £800,000, Credit Share capital £750,000, Credit Share premium £1,950,000

C.Debit Other receivables £800,000, Credit Share capital £150,000, Credit Share premium £650,000

D. Debit Suspense £1,900,000, Debit Other receivables £800,000, Credit Share capital £150,000, Credit Share premium £2,550,000

11. 17 Hope Ltd. had 50,000 5% preference shares of £1 each and 300,000 ordinary shares of £1 each. From years 20×1 to 20×5, profits after tax are £8,500, £12,500, £23, 500, £48,500 and £37,500. The ordinary dividend rate was 2%, 3%, 5.5%, 13% and 7.5% of the total ordinary share capital each year. Please show the movement of retained earnings of the company for year 20×1-20×5.

11. 18 * IDC Ltd. starts business from year 20×9 and has share capital of 400,000 ordinary shares of £1 each and 200,000 5% preference shares of £1 each.

—The profits for the first three years of business ended 31 December are: 20×9, £109,678; 20Y0, £148,640 and 20Y1, £158,220.

—Transfers to reserves are made as follows: 20×9, nil; 20Y0, general reserve, £10,000; and 20Y1, non-current assets replacement reserve, £22,500.

—Dividends were paid for each year on the preference shares at per cent and on the ordinary share at 20×9, 10%; 20Y0, 12.5%, and 20Y1, 15%

You are required to show the movement of retained earnings of the company for the year to 31 December 20×9, 20Y0 and 20Y1.

11. 19 Exhibit 11. 4 gives the statement of financial position of Canvat plc at 31 December 20×1.

Exhibit 11. 4

Canvat plc	
Statement of financial position as at 31 December 20×1	
	£000
ASSETS	2,000
EQUITY AND LIABILITIES	
Equity	
Share capital: 800,000 50p ordinary shares	400
Share premium	500
Retained earnings	300
Total equity	1,200
Total liabilities	800
Total equity and liabilities	2,000

The directors decide to make a 1 for 5 bonus issue, followed by a 1 for 3 rights issue at £1. 60 per share.

Requirement

Show the revised statement of financial position of Canvat plc after both share issues have taken place.

11. 20 * At 30 June 20×2 Brandon plc's capital structure was as follows:

	£
500,000 ordinary shares of 25p each	125,000
Share premium	100,000

In the year ended 30 June 20×3 the company made a 1 for 2 rights issue at £1 per share and this was taken up in full. Later in the year the company made a 1 for 5 bonus issue, using the share premium for the purpose.

Requirement

What was the company's capital structure at 30 June 20×3?

Reference

1. ACCA FA Financial Accounting/FIA FFA Interactive Text 2020, BPP Learning Media.

2. ACCA FA Financial Accounting/FIA FFA Practice & Revision Kit 2020, BPP Learning Media.

3. Accounting (Study Manual 2020), The Institute of Chartered Accountants in England and Wales.

4. Accounting (Question Bank 2020), The Institute of Chartered Accountants in England and Wales.

5. Andrew Thomas and Anne Marie Ward. Introduction to Financial Accounting (2019), McGraw-Hill Education.

Chapter 12

Preparation of Financial Statements for Companies

┌──── ■Learning Objectives ───┐

· Understand the minimum disclosure requirement of the statement of financial position.

· Distinct between profit and loss and other comprehensive income.

· Apply the method for presenting the statement of profit or loss-analysing expenses by nature or function.

· Identify the components of the statement of changes in equity.

· Draw up the three main financial statements in accordance with the requirements of IAS 1, including alternative presentations where permitted.

· Explain the underpinning principles relating to presentation contained in IAS 1.

· Understand the purpose and nature of notes to the financial statements.
└───┘

12. 1 IAS 1: Presentation of Financial Statements

Company financial statements prepared for external publication are extensively regulated to protect investors who use information to make economic decisions, especially when comparing different companies. Published financial statements are therefore prepared on the same basis by all companies so investors can make meaningful comparisons. We have already covered most of what you need to know at this stage of your studies regarding the content, concepts and presentation of financial statements prepared under IFRS. We now need to draw it all together into the IAS 1.

IAS 1 lists the required contents of a company's financial statements. It also gives guidance on how items should be presented in the financial statements.

As well as covering accounting policies and other general considerations governing financial statements, IAS 1 Presentation of Financial Statements gives substantial guidance on the form and content of published financial statements.

A complete set of financial statements includes the following.

· Statement of financial position.

· Statement of profit or loss and other comprehensive income.

· Statement of changes in equity.

· Statement of cash flows.

· Notes, including a summary of significant accounting policies and other explanatory information.

IAS 1 gives guidance on the format and content of all of these, apart from the statement of cash flows, which is covered by IAS 7. We will consider each of these in this chapter.

IAS 1 also requires disclosure of the following information in a prominent position. If necessary it should be repeated wherever it is felt to be of use to the readers in their understanding of the information presented:

· Name of the company.

· Whether the accounts cover the single entity only or a group of entities.

· The reporting date or the period covered by the financial statements (as appropriate).

· The reporting currency used in presenting the figures in the financial statements.

The statement of financial position must distinguish between current and non-current assets and current and non-current liabilities. Current items are to be settled within 12 months of the date of the statement of financial position.

In the accounting policies note to the financial statements the entity must disclose the measurement basis used in their preparation (historical cost or net realisable value, for instance), and the other accounting policies used that are relevant to an understanding of the financial statements.

12. 2　The Statement of Financial Position

IAS 1 specifies what should be included in a statement of financial position and gives the following suggested format for a statement of financial position (Exhibit 12. 1).

Exhibit 12. 1

ABC Co.		
Statement of financial position as at 31 December 20×3		
	£	£
ASSETS		
Non-current assets		

Exhibit 12. 1(continued)

Property, plant and equipment	X	
Goodwill	X	
Other intangible assets	X	
Investments	X̲	
		X
Current Assets		
Inventories	X	
Trade and other receivables	X	
Other current assets (e.g., prepayment)	X	
Cash and cash equivalents	X̲	
		X̲
Total assets		X̲̲
EQUITY AND LIABILITIES		
Equity		
Share capital: Ordinary shares		X
Share capital: Preference shares		X
Share premium		X
Retained earnings		X
Other reserves		X̲
		X
Non-current Liabilities		
Long term borrowings	X	
Deferred tax	X	
Long-term provisions	X̲	
		X
Current Liabilities		
Trade and other payables (including accruals)	X	
Short term borrowings	X	
Current portion of long-term borrowings	X	
Income tax payable	X	
Short term provisions	X̲	
		X̲
Total Equity and Liabilities		X̲̲

The statement of financial position is prepared according to the business entity convention, that a business is separate from its owners. There are some points to note:

· IAS 1 does not prescribe the format of the statement of financial position. Assets can be presented as: total assets = total equity + liabilities. A net asset presentation (assets—liabilities) is also allowed. Both assets and liabilities must show the current/non-current split. Assets can be presented current then non-current, or vice versa, and liabilities and equity can be presented current then non-current then equity, or vice versa

· All tangible assets (including land and buildings) are combined under the heading 'property, plant and equipment'.

· Trade receivables and any other receivables are combined as 'trade and other receivables', and the allowance for receivables is set off here; prepayments are included in the heading 'other current assets'.

· Cash in hand and at bank are combined as 'cash and cash equivalents'.

· Any long-term liabilities such as bank loans or debentures that are not repayable within 12 months are combined as 'long-term borrowings' under 'non-current liabilities'. Redeemable preference shares would be included here.

· Bank overdrafts, which are technically repayable on demand, are called 'short-term borrowings'. They are not offset against any cash and cash equivalent asset balances, unless a right of set-off exists.

· Trade payables and other payables (including interest payable and accruals) are combined as 'trade and other payables'.

· Amounts of income tax payable are each shown as a separate item under current liabilities.

12.3   The Statement of Profit or Loss and Other Comprehensive Income

1. Other Comprehensive Income and Basic Requirements

You have learned how to prepare a statement of profit or loss for a sole trader. However, IAS 1 requires entities to present a **statement of profit or loss and other comprehensive income.** For a limited company, you need to understand what other comprehensive income is.

Other comprehensive income is defined as comprising "items of income and expense (including reclassification adjustments) that are not recognised in profit or loss as required or permitted by other IFRSs". The statement of profit or loss and other comprehensive income therefore reports total comprehensive income which is the profit or loss adjusted for other comprehensive income. The idea is to present all gains and losses, both those recognised in profit or loss (in the statement of profit or loss) as well as those recognised directly in equity, such as the revaluation surplus (in other comprehensive income). Note in this textbook, the only items of other comprehensive income are the gains on revaluations of property, plant and equipment.

Comprehensive income for the period = Profit or loss + Other comprehensive income

IAS 1 gives an entity a choice of presenting:

· A single statement of profit or loss and other comprehensive income, with profit or loss and other comprehensive income presented in two sections.

· Or two statements:

—A separate statement of profit or loss

—A statement of comprehensive income, immediately following the statement of profit or loss and beginning with profit or loss

Exhibit 12. 2 below is a sample of a single statement of profit or loss and other comprehensive income.

Exhibit 12. 2

ABC Co.	
Statement of profit or loss and other comprehensive income for the year ended 31 December 20×3	
	£
Revenue	X
Cost of sales	(X)
Gross profit	X
Other income	X
Distribution costs	(X)
Administrative expenses	(X)
Operating profit	X
Finance costs	(X)
Profit before taxation	X
Income tax expense	(X)
Profit for the year	X
Other comprehensive income	
Gains on property revaluation	X
Total comprehensive income for the year	X

IAS 1 specifies what should be included in a statement of profit or loss and other comprehensive income. As a minimum, IAS 1 requires the following items to be disclosed on the face of the statement of profit or loss and other comprehensive income.

· Revenue.

· Finance costs.

· Share of profits and losses of associates and joint ventures accounted for using the equity method.

- Pre-tax gain or loss attributable to discontinued operations.
- Tax expense.
- Profit or loss.
- Each component of other comprehensive income classified by nature.
- Share of the other comprehensive income of associates and joint ventures.
- Total comprehensive income.

Note that associates and joint ventures, discontinued operations are not included in this textbook.

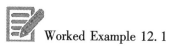 Worked Example 12. 1

An asset originally cost £10,000 and was revalued to £15,000. The gain on the revaluation is recognised in the statement of profit or loss and other comprehensive income (in the other comprehensive income section) as Exhibit 12. 3 and then shown as a movement in the revaluation surplus in the statement of changes in equity which will be discussed in Section 12. 4.

Exhibit 12. 3

Statement of profit or loss and other comprehensive income	
for the year ended...(Extract)	
	£000
...	...
Profit for the year	X
Other comprehensive income	
Gains on property revaluation(15,000 −10,000)	5
Total comprehensive income for the year	X

2. Cost of Sales, Distribution Costs and Administrative Expenses

The allocation of expenses to each of these three headings calls for judgement. In practice the rules are not rigid. IAS 1 states that an entity shall present an analysis of expenses using a classification based on either the nature of expenses or their functions within the entity, whichever provides information that is reliable and more relevant. The format and classification used here is the functional one and you can refer to Exhibit 12. 4. Additional disclosures on the nature of expenses, including depreciation and amortisation, are required.

Exhibit 12. 4 **Analysing expenses by function**

Cost of sales	Distribution costs	Administrative expenses
· Purchases (net of discounts received) · delivery inwards adjusted for opening and closing inventory · Any substantial losses of inventory In a manufacturing company · Wages of production staff · Maintenance and depreciation expenses of production non-current assets · Losses on their disposal	· Wages etc. of marketing and distribution staff · Sales commission · Distribution expenses such as vehicle running costs and carriage outwards · Depreciation of motor vehicles used for distribution, marketing costs such as advertising and promotion, and any loss on disposal of such assets · Depreciation of other non-current assets used by distribution operations and any loss on disposal of such assets · The cost of advertising and selling activities	· Wages of administrative staff · Depreciation of non- current assets used by non-production and non-distribution operations · Any loss on disposal of such assets · Amortisation of intangible assets · Irrecoverable debts expense

3. Other Income

Income other than income classified as revenue should be shown separately. Examples of other income include:

· Dividends received on investments.

· Interest received on savings.

· Rent received from property.

· Insurance claim proceeds.

· Profits on disposal of non-current assets.

12. 4　The Statement of Changes in Equity

The statement of profit or loss and other comprehensive income is a straightforward measure of the financial performance of the entity, in that it shows all items of income and expense recognised in a period. It is then necessary to link this result with the results of transactions with owners of the business, such as share issues and dividends. The statement making the link is the statement of changes in equity.

The statement of changes in equity simply takes the equity section of the statement of financial position and shows the movements during the year. The first line shows the opening balance of individual capital and reserves. The bottom line shows the closing balance of each item, which are the amounts for the current statement of financial position. As we saw above, the total comprehensive income for the year is split between the gains on revaluation of property, which is credited to the revaluation surplus, and the profit for the year, which is credited to retained earnings.

An example statement of changes in equity is shown below (Exhibit 12.5).

Exhibit 12.5

ABC Co					
Statement of changes in equity for the year ended 31 December 20×3					
	Share Capital	Share Premium	Revaluation Surplus	Retained Earnings	Total
	£	£	£	£	£
Balance b/fwd	X	X	X	X	X
Changes in accounting policy	—	—	—	(X)	(X)
Restated balance	X	X	X	X	X
Total comprehensive income for the year			X	X	X
Dividends				(X)	(X)
Issue of share capital	X	X	—	—	X
Balance c/fwd	X	X	X	X	X

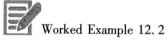 Worked Example 12.2

Last plc had the following share capital and reserves at 1 January 20×4

	£000
Share Capital	2,500
Share Premium	250
Revaluation Surplus	500
Retained Earnings	740
Total Equity	3,990

· Profit after tax for the year ended 31 December 20×4 was £71,000.

· During 20×4, non-current assets were revalued upwards by £50,000.

· An ordinary dividend of £300,000 was paid.

· 200,000 £1 ordinary shares were issued at a premium of 75p per share.

Requirement

Prepare a statement of changes in equity for the year ended 31 December 20×4.

Solution

Last plc's statement of changes in equity is presented as Exhibit 12.6.

Exhibit 12.6

Last plc					
Statement of changes in equity for the year ended 31 December 20×4					
	Share Capital	Share Premium	Revaluation Surplus	Retained earnings	Total
	£000	£000	£000	£000	£000
Balance at 1/1/×4	2,500	250	500	740	3,990
Comprehensive income for the year			50	71	121
Dividends				(300)	(300)
Issue of share capital	200	150	—		350
Balance at 31/12/×4	2,700	400	550	511	4,161

12.5 Notes to the Financial Statements

Notes to the financial statements provide more detail for the users of the accounts about the information in the statement of profit or loss and other comprehensive income, the statement of financial position, the statement of cash flows and the statement of changes in equity. For example, the statement of financial position shows just the total carrying amount of property, plant and equipment owned by an entity. The notes to the financial statements then break down this total into the different categories of assets, the cost, any revaluation, the accumulated depreciation and the depreciation charge for the year.

Those most commonly examined at the introductory level comprise the following:

· Tangible non-current assets (Chapter 9).

A note on the composition of property, plant and equipment and the related accumulated depreciation is necessary to provide detail on the single figure that is reported in the statement of financial position. In addition, this note must include the cost of acquisitions and disposals, any revaluation, diminution in value, the depreciation charges for the year and the accumulated depreciation on disposals. The information on revalued assets should also be disclosed. An illustration is given in Section 9.5 Chapter 9.

· Intangible non-current assets (Chapter 10).

A note on intangible non-current assets shows the reconciliation of the carrying amount at the beginning and the end of the period of the additions (business combinations separately), assets held for sale, retirements and other disposals, revaluations, impairments reversals of impairments, amortisation for the year and other changes. An illustration is given in Section 10.3 Chapter 10.

· Provisions (Chapter 8).

Disclosures required in the financial statements for provisions fall into two parts. Disclose the details of the change in carrying amount of a provision from the beginning to the end of the year, including additional provisions made, amounts used and other movements. For each class of provision, disclose the background to the making of the provision and the uncertainties affecting its outcome.

· Events after the reporting period.

Events after the reporting period are those events, both favourable and unfavourable, that occur between the reporting date and the date on which the financial statements are authorised for issue (IAS 10). Events that provide further evidence of conditions that **existed at the reporting date should be adjusted for** in the financial statements. Events which do not affect the situation at the reporting date should not be adjusted for, but should be **disclosed** in the financial statements.

In respect of non-adjusting events after the reporting period disclose: the nature of the event and an estimate of its financial effect (or a statement that an estimate cannot be made).

Examples of **adjusting events** are:

—Evidence of a permanent diminution in property value prior to the year end

—Sale of inventory after the end of the reporting period for less than its carrying value at the year end

—Insolvency of a customer with a balance owing at the year end

—Determination after the year end of the sale or purchase price of assets sold or purchased before the year end

—Evidence of a permanent diminution in the value of a long-term investment prior to the year end

—Discovery of fraud or errors that show that the financial statements are incorrect

Examples of **non-adjusting events** are:

—Acquisition of, or disposal of, a subsidiary after the year end

—Value of an investment falls between the reporting date and the date the financial statements are authorized for issue

—Major purchases and disposals of assets

—Destruction of a production plant by fire after the end of the reporting period

—Share transactions after the end of the reporting period

—Dividends proposed or declared after the end of the reporting period

· Inventory (Chapter 4).

The financial statements should disclose the accounting policies adopted in measuring inventories, total carrying amount of inventories, the carrying amount in classifications appropriate to the entity and carrying amount of inventories carried at net realisable value (NRV).

· Share capital and reserves (Chapter 11).

There will be separate account for:

—Each different class of share capital (always a credit balance b/d)

—Each different type of reserve (nearly always a credit balance b/d)

12. 6　A Worked Example

To draw together everything we have covered so far we shall work through a full example of how to use final trial balance to prepare an IAS 1 format statement of profit or loss, statement of changes in equity and statement of financial position.

The chief accountant of Format plc has extracted the following initial trial balance as Exhibit 12. 7 from the ledger accounts as at 31 December 20×2.

Exhibit 12. 7

Format plc		
Trial balance as at 31 December 20×2		
	£000	£000
	Dr	Cr
Issued ordinary shares of £1		800
Share premium		200
Trade receivables and trade payables	1,820	1,866
Bank	80	
Inventory at 1 January ×2	1,950	
6% debentures		1,000
Sales		9,500
Rental income		200
Debenture interest (six months to 30 June ×2)	30	
Administration and general expenses, excluding salaries	650	
Administration salaries	275	
Distribution expenses	616	
Purchases	5,125	
Salaries associated with manufacture of goods	300	
Delivery inwards	100	
Sundry costs	300	
Retained earnings		1,100
Freehold land, at cost	2,120	
Fixtures and fittings, at cost	2,000	

Exhibit 12. 7(continued)

Accumulated depreciation, fixtures and fittings		900
Allowance for receivables		100
Goodwill	300	—
	15,666	15,666

The following items have yet to be dealt with:

(1) An inventory count has revealed the closing inventory figure to be £2,020,000.

(2) The company depreciates fixtures and fittings at 20% on the straight-line basis.

(3) The credit controller has said that a debt of £15,000 should be written off as irrecoverable, and the allowance for receivables should be increased to £200,000.

(4) The income tax due on profits for the year is estimated at £750,000.

(5) The allocation of expenditure between cost of sales, distribution costs and administrative expenses should be as follows.

	Distribution	Administrative
	%	%
Sundry costs	25	75
Depreciation	50	50

(6) The debentures are repayable in full in 10 years' time. Interest is paid in two equal instalments per annum.

Requirement

Prepare a statement of profit or loss and a statement of changes in equity for Format plc for the year ended 31 December 20×2 and a statement of financial position as at that date.

Solution

Format plc's statement of profit or loss is presented as Exhibit 12. 8.

Exhibit 12. 8

Format plc	
Statement of profit or loss for the year ended 31 December 20×2	
	£000
Revenue	9,500
Cost of sales (W4)	(5,455)
Gross profit	4,045
Other income	200
Administrative expenses (W5)	(1,465)
Distribution costs (W6)	(891)

Exhibit 12. 8(continued)

Format plc	
Finance costs (6%× 1,000)	(60)
Profit before tax	1,829
Income tax	(750)
Profit for the period	1,079

Format plc's statement of changes in equity is presented as Exhibit 12. 9.

Exhibit 12. 9

Format plc				
Statement of changes in equity for the year ended 31 December 20×2				
	Ordinary shares	Share premium	Retained earnings	Total
	£000	£000	£000	£000
Balance at 1/1/×2	800	200	1,100	2,100
Comprehensive income for the year			1,079	1,079
Balance at 31/12/×2	800	200	2,179	3,179

Format plc's statement of financial position is presented as Exhibit 12. 10.

Exhibit 12. 10

Format plc		
Statement of financial position as at 31 December 20×2		
ASSETS	£000	£000
Non-current assets		
Property, plant and equipment (W7)		2,820
Goodwill		300
Current assets		3,120
Inventories	2,020	
Trade and other receivables (1,805 − 200 allowance)	1,605	
Cash and cash equivalents	80	
		3,705
Total assets		6,825
EQUITY AND LIABILITIES		
Equity		
Ordinary share capital: £1 equity shares		800

Exhibit 12. 10(continued)

Format plc		
Share premium		200
Retained earnings		2,179
		3,179
Non-current liabilities		
Long-term borrowings: 6% debentures		1,000
Current liabilities		
Trade and other payables (1,866+30)	1,896	
Income tax payable	750	
		2,646
Total equity and liabilities		6,825

WORKINGS

(1) Depreciation—fixtures and fittings: £2,000× 20% = £400

(2) Interest accruals:

	£000	£000
DEBIT	Finance cost (6%×1,000 − 30)	30	
CREDIT	Trade and other payable		30

(3) Taxation:

	£000	£000
DEBIT	Income tax	750	
CREDIT	Income tax payable		750

(4) Cost of sales

	£000
Opening inventory	1,950
Purchases	5,125
Closing inventory	(2,020)
Salaries	300
Delivery costs	100
	5,455

(5) Administration expenses

	£000
Per trial balance	650
Administration salaries	275

	£ 000
Irrecoverable debt	15
Allowance for receivables (200−100)	100
Depreciation—Fixtures and fitting (50%× 400)	200
Sundry costs (75%×300)	225
	1,465

(6) Distribution expenses

	£ 000
Per trial balance	616
Depreciation—Fixtures and fitting (50%× 400)	200
Sundry costs (25%× 300)	75
	891

(7) Property, plant and equipment note

	Freehold land	Fixtures and fittings	Total
Cost	£ 000	£ 000	£ 000
At 1. 1. 20×2	2,120	2,000	4,120
Additions			
Disposals			
At 31. 12. 20×2	2,120	2,000	4,120
Accumulated depreciation			
At 1. 1. 20×2		900	900
Charge for the year (£2,000×20%)		400	400
Disposals			
At 31. 12. 20×2		1,300	1,300
Carrying amount			
At 31. 12. 20×2	2,120	700	2,820
At 1. 1. 20×2	2,120	1,100	3,220

Summary

· IAS 1 lists the required contents of a company's financial statements. It also gives guidance on how items should be presented in the financial statements.

· A complete set of financial statements includes a statement of financial position, a statement of profit or loss and other comprehensive income, a statement of changes in equity, a statement of cash flows and disclosures notes.

· IAS 1 specifies what should be included in a statement of financial position and includes suggested format.

· IAS 1 specifies what should be included in a statement of profit or loss and other comprehensive income and includes a suggested format. Some items must be disclosed on the face of the statement.

· IAS 1 requires an entity to provide a statement of changes in equity. The statement of changes in equity shows the movements in the entity's equity for the period.

· Disclosure notes are included in a set of financial statements to give users extra information.

Exercise

12. 1 According to IAS 1, which of the following items must appear on the face of the statement of profit or loss and other comprehensive income? (   )

1 Tax expense

2 Revenue

3 Cost of sales

4 Profit or loss

   A.4 only

   B.2 and 4 only

   C.1, 2 and 4 only

   D.2 and 3 only

12. 2 According to IAS 1, which of the following items make up a complete set of financial statements? (   )

1 Statement of changes in equity

2 Statement of cash flows

3 Notes to the accounts

4 Statement of financial position

5 Statement of profit or loss and other comprehensive income

6 Chairman's report

   A.All of the items

   B.1, 2, 4 and 5 only

   C.1, 2, 3, 4 and 5 only

   D.3, 4 and 5 only

12. 3 Which of the following statements is/are correct? ( )

1 IAS 1 requires that some items must appear on the face of the statement of financial position.

2 IAS 1 requires that a company must present a combined statement of profit or loss and other comprehensive income.

A.1 only

B.2 only

C.Both 1 and 2

D.Neither 1 or 2

12. 4 Where are the following items shown in a company's financial statements? ( )

1 Gains on property revaluations

2 Dividends paid

3 Bonus issue of shares

	Statement of profit or loss and other comprehensive income	Statement of changes in equity
A.	1 and 2 only	2 and 3 only
B.	1 and 3 only	1 and 2 only
C.	1 only	1, 2 and 3
D.	1 only	2 and 3 only

12. 5 Which of the following is/are required for disclosure of revalued assets in a company's financial statements? ( )

1 The methods and significant assumptions applied in estimating the value

2 Whether an independent valuer was involved in the valuation

3 How certain the directors are that the valuation will not change in the next five years

A.1 only

B.1 and 2 only

C.2 only

D.All three are required

12. 6 Which of the following items may appear as current liabilities in a company's statement of financial position? ( )

1 Revaluation surplus

2 Loan due for repayment within one year

3 Taxation

4 Preference dividend payable on redeemable preference shares

A.1, 2 and 3

B.1, 2 and 4

C.1, 3 and 4

D.2, 3 and 4

12. 7 Which of the following might appear as an item in a company's statement of changes in equity? (   )

1 Profit on disposal of properties

2 Surplus on revaluation of properties

3 Equity dividends proposed after the reporting date

4 Issue of share capital

    A.1, 3 and 4 only

    B.2 and 4 only

    C.1 and 2 only

    D.3 and 4 only

12. 8 For which class or classes of assets should a company disclose in the notes to the financial statements a reconciliation of the opening carrying amount to the closing carrying amount, showing the movements in the period? (   )

1 Cash

2 Intangible assets

3 Tangible non-current assets

4 Trade receivables

    A.3 only

    B.2 and 3 only

    C.1 and 4 only

    D.1 only

12. 9 What disclosure is required when it is not possible to estimate the financial effect of an event not requiring adjustment? (   )

    A. No disclosure

    B. A note to the accounts giving what information is available and a statement that an estimate cannot be made

12. 10 Which of the following items are adjusting events? (   )

1 Dividends proposed at the year end

2 A plant destroyed by fire after the reporting date

3 Inventory found to have deteriorated (less than its carrying value at the year end)

    A. 1 only

    B. 2 only

    C. 3 only

D. None of the above

12. 11 Which of the following items are non-adjusting events? (　　　)

1 Inventory destroyed by flood two days before the reporting date

2 A customer goes bankrupt

3 Fall in value of an investment between the reporting date and the date the financial statements are finalised

     A. 1 only

     B. 2 only

     C. 3 only

     D. None of the above

12. 12 The trial balance of Hobo Ltd as at 30 September 20×6 was given as Exhibit 12. 11:

Exhibit 12. 11

Hobo Ltd's trial balance as at 30 September 20×6		
	Dr	Cr
	£	£
Audit fee	1,200	
Irrecoverable debts	5,320	
Accounts receivables and payables	92,360	111,450
Delivery expenses	22,060	
Production wages	32,300	
Warehouse wages	30,200	
Administrative salaries	15,200	
Purchases and Sales	426,500	623,300
Administration expenses	5,600	
Rents administration	12,600	
Inventory 1. 10. 20×5	18,950	
Ordinary 50p shares		100,000
Share premium account		50,000
Accumulated profits 1. 10. 20×5		26,000
Premises	275,000	
Vehicles	18,500	
Equipment	12,000	
Depreciation as at 1. 10. 20×5		

Exhibit 12. 11(continued)

Premises		3,750
Equipment		3,600
Vehicles		6,500
7% debentures		95,000
Bank	51,810	
	1,019,600	1,019,600

The following additional information is available:

(1) Inventory as at 30 September 20×6 was valued at cost £20,650. The net realisable value of the inventory was £19,840.

(2) Premises and equipment are used at 50% production and 50% distribution, and are to be depreciated at the rate of 1 % and 10% straight line respectively.

(3) Vehicles are only used for distribution, and are depreciated at 20% reducing balance.

(4) An allowance for receivables of 5% is to be allowed for.

(5) £500 was prepaid for rent and £600 is owing for production wages as at 30 September 20×6.

(6) Taxation for the year is estimated at £22,680.

Prepare the statement of profit or loss and statement of financial position for Hobo Ltd as at 30 September 20×6 in a form suitable for publication.

12. 13 * The following trial balance (Exhibit 12. 12) was extracted from the books of Cuddly Toy Ltd as at 31 December 20×5.

Exhibit 12. 12

Cuddly Toy Ltd's trial balance as at 31 December 20×5		
	Dr	Cr
	£000	£000
Sales		1,562
Inventory 1 January 20×5	660	
Purchases	885	
Land	1,010	
Buildings	980	
Equipment	55	
Vehicles	72	
Depreciation: Buildings		390
Equipment		18

Exhibit 12. 12(continued)

Cuddly Toy Ltd's trial balance as at 31 December 20×5		
Vehicles		25
Accounts receivables and payables	180	235
Bank	121	
£1 ordinary shares		900
Share premium		350
Distribution Expenses	98	
Administration expenses	24	
Accumulated profits 1 January 20×5		185
5% debentures	—	420
	4,085	4,085

The following information has not yet been accounted for:

(1) Closing Inventory 31 December 20×5 is valued at £560,000.

(2) Depreciation is to be charged as follows:

—2% straight line on buildings

—20% straight line on equipment

—25% reducing balance on vehicles

(3) Assets are used as follows:

—buildings: 50% cost of sales, 25% distribution and 25% administration

—equipment: all cost of sales

—vehicles: all distribution

(4) Taxation to be charged for the year is estimated at £200,000.

(5) Dividend has been declared but not yet paid for 6p per share.

(6) Land was revalued to £1,300,000.

Requirement

Prepare the published statement of comprehensive income, statement of changes in equity and statement of financial position for the company as at 31 December 20×5. Disclosure note for non-current assets is not required.

12. 14 You are required to prepare the statement of profit or loss, statement of changes in equity for the year ended 31 March 20×6 and the statement of financial position as at that date for the following company, for internal use. Exhibit 12. 13 gives the trial balance of Gerry ltd.

Exhibit 12. 13

Trial balance of Gerry ltd as at 31 March 20×6		
	Dr	Cr
	£	£
Ordinary shares £1		100,000

Exhibit 12. 13(continued)

6% preference shares £1		20,000
8% debentures		30,000
Share premium		9,500
Revaluation reserve		10,000
General reserve		12,000
Accumulated profit b/f 1 April 20×5		976
Non-current assets (cost £210,000)	191,000	
Inventory 1 April 20×5	14,167	
Accounts receivables and payables	11,000	7,500
Allowances for receivables		324
Bank	9,731	
Purchases and sales	186,000	271,700
Wages and salaries	31,862	
General expenses	15,840	
Debenture interest	1,200	
Preference dividend	1,200	
	462,000	462,000

You are also given the following information:

(1)Inventory 31 March 20×6 £23,483.

(2)Depreciation of non-current assets is to be provided at the rate of 10% per annum on cost.

(3)The allowance for receivables is to be 5% of accounts receivables.

(4)£1,200 of debenture interest and £1,437 of general expenses are to be accrued.

(5)£925 of general expenses have been paid in advance.

(6)Provision is to be made for taxation on this year's profits of £9,700.

(7)The directors have decided to increase the general reserve by a further £3,000.

12. 15 * Prepare the statement of comprehensive income for the year ended and the statement of financial position as at 31 October 20×5 following IAS 1. Exhibit 12. 14 presents the trial balance of Fresher ltd.

Exhibit 12. 14

Fresher ltd trial balance at 31 October 20×5		
	£000	£000
Property	8,900	
Factory	2,700	
Administration building	1,200	
Delivery vehicles	500	10

Exhibit 12. 14(continued)

Sales		10,300
Inventory at 1 November 20×4	1,195	
Purchases	6,350	
Factory wages	575	
Administration expenses	140	
Distribution costs	370	
Interests paid (6 months to 30 April 20×5)	100	
Accumulated profit at 1 November 20×4		3,701
10% loan		2,000
£1 Ordinary shares		4,000
Share premium		1,500
Dividends paid	400	
Revaluation reserve		2,500
Cash	1,200	
Trade receivables and payables	947	566
	24,577	24,577

Other relevant information:

(1) The cost of the inventory at 31 October 20×5 was £1,150,000. The net realisable value of the inventory was £1,080,000.

(2) The property has been further revalued at 31 October 20×5 at the market price of £9,200,000.

(3) A current tax provision for £350,000 is required for the period ended 31 October 20×5.

(4) Depreciation rates are:

    Factory—5% straight-line

    Administration building—3% straight-line

    Delivery vehicles—25% reducing balance

(5) It is agreed that £215,000 of the trade receivables should be written off since one customer has gone into liquidation.

12.16 The trial balance of Burn Ltd. as at 31 December 20 × 9 was as given in Exhibit 12.15:

Exhibit 12.15

Trial balance of Burn Ltd as at 31 December 20×9		
	Dr	Cr
	£	£
Purchases and sales	15,260	83,460

Exhibit 12. 15(continued)

Inventory 1 January 20×9	6,230	
Accounts receivables and payables	8,240	7,210
Production salaries and wages	12,320	
Production expenses	7,210	
Warehouse expenses	950	
Warehouse wages	10,100	
Administration salaries	14,200	
Administration expenses	950	
Ordinary £1 shares		100,000
Share premium account		20,000
Accumulated profits 1 January 20×9		62,000
Premises	200,000	
Equipment	50,000	
Vehicles	15,000	
Accumulated depreciation: Premises		20,000
Equipment		15,000
Vehicles		6,560
6% Debentures		50,000
Bank	103,520	
Cash	250	
New capital (Note 5)	____	80,000
	444,230	444,230

The following additional information is available none of which has been accounted for in the trial balance:

(1) Inventory 31 December 20×9 £4,560.

(2) Premises and equipment are used 50% production, 25% distribution and 25% administration and are depreciated at the rate of 2% and 10% respectively.

(3) Vehicles are only used by distribution and are depreciated at 20% reducing balance.

(4) The allowance for receivables of 5% is to be made.

(5) The new capital consists of the issue on 1 December 20×9 of 40,000 £1 shares; the ledger clerk did not know how to treat this item in the ledgers.

(6) Tax for the year is estimated at £1,200.

(7) A vehicle, purchased 1 January 20×7 for £7,000 was sold on 1 August 20×9 for £3,750. The proceeds had been credited to sales. The policy of the company is to provide a full year's depreciation in the year of purchase and none in the year of sales.

(8) 5% Debentures were issued on 1 January 20×9 at par value £10,000. The £10,000 has been credited to accumulated profits 1 January 20×9 account.

Requirement

Prepare the statement of profit or loss, statement of changes in equity and statement of financial position for Burn Ltd. as at 31 December 20×9 in a form suitable for publication. Disclosure note for non-current assets is not required.

12. 17* The trial balance of Black Ltd as at 31 December 20×5 was shown as Exhibit 12. 16:

Exhibit 12. 16

Trial balance of Black Ltd as at 31 December 20×5		
	Dr	Cr
	£	£
Accounts receivables and payables	46,800	34,200
Return inwards	2,450	
Productive wages	74,000	
Distributive expenses	32,870	
Administrative salaries	61,230	
Purchases and Sales	321,700	552,600
Office expenses	5,630	
Return outwards		4,670
Inventory	22,300	
Ordinary £1 shares		150,000
Debentures 6%		50,000
Accumulated profits 1 January 20×5		9,870
Premises	150,000	
Vehicles	85,000	
Equipment	70,000	
Depreciation as at 1 January 20×5		
Premises		11,600
Equipment		27,500
Vehicles		29,250
Bank		2,290
	871,980	871,980

The following additional information is available none of which has been taken account of in the preparation of the trial balance above:

(1) Inventory as at 31 December 20×5 is valued at £22,000.

(2) Vehicles are primarily used for distribution, premises equally between production, distribution and administration and equipment equally between production and administration.

(3) Premises are to be depreciated 1% straight line, equipment 20% straight line and vehicles 25% reducing balance.

(4) Equipment was sold on the 31 August 20×5 for £15,000. This had been credited to sales. The original cost was £20,000 and it had been purchased on 1 January 20×3. No further entries than cash and sales had been made in the books. The policy of the company is to provide a full year's depreciation in the year of purchase and none in the year of sales.

(5) Irrecoverable debts of £2,600 need writing off and the allowance for receivables at the rate of 5% is to be introduced.

(6) Taxation for the year is estimated at £9,860.

(7) Accruals of £3,500 for administration expense are required and prepayments of £5,600 have been identified within distribution expenses.

(8) The interest on the debentures has not yet been paid.

Requirement

Prepare the statement of profit or loss for the year ended 31 December 20×5 and statement of financial position as at that date in a form suitable for publication.

12.18 * The following information (Exhibit 12.17) has been extracted from the books of Tonson, a limited liability company, as at 31 October 20×6.

Exhibit 12.17

Tonson's trial balance as at 31 October 20×6		
	Dr	Cr
	£000	£000
Cash	15	
Insurance	75	
Inventory at 1 November 20×5	350	
General expenses	60	
Energy expenses	66	
Marketing expenses	50	
Wages and salaries	675	
Discounts received		50
Share premium account		200
Retained earnings at 1 November 20×5		315
Allowance for receivables at 1 November 20×5		40

Exhibit 12. 17(continued)

Sales revenue		5,780
Telephone expenses	80	
Property expenses	100	
Bank		94
Returns inward	95	
Trade payables		290
Loan note interest	33	
Trade receivables	900	
Purchases	3,570	
7% loan notes		470
Irrecoverable debts	150	
£1 ordinary shares		1,800
Accumulated depreciation at 1 November 20×5		
Buildings		360
Motor Vehicles		80
Furniture and equipment		420
Land at cost	740	
Buildings at cost	1,500	
Motor vehicles at cost	240	
Furniture and equipment at cost	1,200	
	9,899	9,899

You have also been provided with the following information:

(1) Inventory at 31 October 20×6 was valued at £275,000 based on its original cost. However, £45,000 of this inventory has been in the warehouse for over two years and the directors have agreed to sell it in November 20×6 for a cash price of £20,000.

(2) The marketing expenses include £5,000 which relates to November 20×6.

(3) The allowance for receivables is to be increased to 5% of trade receivables.

(4) There are wages and salaries outstanding of £40,000 for the year ended 31 October 20×6.

(5) Buildings are depreciated at 5% of cost. At 31 October 20×6 the buildings were professionally valued at £1,800,000 and the directors wish this valuation to be incorporated into the accounts.

(6) Depreciation is to be charged as follows:

—Motor vehicles at 20% of written down value

—Furniture and equipment at 20% of cost

(7) No dividends have been paid or declared.

(8) Tax of £150,000 is to be provided for the year.

(9) During October 20×6 a bonus issue of one for ten shares was made to ordinary shareholders. This has not been entered into the books. The share premium account was used for this purpose.

Requirement

Prepare following statements, for internal use: statement of comprehensive income for the year ended 31 October 20×6 and statement of financial position as at 31 October 20×6.

Reference

1. ACCA FA Financial Accounting/FIA FFA Interactive Text 2020, BPP Learning Media.

2. ACCA FA Financial Accounting/FIA FFA Practice & Revision Kit 2020, BPP Learning Media.

3. Accounting (Study Manual 2020), The Institute of Chartered Accountants in England and Wales.

4. Accounting (Question Bank 2020), The Institute of Chartered Accountants in England and Wales.

Chapter 13

Statement of Cash Flows

┌┈┈┈ ■Learning Objectives ┈┈┈┈┈┈┈┈┈┈┈┈┈┈┈┈┈┈┈┈┈┈┈┈┈┈┈┐
· Understand the difference between cash and profit.

· Distinguish between operating activities, investing activities and financing activities.

· Apply direct method and indirect method of determining cash flows from operating activities.

· Define the terms cash and cash equivalents.

· Identify non-cash transactions.

· Prepare abasic statement of cash flows.
└┈┈┘

13.1 Introduction to the Statement of Cash Flows

In the past, the statement of profit or loss and the statement of financial position were considered to be sufficient for financial reporting purposes. However, people recognised the importance of the statement of cash flows and the need for companies to publish this information. The provision of information on cash receipts and cash payments for a given period, i.e. the financial year in question, gives a picture of the cash inflows and cash outflows of the company. The importance of this information is evident when we consider that a company must have cash in order to survive. For this reason a statement of cash flows is needed, so that a reconciliation between the company's profit for the year and its cash can be presented. This reconciliation demonstrates by how much cash has gone up or down for a given financial period.

1. Purpose of the Statement of Cash Flows ├────────────────────

The statements of cash flows are given as an additional statement, supplementing the statement of financial position, statement of profit or loss and related notes. Users can gain further appreciation of the change in net assets, of the entity's financial position (liquidity and solvency) and the entity's ability to adapt to changing circumstances by adjusting the amount and timing of cash flows. Statements of cash flows enhance comparability, as they are not affected by differing accounting policies used for the same type of transactions or events. Cash flow information of a historical nature can be used as an indicator of the amount, timing and certainty of future cash flows. Past forecast cash flow information can be checked for accuracy as actual figures emerge. The relationship between profit and cash flows can be analysed, as can changes in prices over time. All this information helps management to control costs by controlling cash flow.

This chapter seeks to focus on the cash inflows and cash outflows that make up the statement of cash flows. The group aspects of statements of cash flows (and certain complex matters) have been excluded, as they are beyond the scope of this textbook.

2. Cash vs Profit

It has been argued that 'profit' does not always give a useful or meaningful picture of a company's operations. Readers of a company's financial statements might even be misled by a reported profit figure. Consider the following examples.

· Shareholders might believe that if a company makes a profit after tax of, say, £100,000 then this is the amount which it could afford to pay as a dividend. Unless the company has sufficient cash available to stay in business and also to pay a dividend, the shareholders' expectations would be wrong.

· Employees might believe that if a company makes profits, it can afford to pay higher wages next year. This opinion may not be correct: the ability to pay wages depends on the availability of cash.

· Cash is the lifeblood of the business. Survival of a business entity depends not so much on profits as on its ability to pay its debts when they fall due. Such payments might include 'profit and loss' items such as material purchases, wages, interest and taxation etc., but also capital payments for new non-current assets and the repayment of loan capital when this falls due (for example, on the redemption of debentures).

From these examples, it is clear that a company's future performance and prospects depend not so much on the 'profits' earned in a period, but more realistically on liquidity or cash flows.

The following are some of the factors that will result in a company's profit figure being different from its cash figure:

· Timing differences.

The point at which the cash is paid and/or received is often different from when the cash is shown in the statement of profit or loss. This difference is a result of the accruals concept. In the statement of profit or loss we show the effect of transactions as soon as they have taken place. This means that any income earned or cost incurred is shown in the statement of profit or loss immediately. However, we do not show the effect of any income earned or cost incurred in the statement of cash flows until the cash has actually been paid or received.

· Depreciation.

Depreciation will appear in the statement of profit or loss, but it is not a cash movement so will not appear in the statement of cash flows. Depreciation is merely an accounting transaction that has no impact on the physical movement of cash.

· Accounting transactions that bypass the statement of profit or loss.

Any cash transaction that takes place will pass through the statement of cash flows. However, not all transactions pass through the statement of profit or loss. This is because the statement of profit or loss only gives a picture of the company's activities for any given year. As such it focuses on income and expenditure types—those that arise and are incurred in order to support the day-to-day running of the company. The statement of profit or loss does not reflect capital expenditure, which is predominately concerned with a longer-term benefit. For example, expenditure on capital items is a drain on the cash flow but leaves the statement of profit or loss unchanged, because this expenditure is not specific to the revenue generated in that year only.

13. 2   IAS 7: Statement of Cash Flows

1. Objective and Scope

The objective of IAS 7 Statement of Cash Flows is to provide historical information about changes in cash and cash equivalents, classifying cash flows between operating, investing and financing activities. This will provide information to users of financial statements about the entity's ability to generate cash and cash equivalents, as well as indicating the cash needs of the entity.

IAS 7 requires all entities to include a statement of cash flows as an integral part of their financial statement. All types of entity can provide useful information about cash flows as the need for cash is universal, whatever the nature of their revenue-producing activities.

Most computerised accounting systems can automatically produce a statement of cash flows as one of the primary financial statements of a business. It is important that an accountant can understand the underlying approach to preparing the statement of cash flows and how to identify cash movements from transactions.

2. Definitions

· **Cash flows** are inflows and outflows of cash and cash equivalents.
· **Cash** comprises cash on hand and demand deposits.
· **Cash equivalents** are short-term, highly liquid investments that are readily convertible to

known amounts of cash and which are subject to an insignificant risk of changes in value (maturity of three months or less from the date of acquisition).

  • **Operating activities** are the principal revenue-producing activities of the enterprise and other activities that are not investing or financing activities.

  • **Investing activities** are the acquisition and disposal of non-current assets and other investments not included in cash equivalents.

  • **Financing activities** are activities that result in changes in the size and composition of the equity capital and borrowings of the entity.

13. 3   Presentation of the Statement of Cash Flows

IAS 7 requires the items that are normally contained in a statement of cash flows to be classified under three headings. These are net cash flows from operating activities, net cash flows from investing activities and net cash flows from financing activities.

1. Cash Flows from Operating Activities

This is perhaps the key part of the statement of cash flows because it is an indication of how well the entity can generate enough cash flows to maintain its operations and meet its debts without relying on external finance.

Most of the components of cash flows from operating activities will be those items which determine the net profit or loss of the enterprise, i.e. they relate to the main revenue-producing activities of the enterprise. Cash flows from operating activities can consist of:

  • Cash receipts from the sale of goods and the rendering of services.
  • Cash receipts from royalties, fees, commissions and other revenue.
  • Cash payments to suppliers for goods and services.
  • Cash payments to and on behalf of employees.

Cash flows from interest paid and income taxes paid are **usually** dealt with here. IAS 7 allows two possible layouts for cash generated from operations:

  • Direct method: disclose major classes of gross cash receipts and gross cash payments.
  • Indirect method: net profit or loss is adjusted for the effects of transactions of a non-cash nature, any deferrals or accruals of past or future operating cash receipts or payments, and items of income or expense associated with investing or financing cash flows.

IAS 7 encourages direct method as it provides additional information to the users of financial statements which would not otherwise be available, but it is not compulsory. In practice, the majority of businesses use the indirect method, since it is quicker and easier, and can be prepared directly from the statement of financial position and statement of comprehensive income with little additional information.

(1) Direct Method

Using the direct method, cash generated from operations would be analysed as follows (Exhibit 13.1) and shown as a note to the statement of cash flows:

Exhibit 13.1

Cash generated from operations for the year ended December 20×4	
	£
Cash received from customers	X
Cash payments to suppliers	(X)
Cash payments to and on behalf of employees	(X)
Cash generated from operations	X
Interest paid	(X)
Income tax paid	(X)
Net cash flows from operating activities	X

The reasons for certain items being added and others being deducted is very straightforward with this method—cash inflows are added and cash outflows are deducted.

 Worked Example 13.1

Hail plc commenced trading on 1 January 20×7 following a share issue which raised £35,000. During the year the company entered into the following transactions:

· Purchases from suppliers were £19,500, of which £2,550 was unpaid at the year end
· Wages and salaries amounted to £10,500, of which £750 was unpaid at the year end
· Sales revenue was £29,400, including £900 receivables at the year end

Requirement

Calculate the cash generated from operations using direct method.

Solution

Cash generated from operations would be calculated and disclosed as follows:

Operating cash flows for the year ended 31 December 20×7

	£
Cash received from customers (29,400 – 900)	28,500
Cash paid to suppliers and employees (W)	(26,700)
Cash generated from operations	1,800

WORKING

	£
Cash paid to suppliers (19,500 − 2,550)	16,950
Cash paid to and on behalf of employees (10,500 − 750)	9,750
Cash paid to suppliers and employees	26,700

(2) Indirect Method

Indirect method should include all amounts received and paid as a result of the company's trading activities. This means adjusting the operating profit before tax so that it reflects the cash effect of the company's trading/operating activities only.

Using the indirect method, cash generated from operations is calculated by performing a reconciliation between:

· Profit before tax as reported in the statement of profit or loss.

· Cash generated from operations.

The net profit or loss for the period is adjusted for the following:

· Changes during the period in inventories, operating receivables and payables.

· Non-cash items, e.g. depreciation, provisions, profits/losses on the sales of assets.

· Other items, the cash flows from which should be classified under investing or financing activities.

A proforma of such a calculation is as follows (Exhibit 13. 2).

Exhibit 13. 2

Cash generated from operations for the year ended December 20×4	
	£
Profit/(loss) before tax	X
Finance cost	X
Investment income	(X)
Depreciation charge	X
Amortisation charge	X
Loss/(profit) on disposal of non-current assets	X/(X)
(Increase)/decrease in inventories	(X)/X
(Increase)/decrease in trade and other receivables	(X)/X
(Increase)/decrease in prepayments	(X)/X
Increase/(decrease) in trade and other payables	X/(X)
Increase/(decrease) in accruals	X/(X)
Increase/(decrease) in provisions	X/(X)
Cash generated from operations	X

Exhibit 13. 2(continued)

Interest paid	(X)
Income tax paid	(X)
Net cash flows from operating activities	X

It is important to understand why certain items are added and others subtracted. Note the following points.

· Depreciation is not a cash expense, but is deducted in arriving at the profit figure in the statement of profit or loss. It makes sense, therefore, to eliminate it by adding it back.

· By the same logic, a loss on a disposal of a non-current asset needs to be added back and a profit on disposal needs to be deducted.

· An increase in inventory means less cash—you have spent cash on buying inventory.

· An increase in receivables means receivables have not been received as much, therefore less cash.

· If we pay off payables, causing the figure to decrease, again we have less cash.

Most of the adjustments involve comparing the statement of financial positions for the last two years to determine the adjustments. The net operating cash flows is often the hardest figure to arrive at in the cash flow statement, so it is worth working through a basic example.

 Worked Example 13. 2

Planet plc has profit before tax for the year to 31 December 20×9 of £115. 5m, after charging £28. 7m for depreciation.

The statement of financial position for the year shows the following entries:

	20×9	20×8
	£ m	£ m
Inventory	16. 1	15. 4
Trade and other receivables	14. 7	12. 6
Trade and other payables	11. 9	10. 5

Requirement

Calculate the cash generated from operations using indirect method.

Solution

Refer to Exhibit 13. 3.

Exhibit 13. 3

Cash generated from operations for the year ended December 20×9	
	£ m
Profit before tax	115. 5
Add back depreciation	28. 7
	144. 2
Increase in inventory	(0. 7)
Increase in receivables	(2. 1)
Increase in payables	1. 4
Cash generated from operations	142. 8

 Question

Quest plc has profit before tax for the year to 31 December 20×6 of £850, after charging £650 for depreciation and making a profit on sale of a car of £120.

The statement of financial position for the year shows the following entries:

	20×6	20×5
Inventories	586	763
Trade and other receivables	1,021	589
Trade and other payables	443	1,431

Requirement

Calculate the cash generated from operations.

2. Cash Flows from Investing Activities

The cash flows classified under this heading show the extent of new investment in assets which will generate future profit and cash flows. These are the acquisition and disposal of long-term assets and other investments not included in cash equivalents.

This could include the following items:

· Cash payments to acquire property, plant and equipment, intangibles and other non-current assets, including those relating to capitalised development costs and self-constructed property, plant and equipment.

· Cash receipts from sales of property, plant and equipment, intangibles and other non-current assets.

· Cash payments to acquire equity or debt of other entities.

· Cash receipts from sales of equity or debt of other entities.

Interest received and dividends received are **usually** shown as investing cash flows.

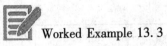
Worked Example 13. 3

Plant with a net book value of £12,000 (cost £23,500) was sold during the year 20×8 for £7,800. The loss on sale has been included in the profit before interest and tax.

Statement of financial position (extract) as at 31 March 20×8

	20×8 £	20×7 £
Non-current assets		
Plant at cost	84,600	70,000
Plant accumulated depreciation	37,600	22,500
Investments	–	16,900

Requirement

Calculate the cash generated from investing activities.

Solution

From the above extracts we can calculate the cash effect of this transaction, by looking at the movement in non-current assets from one year to the next.

Plant cost

	£		£
Balance b/d	70,000	Disposal	23,500
Additions (balancing figure)	38,100	Balance c/d	84,600
	108,100		108,100

The cash amount that has been spent on non-current assets is £38,100 and this should be shown in statement of cash flows under the heading 'Cash flows from investing activities' as a cash outflow. Equally the cash received for the disposal during the year amounting to £7,800 should be shown as a cash inflow under the same heading. Cash generated from investing activities is shown as Exhibit 13. 4.

Exhibit 13. 4

Cash generated from investing activities	
	£
Purchase of non-current assets	(38,100)
Proceeds from sale of non-current assets	7,800
Proceeds from sale of investments	16,900
Net cash flows from investing activities	(13,400)

Question

The following information is available for Sun plc's non-current assets:

	20×7 £m	20×6 £m
Property, plant and equipment at NBV	125	50

· During the year there was a £10m depreciation charge.

· A revaluation surplus of £30m existed.

· Assets with a net book value of £7.5m were disposed of.

Requirement

How much cash was spent on non-current assets in the year?

3. Cash Flows from Financing Activities

This section of the statement of cash flows shows the share of cash which the entity's capital providers have claimed during the period. This is an indicator of likely future interest and dividend payments. The standard gives the following examples of cash flows which might arise under this heading.

· Cash proceeds from issue of shares.

· Cash payments to owners to acquire or redeem the enterprise's shares.

· Cash proceeds from issuing debentures, loans, notes, bonds, mortgages and other short-or long-term borrowings.

· Cash repayments of amounts borrowed.

Dividends paid is **usually** presented as a financing cash flow, showing the cost of obtaining financial resources.

 Worked Example 13.4

Rustler plc's annual accounts for the year to 31 December 20×7 show the following figures.

	At 31 December 20×7 £000	At 31 December 20×6 £000
Share capital: Ordinary shares of 50p	6,750	5,400
Share premium	12,800	7,300

There were no bonus issues of shares during the year.

Requirement

What amount of cash was raised from shares issued during the year?

Solution

Share capital and premium

	£000		£000
		Balance b/d (5,400+7,300)	12,700
Balance c/d (6,750+12,800)	19,550	**Cash receipt** (balancing figure)	6,850
	19,550		19,550

 Question

Spear Plc issued 87,500 £1 shares at par during the year to 31 December 20×6. Loans taken out increased from £18,000 at the beginning of the year to £30,000 at the end of the year. The company declared a dividend of 10p per share.

Requirement

Calculate the cash flows from financing activities.

4. Cash and Cash Equivalents

IAS 7 defines cash equivalents are not held for investment or other long-term purposes, but rather to meet short-term cash commitments. To fulfil the above definition, an investment's maturity date should normally be three months from its acquisition date. Usually equity investments (i.e. shares in other companies) are not cash equivalents.

Loans and other borrowings from banks are classified as financing activities. In some countries, however, bank overdrafts are repayable on demand and are treated as part of an enterprise's total cash management system. In these circumstances an overdrawn balance will be included in cash and cash equivalents.

The components of cash and cash equivalents should be disclosed and a reconciliation should be presented, showing the amounts in the statement of cash flows reconciled with the equivalent items reported in the statement of financial position.

It is also necessary to disclose the accounting policy used in deciding the items included in cash and cash equivalents, in accordance with IAS 1 Presentation of Financial Statements, but also because of the wide range of cash management practices world wide. Please see a full format of a statement of cash flows in Exhibit 13.5.

Exhibit 13.5

Company XYZ		
Statement of cash flows for the year ended 31 December 20××		
	£	£
Cash flows from operating activities		

Exhibit 13. 5(continued)

Profit before tax	X	
Adjusted for		
Depreciation	X	
Investment loss/(income)	X/(X)	
Interest Expense/(Income)	X/(X)	
Loss/(profit) on disposal of NCA	X/(X)	
Operating profit before working capital changes	X	
Decrease/(increase) in inventories	X/(X)	
Decrease/(increase) in trade receivables	X/(X)	
Increase/(decrease) in trade payables	X/(X)	
Cash generated from operations	X	
Interest paid	(X)	
Tax paid	(X)	
Net cash flows from operating activities		XX
Cash flows from investing activities		
Payments to acquire NCA and other investments	(X)	
Proceeds from disposal of NCA	X	
Dividends received	X	
Interest received	X	
Net cash flows from investing activities		XX
Cash flows from financing activities		
Issue of shares	X	
Issue of loan notes	X	
Repayment of loans	(X)	
Dividends paid	(X)	
Net cash flows from financing activities		XX
Increase/(decrease) in cash and cash equivalents		XX(XX)
Cash and cash equivalents at beginning of period		XX
Cash and cash equivalents at end of period		XX

13.4 An Example: Preparing a Statement of Cash Flows

In essence, preparing a statement of cash flows is very straightforward. You should therefore simply use the format you learned in previous sections. Now let's see an example on preparing a full statement of cash flows.

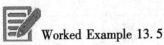 Worked Example 13.5

Kane plc's statement of profit or loss for the year ended 31 December 20×2 (Exhibit 13.6) and statement of financial position at 31 December 20×1 and 31 December 20×2 (Exhibit 13.7) were as follows.

Exhibit 13.6

kane plc	
Statement of profit or loss for the year ended 31 December 20×2	
	£000
Revenue	720
Cost of sales	(188)
Gross profit	532
Distribution costs	(18)
Administrative expenses	(94)
Profit from operations	420
Finance costs	(28)
Profit before tax	392
Income tax expense	(124)
Profit for the period	268

Exhibit 13.7

	kane plc			
Statement of financial position as at 31 December				
	20×2		20×1	
	£000	£000	£000	£000
Non-current assets				
Cost		1,596		1,560
Depreciation		(318)		(224)

Exhibit 13. 7(continued)

		1,278		1,336
Current assets				
Inventory	24		20	
Trade receivables	66		50	
Bank	48	138	56	126
Total assets		1,416		1,462
Equity				
Share capital		360		340
Share premium		36		24
Retained earnings		716		514
Non-current liabilities				
Borrowings		200		500
Trade payables	12		6	
Taxation	92	104	78	84
		1,416		1,462

Dividends totalling £66,000 were paid during the year.

During the year, the company paid £90,000 for a new piece of machinery.

Included in the cost of sales is depreciation of £118,000. A loss on disposal of £18,000 has been included in distribution costs.

Requirement

Prepare a statement of cash flows for Kane plc for the year ended 31 December 20×2 in accordance with the requirements of IAS 7.

Solution

Kane plc's statement of cash flows is shown in Exhibit 13. 8.

Exhibit 13. 8

Kane plc		
Statement of cash flows for the year ended 31 December 20×2 (indirect method)		
Cash flows from operating activities	£000	£000
Profit before taxation	392	
Loss on sale of property, plant and equipment	18	
Depreciation	118	
Interest expense	28	
Increase in trade and other receivables	(16)	

Exhibit 13. 8(continued)

Increase in inventories	(4)	
Increase in trade payables	<u>6</u>	
Cash generated from operations	542	
Interest paid	(28)	
Income taxes paid (W1)	<u>(110)</u>	
Net cash from operating activities		404
Cash flows from investing activities		
Purchase of property, plant and equipment	(90)	
Proceeds from sale of equipment (W2)	<u>12</u>	
Interest received		
Net cash used in investing activities		(78)
Cash flows from financing activities		
Proceeds from issue of share capital (360 + 36 − 340 − 24)	32	
Repayment for long-term borrowings (500 − 200)	(300)	
Dividends paid	<u>(66)</u>	
Net cash used in financing activities		<u>(334)</u>
Net increase in cash and cash equivalents		(8)
Cash and cash equivalents at beginning of period		<u>56</u>
Cash and cash equivalents at end of period		<u>48</u>

WORKINGS

(1) Income tax paid

	£ 000
Opening tax payable	78
Charge for year	124
Closing tax payable	(92)
Tax paid	<u>110</u>

(2) Non-current asset disposal

Cost

	£ 000		£ 000
Balance b/d	1,560	**Disposal** (balancing figure)	54
Additions	<u>90</u>	Balance c/d	<u>1,596</u>
	<u>1,650</u>		<u>1,650</u>

Accumulated depreciation

	£000		£000
Disposal (balancing figure)	24	Balance b/d	224
Balance c/d	318	Charge	118
	342		342

	£000
Carrying amount of disposals(54−24)	30
Net loss reported	(18)
Proceeds of disposals	12

Summary

· The statement of profit or loss is prepared on an accrual basis, but the statement of cash flows is prepared on a cash basis. Therefore profit and cash is not the same thing.

· The statement of cash flows shows movements in cash and cash equivalents and is a useful addition to the financial statements of companies.

· The statement of cash flows concentrates on the sources and uses of cash and are a useful indicator of a company's liquidity and solvency.

· You need to be aware of the layout and structure of the statement as laid out in IAS 7.

Exercise

13. 1 Which one of the following options best describes the objective of IAS 7, Statement of Cash Flows? (   )

　　A.To aid comparison of cash flows between entities

　　B.To assist users to understand the cash management and treasury practices of an entity

　　C.To assist users to confirm the going concern of an entity

　　D.To enable entities to report cash inflows and outflows analysed under standard headings

13. 2 Which one of the following statements gives the best definition of cash equivalents as set out in IAS 7, Statement of Cash Flows? (   )

　　A.Cash equivalents are cash, overdrafts, short-term deposits, options and other financial instruments and equities traded in an active market

　　B.Cash equivalents are short-term highly liquid investments subject to insignificant risks of change in value

　　C.Cash equivalents are readily disposable investments

D.Cash equivalents are investments which are traded in an active market

13. 3 In a company's statement of cash flows prepared in accordance with IAS 7, Statement of Cash Flows, a revaluation of non-current assets during the year will be( ).

A.Entirely excluded

B.Shown under cash flows from operating activities

C.Disclosed under investing activities

D.Shown as a cash inflow

13. 4 A company has the following information about property, plant and equipment.

	20×7	20×6
	£000	£000
Cost	750	600
Accumulated depreciation	250	150
Carrying amount	500	450

Plant with a carrying amount of £75,000 (original cost £90,000) was sold for £30,000 during the year.

What is the cash flow from investing activities for the year? ( )

A.£95,000 inflow

B.£210,000 inflow

C.£210,000 outflow

D.£95,000 outflow

13. 5 Waterloo plc acquired a freehold building for cash, financed in full by issuing for cash 166,000 £1 ordinary shares at a premium of £2 per share.

In its statement of cash flows prepared in accordance with IAS 7 Statement of Cash Flows this transaction should be stated as( ).

A.Inflow £498,000, outflow nil

B.Inflow nil, outflow nil

C.Inflow £498,000, outflow £498,000

D.Inflow nil, outflow £498,000

13. 6 Information concerning the non-current assets of Ealing plc is detailed in the table. During the year non-current assets which had cost £80,000 and which had a carrying amount of £30,000 were sold for £20,000. Net cash from operating activities for the year was £300,000.

	Start of year	End of year
	£	£
Cost	180,000	240,000
Accumulated depreciation	(120,000)	(140,000)
Carrying amount	60,000	100,000

There was no other cash activity. As a result of the above, cash increased over the year by
(   ).

    A.£240,000

    B.£260,000

    C.£320,000

    D.£180,000

13. 7 Which of the following items could appear in a company's statement of cash flows?
(   )

1 Surplus on revaluation of non-current assets

2 Proceeds of issue of shares

3 Proposed dividend

4 Irrecoverable debts written off

5 Dividends received

    A.1, 2 and 5 only

    B.2, 3, 4, 5 only

    C.2 and 5 only

    D.3 and 4 only

13. 8 Part of the process of preparing a company's statement of cash flows is the calculation of cash inflow from operating activities.

Which of the following statements about that calculation (using the indirect method) are correct? (   )

1 Loss on sale of operating non-current assets should be deducted from net profit before taxation

2 Increase in inventory should be deducted from operating profits

3 Increase in payables should be added to operating profits

4 Depreciation charges should be added to net profit before taxation

    A.1, 2 and 3

    B.1, 2 and 4

    C.1, 3 and 4

    D.2, 3 and 4

13. 9 In the course of preparing a company's statement of cash flows, the following figures are to be included in the calculation of net cash from operating activities.

	£
Depreciation charges	980,000
Profit on sale of non-current assets	40,000
Increase in inventories	130,000
Decrease in receivables	100,000
Increase in payables	80,000

What will the net effect of these items be in the statement of cash flows? (   )

	£
A.Addition to operating profit	890,000
B.Subtraction from operating profit	890,000
C.Addition to operating profit	1,070,000
D.Addition to operating profit	990,000

13. 10 Part of a company's draft statement of cash flows is shown below:

	£000
Net profit before tax	8,640
Depreciation charges	(2,160)
Proceeds of sale of non-current assets	360
Increase in inventory	(330)
Increase in accounts payable	440

The following criticisms of the above extract have been made:

1 Depreciation charges should have been added, not deducted

2 Increase in inventory should have been added, not deducted

3 Increase in accounts payable should have been deducted, not added

4 Proceeds of sale of non-current assets should not appear in this part of the statement of cash flows

Which of these criticisms are valid? (   )

A.2 and 3 only

B.1 and 4 only

C.1 and 3 only

D.2 and 4 only

13. 11 In preparing a company's statement of cash flows complying with IAS 7, which, if any, of the following items could form part of the calculation of cash flow from financing activi-

ties? (   )

1 Proceeds of sale of premises

2 Dividends received

3 Bonus issue of shares

    A.1 only

    B.2 only

    C.3 only

    D.None of them

13. 12 IAS 7 requires the statement of cash flows to open with the calculation of net cash from operating activities, arrived at by adjusting net profit before taxation.

Which one of the following lists consists only of items which could appear in such a calculation? (   )

    A.Depreciation, increase in receivables, decrease in payables, proceeds from sale of equipment, increase in inventories

    B.Increase in payables, decrease in inventories, profit on sale of plant, depreciation, decrease in receivables

    C.Increase in payables, proceeds from sale of equipment, depreciation, decrease in receivables, increase in inventories

    D.Depreciation, interest paid, proceeds from sale of equipment, decrease in inventories

13. 13 The following extract is from the financial statements of Pompeii, a limited liability company at 31 October:

	20×9	20×8
Equity and liabilities	£000	£000
Share capital	120	80
Share premium	60	40
Retained earnings	85	68
	265	188
Non-current liabilities		
Bank loan	100	150
	365	338

What is the cash flow from financing activities to be disclosed in the statement of cash flows for the year ended 31 October 20×9? (   )

    A.£60,000 inflow

    B.£10,000 inflow

C.£110,000 inflow

D.£27,000 inflow

13.14 Which one of the following statements is correct, with regard to the preparation of a statement of cash flows that complies with IAS 7 Statements of Cash Flows? ( )

  A.A statement of cash flows prepared using the direct method produces the same figure for net cash from operating activities as a statement produced by the indirect method

  B.An increase in a bank overdraft during the accounting period is included within cash flows from financing activities

  C.A profit on the sale of equipment is included within cash flows from investing activities

  D. A surplus on the revaluation of property will appear within cash flows from investing activities

13.15 A company sold warehouse premises at a loss during a financial period. How would this transaction be included in a statement of cash flows for the period that complies with IAS 7 Statements of Cash Flows and that uses the indirect method to present cash flows from operating activities? ( )

	Loss on disposal	Proceeds from sale
A.	Deduct as an adjustment in the calculation of cash flows from operating activities	Include in cash flows from investing activities
B.	Deduct as an adjustment in the calculation of cash flows from operating activities	Include in cash flows from operating activities
C.	Add as an adjustment in the calculation of cash flows from operating activities	Include in cash flows from investing activities
D.	Add as an adjustment in the calculation of cash flows from operating activities	Include in cash flows from operating activities

13.16 Which one of the following statements is correct? ( )

  A.If a business makes a profit, it has positive cash flow

  B.If a business makes a loss, it has negative cash flow

  C.A business may make a profit but have negative cash flow

  D.A business that breaks even has cash inflows equal to cash used

13.17 Toots Co has made healthy profits for the past year, although at times the company has been close to running out of cash. Because Toots Co is profitable, Adam, their accountant is unconcerned by the cash shortage. Jo, the financial controller at Toots Co, is concerned. Jo tells Adam, 'profits are fine on paper, but in the real world cash is king'. Jo believes Toots

Co needs to take a more proactive approach to cash flow management.

Adam and Jo have two different views. Who is correct, and why? (　　)

　　A.Adam is correct. A profitable business should not waste management time on cash flow issues

　　B.Adam is correct. A profitable business will always survive and prosper

　　C.Jo is correct. Proactive cash flow management is required under IAS 7 Statement of cash flows

　　D.Jo is correct. A business that does not have cash available to fund operations is likely to fail

13.18* Flail Co commenced trading on 1 January 20×1 with a medium-term loan of £21,000 and a share issue which raised £35,000. The company purchased non-current assets for £21,000 cash and during the year to 31 December 20×1 entered into the following transactions.

（1）Purchases from suppliers were £19,500, of which £2,550 was unpaid at the year end.

（2）Wages and salaries amounted to £10,500, of which £750 was unpaid at the year end.

（3）Interest on the loan of £2,100 was fully paid in the year and a repayment of £5,250 was made.

（4）Sales turnover was £29,400, including £900 receivables at the year end.

（5）Interest on cash deposits at the bank amounted to £75.

（6）A dividend of £4,000 was proposed as at 31 December 20×1.

You are required to prepare Flail Co's statement of cash flows for the year ended 31 December 20×1.

13.19 You have been given the following information(Exhibit 13.9 & 13.10) relating to a limited liability company called Nobrie. This company is preparing financial statements for the year ended 31 May 20×4.

Exhibit 13.9

Nobrie	
Statement of profit or loss for the year ended 31 May 20×4	
	£000
Revenue	66,600
Cost of sales	(13,785)
Gross profit	52,815
Distribution costs	(7,530)

Exhibit 13.9(continued)

Administrative expenses	(2,516)
Investment income	146
Finance cost	(1,177)
Profit before tax	41,738
Tax	(9,857)
Profit for the year	31,881

Exhibit 13.10

Nobrie				
Statements of financial position as at 31 May				
	20×4		20×3	
	£000	£000	£000	£000
Assets				
Non-current assets Cost		144,844		114,785
Accumulated depreciation		(27,433)		(26,319)
Current assets		117,411		88,466
Inventory	24,931		24,065	
Trade receivables	18,922		13,238	
Cash	3,689		2,224	
		47,542		39,527
Total assets		164,953		127,993
Equity and liabilities				
Ordinary share capital	27,000		23,331	
Share premium	14,569		10,788	
Revaluation surplus	15,395		7,123	
Retained earnings	59,944		28,063	
		116,908		69,305
Non-current liabilities				
6% loan note		17,824		24,068
Current liabilities				
Bank overdraft	5,533		6,973	

Exhibit 13. 10(continued)

Trade payables	16,699		20,324	
Taxation	7,989		7,323	
		30,221		34,620
Total equity and liabilities		164,953		127,993

Additional information

(1) During the year ended 31 May 20×4, the company sold a piece of equipment for £3,053,000, realising a profit of £1,540,000. There were no other disposals of non-current assets during the year.

(2) Depreciation of £5,862,000 has been charged.

(3) There were no amounts outstanding in respect of interest payable or receivable as at 31 May 20×3 or 20×4.

(4) There were no dividends paid or declared during the year.

Requirement

Prepare a statement of cash flows for Nobrie for the year ended 31 May 20×4 in accordance with IAS 7 Statement of cash flows (using indirect method).

Reference

1. Parminder Johal and Beverly Vickerstaff, Financial Accounting(2014). Routledge.

2. Jennifer Maynard. Financial Accounting, Reporting and Analysis (2017). Oxford University Press.

3. ACCA FA Financial Accounting/FIA FFA Interactive Text 2020, BPP Learning Media.

4. ACCA FA Financial Accounting/FIA FFA Practice & Revision Kit 2020, BPP Learning Media.

5. Accounting (Study Manual 2020), The Institute of Chartered Accountants in England and Wales.

6. Accounting (Question Bank 2020), The Institute of Chartered Accountants in England and Wales.

Chapter 14

An Introduction to Financial Analysis

■Learning Objectives

· Explain the purpose of interpretation of ratios.

· Understand the difference of horizontal, vertical and ratio analysis.

· Calculate key accounting ratios: Profitability, Liquidity, Gearing/Leverage, Efficiency and Investment.

· Explain the interrelationships between ratios.

· Calculate and interpret the relationship between the elements of the financial statements with regard to profitability, liquidity, gearing, efficient use of resources and investment position.

· Draw valid conclusions from the information contained within the financial statements and present these to the appropriate user of the financial statements.

14.1　Basics of Financial Analysis

All users of financial statements require information to help them make decisions about providing resources to company or assist them in the decisions in relation to their interactions with a company. An initial look at an income statement and statement of financial position will provide you with some interesting data, but the absolute amount of profit, or assets and liabilities, shown in the financial statements is not usually a particularly meaningful criterion for evaluating the performance or financial position of businesses. Therefore, the accounts will require some interpretation in order to fully understand the data and convert it into meaningful information. One of the first things you need to do when interpreting accounts is to calculate the relevant ratios. Accounting ratios are mathematical comparisons used to highlight the relationships that exist between different figures on the statement of profit or loss and statement of financial position. Once you have calculated the ratios you either need to compare them to previous ratios of the same business in order to establish trends or compare them to the ratios of other organisations to see how the business is performing, in comparison to its competitors.

1. Users of the Ratios

There are a great many parties interested in analysing financial statements, including shareholders, loan creditors, customers, suppliers, employees, government agencies, analyst-advisers, competitors and the public. Yet, in many respects, they will be interested in different things. There is not, therefore, any definitive, all-encompassing list of points for analysis that would be useful to all these stakeholder groups.

· **Shareholders:** if they wish to assess the investment returns, they will focus on dividend payment and the quality of the profits business is making. In addition, they may be more interested in the future prospects of the company to determine whether to make or retain an investment in a particular business.

· **Loan creditors:** they will be more concerned about the profit levels and whether or not the business will be in a position to repay its debts both today and in the future.

· **Customers:** they are interested whether the company will exist in the future and the continuing opportunity to obtain parts or service advice for a product they have purchased.

· **Suppliers:** they will want to know if their invoices are likely to get paid when due.

· **Employees:** they may use the financial information to analyse the possibility of a pay rise and their employment security in the future.

· **Government agencies:** they will analyse financial statements to assess taxation and help plan economic policy, design fiscal policy and provide support for business sectors in need.

· **Analyst-adviser:** this group includes investment analysts, trade union representatives and credit rating agencies. They will need to identify and extract data to look at trends and carry out comparisons with other businesses.

· **Competitors:** they will utilize companies in the same business sector as themselves in order to benchmark their progress.

· **Public:** they are becoming increasingly concerned about the global environment and sustainability and will therefore be interested in the policies of an organisation and how these affect the environment, as well as potential employment opportunities.

2. Overview of Financial Statements

(1) Horizontal Analysis

Horizontal analysis, sometimes referred to as **trend analysis,** is a comparison for the same business over time. The aim of it is to gain a 'feel' for the financial performance and position of the company at least for the later year compared with the previous year.

Absolute differences in figures are off little use unless put in the context of the actual figures themselves, so expressing the changes in percentage terms provides the necessary analytical information. Consider the following example 14. 1.

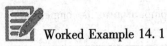 Worked Example 14. 1

	Year 1	Year 2	Year 3	Year 4
Revenue (£m)	630	819	1,046	1,298
Increase over previous year		189	227	252
% increase over previous year		30%	28%	24%

If Year 1 is chosen as base year, the rate of growth in Year 2 is equal to: 189/630×100% =30%. The analysis of Year 3 and Year 4 shows that, although there is a growth in the revenue over the four-year period, the rate of growth is slowing from 30% in Year 2 to 24% in the final period.

(2) Vertical Analysis

Another way of providing an overview of the financial statements is to work vertically: vertical analysis. For each financial statement a key figure is identified, such as revenue for the statement of comprehensive income and total assets or net assets for the statement of financial position, and all other figures are expressed as a percentage of this figure. The following example 14. 2 shows an extract of a common size statement for a statement of financial position.

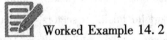 Worked Example 14. 2

The individual statement of financial position figures are shown as a percentage of the net assets of the company in Exhibit 14. 1. In this statement, net assets is the basis of 100%.

Exhibit 14. 1

Statement of Financial Position as at...		
	£000	% of net assets
...	...	...
Current assets		
Inventory	8,600	34%
Receivables	2,600	10%
Cash at bank	600	2%
...	...	...
Net assets	25,300	100%

14. 2   Ratio Analysis

In addition to reviewing and comparing individual line items, the relationships of different figures within a single set of financial statements are of importance and can provide much useful information to a user. A ratio can be calculated using any two or more figures. Calculating the ratios does not involve complicated mathematics as it simply requires one number to be divided by another. The hardest part of calculating ratios is to identify the numbers that are used in the calculations.

Remember that different users require different information from financial statements, so will use different groups of ratios. Appropriate ratios should, therefore, be selected for the purposes of the particular analysis.

A ratio, once calculated, may have some meaning on its own. However, to be really useful, a ratio should be put in context and related to some sort of reference point or standard.

There are numerous ratios that can be calculated but the five most commonly used categories are shown below.

- Profitability.
- Liquidity.
- Gearing/Leverage.
- Efficiency.
- Investment.

1. Profitability Ratios

Profitability ratios can be used to measure the financial performance of a company. Ratios included in this category are:

- Gross profit margin.
- Net profit margin.
- Expenses as a percentage of sales.
- Returned on capital employed.
- Asset turnover.

(1) Gross Profit Margin

Gross profit margin ratio shows gross profit as a percentage of sales and consequently highlights the efficiency in production or buying and has a fundamental impact on the overall profitability of a business. The gross profit percentage shows how much gross profit is made per £1 of sales revenue.

$$\text{Gross profit margin} = \frac{\text{Gross profit}}{\text{Revenue}} \times 100$$

This ratio will vary considerably between different business sectors, for example a supermarket will operate on a low gross profit percentage whereas a manufacturing company is likely to operate on a higher gross profit percentage. Whatever the type of business, gross profit needs to be sufficient to cover the expenses and to provide an acceptable level of net profit.

(2) Net Profit Margin

Net profit margin ratio highlights the net profit the business has made and the extent to which expenses affect profitability. It also shows the amount of net profit made per £1 of sales revenue.

$$\text{Net profit margin} = \frac{\text{Net profit}}{\text{Revenue}} \times 100 \text{ or } \frac{\text{Profit before interest and tax (PBIT)}}{\text{Revenue}} \times 100$$

Just like the gross profit percentage the net profit percentage will vary from business to business. Again, supermarkets are likely to operate on lower margins than manufacturing companies.

(3) Expenses as a Percentage of Sales

This can be calculated for any expense individually or in total, and gives some idea as to whether the business has been controlling expenses in relation to the level of revenue achieved. It is expressed as a percentage.It shows the amount of expense incurred per £1 of sales revenue.

$$\text{Expense}\% = \frac{\text{Expense item}}{\text{Revenue}} \times 100$$

Facts about the business—the type of property will have much influence over these ratios; this should be considered when comparing different businesses, in particular. Within the same business these ratios should, ideally, stay the same from year to year or, as the business grows, the ratios may be expected to decrease as economies of scale are seen.

(4) Return on Capital Employed (ROCE)

ROCE expresses the net profit of the business in relation to the capital employed by the business and is given as a percentage. It is a useful ratio that highlights the performance of the business, showing how much profit is made in comparison to the capital invested. However, there are variations in the calculation of this ratio which stem from how profit and capital employed are defined.

$$\text{ROCE} = \frac{\text{Profit before interest and tax (PBIT)}}{\text{Capital employed}} \times 100$$

$$\text{Capital employed} = \text{Shareholders' equity} + \text{long-term debt}$$
$$(\text{or total assets} - \text{current liabilities})$$

A basic definition is that capital employed is all long-term capital in a business, which includes the shareholders' equity and long-term debt, including the current portion of long-term debt. The ratio then takes a profit figure generated from the use of this capital before the actual return to these providers of capital, in other words this would be profit before interest and tax (PBIT), sometimes called operating profit.

If the ratio is being calculated on behalf of the shareholders, it may be more appropriate to calculate the return on equity only and exclude the long-term borrowings. In this case the relevant profit figure can either be the profit before taxation or the profit after taxation. Therefore, it can be re-written as:

$$\text{Return on equity} = \frac{\text{Profit before /after tax}}{\text{Shareholders' equity}} \times 100$$

There is no best method of calculating the ROCE. You should decide on which you feel is more appropriate for the analysis you are carrying out. The underlying principle is that we must compare like with like. To improve the accuracy of the ratio an average figure can be used for the capital employed if the information is available, by taking an average of the opening and closing capital employed figures.

(5) Asset Turnover

Asset turnover ratio shows the value of revenue generated per £1 of the assets employed in the year and is used to assess the efficiency of the use of net assets during the year.

$$\text{Asset turnover} = \frac{\text{Revenue}}{\text{Capital employed}} \times 100$$

It is strictly an efficiency ratio; however, it is explained here because it is used in the interpretation of ROCE. Generally, a larger figure for this ratio indicates that higher volume of sales has been generated with more efficient use of assets.

Profit margin and asset turnover together explain the ROCE and if the ROCE is the primary profitability ratio, these other two are the secondary ratios. The relationship between the three ratios can be shown mathematically.

$$\text{Profit margin} \times \text{Asset turnover} = \text{ROCE}$$

$$\frac{\text{PBIT}}{\text{Revenue}} \times \frac{\text{Revenue}}{\text{Capital employed}} = \frac{\text{PBIT}}{\text{Capital employed}}$$

2. Liquidity Ratios

Liquidity refers to the ability of a business to quickly turn current assets into the most liquid asset of cash. It is essential that a business can pay its liabilities as they fall due or the company will run the risk of being closed down. Ratios included in this category are:

· Current ratio.

· Quick ratio.

(1) Current Ratio

Current ratio measures how easily a business can meet its current liabilities as they fall due; in other words, for every £1 of current liabilities how much is there in the form of current assets?

$$\text{Current ratio} = \frac{\text{Current assets}}{\text{Current liabilities}}$$

The current ratio is usually expressed in the form of X:1. Although some textbooks may suggest a ratio of 2:1 is ideal, it should be remembered that different business sectors will operate effectively on different ratios. Supermarkets may operate on a comparatively low ratio as they trade in fast-moving, often perishable goods that are usually sold for cash, whereas manufacturing businesses hold stocks of raw materials, work-in-progress and finished goods that get converted into trade receivables before generating cash, thus creating a higher current ratio.

(2) Quick Ratio

Also called the acid test, this is a more pertinent measure of the ability of a business to meet its liabilities as they fall due because it omits the least liquid current asset—inventories—from the numerator.

$$\text{Current ratio} = \frac{\text{Current assets} - \text{Inventory}}{\text{Current liabilities}}$$

This again is usually expressed as a ratio in the form X : 1. It is a variation of the current ratio that excludes inventories as most businesses cannot immediately convert their inventories into cash. This is a more stringent test of liquidity. Textbooks sometimes quote an ideal ratio of 1 : 1 but for the reasons outlined above, there are variations between industries and some businesses can operate with no liquidity worries on a ratio of less than 1 : 1.

3. Gearing/Leverage Ratios

Gearing, or leverage, as it is called in US, is a measure of the balance between the two main types of long-term capital or funding in a business—that provided by equity (i.e. ordinary share capital and reserves) and that provided by debt (i.e. long-term loans, such as debentures). Ratios included in this category are:

· Gearing.
· Interest cover.

(1) Gearing Ratio

Gearing is concerned with a company's long-term capital structure. Two basic gearing ratios are:

$$\text{Gearing} = \frac{\text{Long-term debt}}{\text{Shareholders' equity}} \times 100$$

or

$$\text{Gearing} = \frac{\text{Long-term debt}}{\text{Shareholders' equity} + \text{Long-term debt}} \times 100$$

Whichever way gearing is calculated, a company that has a high proportion of debt finance is considered highly geared, while a company that has mainly equity financing is considered a low-geared company. A company could lower its gearing by boosting its shareholders' capital, either with retained profits or by a new share issue.

(2) Interest Cover

The interest cover ratio shows whether a company is earning enough PBIT to pay its interest costs comfortably, or whether its interest costs are high in relation to the size of its profits.

$$\text{Interest cover} = \frac{\text{PBIT}}{\text{Interest charges}} \times 100$$

A low ratio may indicate the business will have difficulties meeting these requirements, which could, potentially, have serious consequences.

4. Efficiency Ratios

Efficiency ratios may also be referred to as activity ratios. They are designed to provide information about the efficiency with which management controls the business. Ratios included in this category are:

- Asset turnover [discussed in Section 14. 2-1-(5)].
- Inventory turnover period.
- Receivables collection period.
- Payables payment period.

(1) Inventory Turnover Period

Inventory turnover indicates the average number of days that items of inventory are held for. This calculated how quickly the company is turning over its inventory during the year and can give an indication of slow-moving inventories.

$$\text{Inventory turnover period} = \frac{\text{Average inventory}}{\text{Cost of sales}} \times 365$$

It is better to use the average of opening and closing inventory figure for this ratio, but the year-end figure would be acceptable. It is only an approximate estimated figure, but one which should be reliable enough for comparing changes year on year. The nature of the inventories is crucial in interpreting this ratio, for example a greengrocer will have an inventory turnover of a few days, while a furniture shops ratio may be 60-90 days. Businesses generally strive to reduce their inventory turnover period.

(2) Receivables Collection Period

Receivables collection period highlights the average number of days between making a credit sale and receiving the cash from the customer.

$$\text{Receivables collection period} = \frac{\text{Trade receivables}}{\text{Credit sales}} \times 365$$

Credit sales is usually not available from the accounts, so revenue from statement of profit or loss is often used instead. An average of opening and closing receivables may be used, but the year-end receivable is often the figures included in the calculation. Businesses generally strive to keep the trade receivables turnover period to a minimum.

(3) Payables Payment Period

Payables payment period highlights the average number of days between purchasing an item on credit and making a payment to the supplier.

$$\text{Payables payment period} = \frac{\text{Trade payables}}{\text{Credit purchases}} \times 365$$

Similarly, the figure for credit purchases is not available from financial statements, so total purchases or cost of sales is often used instead. An average of opening and closing payables may be used, but the year-end payable is acceptable. Delaying payment too long may cause problems with suppliers' relationships, or deter new suppliers from entering into business arrangements, so a business does not necessarily want this ratio to be as large as possible.

5. Investment Ratios

There are a number of investment ratios that can be calculated to assist investors in assessing the performance of their investment. This section will concentrate on three of the most commonly used ratios.

- Earnings per share.
- Dividend cover.
- Price/earnings ratio.

(1) Earnings per Share

Earnings per share is a key ratio for investors. The ratio measures earnings available to the ordinary shareholder per share and is usually expressed as an amount, pence.

$$\text{Earnings per share} = \frac{\text{Profit attributable to ordinary shareholders}}{\text{Number of ordinary shares in issue}}$$

"Profit attributable to ordinary shareholders" is the profit after taxation less any preference dividend that may be deducted. Companies are required to calculate and disclose EPS on the face of the statement of comprehensive income. Companies and investors like to see this value rising from year to year. The ratio has its own accounting standard IAS 33 Earnings Per Share. There are complex rules for ascertaining the number of equity shares when there are movements in the number of shares during the year but these are beyond the scope of this book.

(2) Dividend Cover

Dividend cover highlights how many times the earnings cover the dividend paid. The dividend includes both the interim and final dividends.

$$\text{Dividend cover} = \frac{\text{Profit after tax and preference dividends}}{\text{Total ordinary dividends}}$$

A high dividend cover shows a business is retaining a considerable proportion of its profits for reinvestment and can easily pay the dividend, whereas a low dividend cover shows a business may be struggling to maintain its level of dividend.

(3) Price/Earnings Ratio(P/E Ratio)

The P/E ratio highlights the relationship between the earnings and the market value of a business. It provides a useful guide to market confidence in the future performance of the company.

$$\text{P/E ratio} = \frac{\text{Market value per share}}{\text{Earnings per share}}$$

The higher the P/E ratio, the greater the confidence the market has in the future earning potential of the business. With this, an informative comparison can be made with other businesses.

14. 3 Interpretating Financial Information

Since we have learned the calculation of ratios, we now can consider a more in-depth example, using the financial statements of a public limited company, to lead us through the main ratios used by analysts in interpreting statement of profit or loss and statement of financial position.

1. A Worked Example

Sharples plc is a company that wholesales non-electrical office equipment, from pens and stationery to filing cabinets. The company has just one warehouse and, during 20×9, replaced much of its shelving, as well as investing in new computer equipment to maintain inventory and other records.Exhibit 14. 2 & 14. 3 are the published financial statements of Sharples plc, for the year ended 31 December 20×9 and 20×8. We will use them throughout this section in application of the analytical techniques and interpretations.

Exhibit 14. 2

Sharples plc.		
Statement of Profit or Loss for the year ended December 20×9 and 20×8		
	20×9	20×8
	£000	£000
Revenue	3,000	2,500
Cost of sales	(1,800)	(1,425)
Gross profit	1,200	1,075
Distribution costs	(544)	(453)
Administrative expenses	(250)	(245)
Profit from operations	406	377
Finance costs	(66)	(60)
Profit before taxation	340	317
Income tax expense	(180)	(122)
Profit after taxation	160	195

Exhibit 14. 3

Sharples plc.		
Statement of Financial Position as at 31 December 20×9 and 20×8		
	20×9	20×8
	£000	£000
ASSETS		

Exhibit 14. 3(continued)

Non-current assets	2,320	2,080
Current assets		
Inventories	400	290
Trade receivables	450	350
Cash at bank	50	200
	900	840
Total assets	3,220	2,920
EQUITY AND LIABILITIES		
Equity		
Ordinary share capital (£1 each)	1,000	1,000
Preference share capital (£1 each)	200	200
Retained earnings	800	740
Total equity	2,000	1,940
Non-current liabilities		
10% Debentures	720	600
Current liabilities		
Trade payables	400	300
Current tax payable	100	80
	500	380
Total liabilities	1,220	980
Total equity and liabilities	3,220	2,920

Note: Dividend paid are as follows.

	20×9	20×8
	£000	£000
Preference dividends paid	20	20
Ordinary dividends paid	80	75

Ratio calculation of the basic five categories for Sharples plc is shown as Exhibit 14. 4.

Exhibit 14. 4

Category	Ratios	Formula	20×9		20×8	
Profitability	Gross profit margin	$\dfrac{\text{Gross profit}}{\text{Revenue}}$	$\dfrac{1,200}{3,000}$	40. 0%	$\dfrac{1,075}{2,500}$	43. 0%
	Net profit margin	$\dfrac{\text{PBIT}}{\text{Revenue}}$	$\dfrac{406}{3,000}$	13. 5%	$\dfrac{377}{2,500}$	15. 1%
	Administration expenses %	$\dfrac{\text{Admin. costs}}{\text{Revenue}}$	$\dfrac{544}{3,000}$	18. 1%	$\dfrac{453}{2,500}$	18. 1%
	Distribution costs %	$\dfrac{\text{Distr. costs}}{\text{Revenue}}$	$\dfrac{250}{3,000}$	8. 3%	$\dfrac{245}{2,500}$	9. 8%
	ROCE	$\dfrac{\text{PBIT}}{\text{Capital employed}}$	$\dfrac{406}{2,000 + 720}$	14. 9%	$\dfrac{377}{1,940 + 600}$	14. 8%
	Asset turnover	$\dfrac{\text{Revenue}}{\text{Capital employed}}$	$\dfrac{3,000}{2,000 + 720}$	1. 10	$\dfrac{2,500}{1,940 + 600}$	0. 98
Liquidity	Current ratio	$\dfrac{\text{Current assets}}{\text{Current liabilities}}$	$\dfrac{900}{500}$	1. 8	$\dfrac{840}{380}$	2. 2
	Quick ratio	$\dfrac{\text{Current assets} - \text{Inventory}}{\text{Current liabilities}}$	$\dfrac{900 - 400}{500}$	1. 0	$\dfrac{840 - 290}{380}$	1. 4
Gearing	Gearing ratio	$\dfrac{\text{Long} - \text{term debt}}{\text{Equity} + \text{Long} - \text{term debt}}$	$\dfrac{720}{2,000 + 720}$	26. 5%	$\dfrac{600}{1,940 + 600}$	23. 6%
	Interest cover	$\dfrac{\text{PBIT}}{\text{Interest charges}}$	$\dfrac{406}{66}$	6. 2	$\dfrac{377}{60}$	6. 3
Efficiency	Inventory turnover period	$\dfrac{\text{Average inventory}}{\text{Cost of sales}} \times 365$	$\dfrac{400}{1,800} \times 365$	81	$\dfrac{290}{1,425} \times 365$	74
	Receivables collection period	$\dfrac{\text{Trade receivables}}{\text{Credit sales}} \times 365$	$\dfrac{450}{3,000} \times 365$	55	$\dfrac{350}{2,500} \times 365$	51
	Payables payment period	$\dfrac{\text{Trade payables}}{\text{Credit purchases}} \times 365$	$\dfrac{400}{1,800} \times 365$	81	$\dfrac{400}{1,425} \times 365$	77
Investment	Earnings per share	$\dfrac{\text{Profit after tax and preference dividends}}{\text{No. of ordinary shares}}$	$\dfrac{160 - 20}{1,000}$	£0. 14	$\dfrac{195 - 20}{1,000}$	£0. 175
	Dividend cover	$\dfrac{\text{Profit after tax and preference dividends}}{\text{Ordinary dividends}}$	$\dfrac{160 - 20}{80}$	1. 75	$\dfrac{195 - 20}{75}$	2. 33
	Price/earnings ratio	$\dfrac{\text{Market value per share}}{\text{Earnings per share}}$	$\dfrac{1. 80}{0. 14}$	12. 9	$\dfrac{1. 65}{0. 175}$	9. 4

The ratios calculated for Sharples plc.

Assume that market prices per share at 31 December 20×9 and 20×8 are £1. 80 and £1. 65 respectively.

Interpretation of the profitability ratios

· A fall in the net profit margin from 15. 1% to 13. 9% shows it has been caused by a fall in gross profit margin from 43% to 40%, slightly mitigated by distribution costs being a smaller percentage of sales.

· The fall in gross profit margin could be as a result of any, or all, of the following:

—increase in the cost of purchases (e.g. different suppliers, delivery charges, exchange rates) not passed on to customers

　　—a reduction in sales prices (possibly unlikely)

　　—special deals with the new high street customer in order to gain the contract

　　· ROCE is fairly constant over the two years. Both PBIT and capital employed have increased in 20×9. Both equity and long-term debt have increased. Is this a reasonable return for this type of business?

　　· More sales have been generated from the use of assets (has the company been more efficient in 20×9?)

Interpretation of the liquidity ratios

　　· No apparent liquidity problems are indicated by these ratios with the company able to pay its liabilities as they fall due.

　　· Cash balances and the two liquidity ratios have fallen, but the company is still able to cover its current liabilities from its liquid assets (receivables and cash).

　　· The key question is why have cash balances fallen? (It may be due to company's investment in a new computer equipment).

Interpretation of the gearing ratios

　　· Although gearing has increased, the company is not very highly geared.

　　· Both long-term borrowings (additional debenture issued) and equity have increased, but cash balances have fallen significantly—all contributing to the increase in gearing.

　　· Although the company issued more debentures, the company can comfortably meet its interest payment, so the ordinary shareholders face little risk in their investment.

Interpretation of the efficiency ratios

　　· The efficiency ratios have all increased, indicating that the company is holding onto inventories longer, is taking longer to collect its receivables, and is taking longer to pay its payables.

　　· Why? Possible reasons may be:

　　—The company is building up inventories to supply a new customer

　　—There is a large debt uncollected at the 20×9 year end

　　—The company has negotiated longer payment terms with customer

Interpretation of the investment ratios

　　· Earnings per share has fallen owing to the fall in profit for the year. Reasons for this are not evident from the financial statements.

　　· Despite this, the company has marginally increased the dividend per share, with the result that dividend cover has fallen. However, this ratio should be monitored closely, as shareholders may be concerned that the ratio has fallen because of more of profits being paid out through dividends.

　　· The P/E ratio has increased significantly because the share price has risen, while EPS has fallen. This does indicate that the markets have confidence in the company.

2. Limitations of Ratio Analysis

Although ratio analysis is a useful technique, users must be aware of its limitations. Ratios are only as good as the information on which they are based. Consequently if accounting information has been manipulated through 'window dressing', the ratios will be unreliable. It must also be remembered that the statement of financial position is only a snapshot of a business on a particular day; it may not be representative of the business's year-round position, for example, a retail outlet selling surfing equipment is likely to have a far higher inventory at the end of June than at the end of December.

The financial statements used for ratio analysis are based upon historical data. In order to carry out a full analysis of a business, information is required about its future aims and objectives, its product development and budgeted cash flows. Some of this information is likely to be found in the chairman's statement or director's report.

If ratios are being compared to those of other businesses it must be remembered that companies can choose their own accounting policies, such as the method of depreciation and the rate, and these variations may distort the comparison. In addition, no two businesses are identical in terms of structure or activities so like-for-like comparisons are difficult to make.

When carrying out trend analysis it is important to consider the impact the economic climate will have on the data. In times of high inflation, comparisons of sales revenue, profit and asset values will be distorted. New accounting standards and changes in the business activities will also reduce the usefulness of year-on-year comparisons.

Summary

· Users of financial statements can gain a better understanding of the significance of the information in financial statements by comparing it with other relevant information.

· Ratios provide information through comparison.

· Profitability ratios include:

—Gross/Net profit margin

—Expenses as a percentage of sales

—Return on capital employed

—Asset turnover

· Liquidity ratios include:

—Current ratio

—Quick ratio

· Gearing/Leverage ratios include:

—Gearing ratio

—Interest cover

· Efficiency ratios include:

—Inventory turnover period

—Receivables collection period

—Payables payment period

· Investment ratios include：

—Earnings per share

—Dividend cover

—P/E ratio

· You must be able to interpret financial data as well as calculate ratios.

· Ratio analysis has limitations.

Exercise

14. 1 Which one of the following would help a company with high gearing to reduce its gearing ratio? (　　)

    A.Making a rights issue of equity shares

    B.Issuing further long-term loan notes

    C.Making a bonus issue of shares

    D.Paying dividends on its equity shares

14. 2 A company's gross profit as a percentage of sales increased from 24% in the year ended 31 December 20×1 to 27% in the year ended 31 December 20×2.

Which of the following events is most likely to have caused the increase? (　　)

    A.An increase in sales volume

    B.A purchase in December 20×1 mistakenly being recorded as happening in January 20×2

    C.Overstatement of the closing inventory at 31 December 20×1

    D.Understatement of the closing inventory at 31 December 20×1

14. 3 Which of the following transactions would result in an increase in capital employed? (　　)

    A.Selling inventory at a profit

    B.Writing off an irrecoverable debt

    C.Paying a payable in cash

    D.Increasing the bank overdraft to purchase a non-current asset

14. 4 From the following information regarding the year to 31 August 20×6, what is the accounts payable payment period? You should calculate the ratio using purchases as the denominator.(　　)

	£
Sales	43,000
Cost of sales	32,500
Opening inventory	6,000
Closing inventory	3,800
Trade accounts payable at 31 August 20×6	4,750

A.40 days

B.50 days

C.53 days

D.57 days

14. 5 Quality Co are drafting their financial statements. An extract from their draft statement of financial position at 31 March 20×8 is set out below.

	£	£
Non-current assets		450
Current assets: Inventory	65	
Receivables	110	
Prepayments	30	
	205	
Current liabilities: Payables	30	
Bank overdraft (Note)	50	
	80	
		125
		575
Non-current liability: Loan		(75)
		500
Ordinary share capital		400
Retained earnings		100
		500

Note: The bank overdraft first occurred on 30 September 20×7.

What is the gearing of the company? You should calculate gearing using capital employed as the denominator.(   )

A.13%

B.16%

C.20%

D.24%

14. 6 Which of the following is a ratio which is used to measure how much a business owes in relation to its size? (　　)

　　A.Asset turnover

　　B.Profit margin

　　C.Gearing

　　D.Return on capital employed

14. 7 A business operates on a gross profit margin of $33\frac{1}{3}$ %. Gross profit on a sale was £800, and expenses were £680.

　　What is the net profit margin? (　　)

　　A.3. 75%

　　B.5%

　　C.11. 25%

　　D.22. 67%

14. 8 A company has the following details extracted from its statement of financial position:

	£000
Inventories	1,900
Receivables	1,000
Bank overdraft	100
Payables	1,000

The industry the company operates in has a current ratio norm of 1. 8. Companies who manage liquidity well in this industry have a current ratio lower than the norm.

Which of the following statements accurately describes the company's liquidity position? (　　)

　　A.Liquidity appears to be well managed as the bank overdraft is relatively low

　　B.Liquidity appears to be poorly controlled as shown by the large payables balance

　　C.Liquidity appears to be poorly controlled as shown by the company's relatively high current ratio

　　D.Liquidity appears to be poorly controlled as shown by the existence of a bank overdraft

14. 9 Why is analysis of financial statements carried out? （　　）

A. So that the analyst can determine a company's accounting policies

B. So that the significance of financial statements can be better understood through comparisons with historical performance and with other companies

C. To get back to the 'real' underlying figures, without the numbers being skewed by the requirements of International Financial Reporting Standards

D. To produce a report that can replace the financial statements, so that the financial statements no longer need to be looked at

14. 10 Z has a current ratio of 1. 5, a quick ratio of 0. 4 and a positive cash balance. If it purchases inventory on credit, what is the effect on these ratios? （　　）

	Current ratio	Quick ratio
A.	Decrease	Decrease
B.	Decrease	Increase
C.	Increase	Decrease
D.	Increase	Increase

14. 11 HJ has an asset turnover of 2. 0 and an operating profit margin of 10%. The entity is about to launch a new product which is expected to generate additional sales of £1. 6m and additional profit of £120,000 in its first year. To manufacture the new product HJ will need to purchase additional assets of £500,000.

What will be the effect of the new product on the following ratios of HJ? （　　）

	Operating profit margin	Return on capital employed
A.	Decrease	Decrease
B.	Decrease	Increase
C.	Increase	Decrease
D.	Increase	Increase

14. 12 Justin is a sole trader who prepares accounts to 31 December each year. For the year ended 31 December 20×3 his income statement (Exhibit 14. 5) and statement of financial position (Exhibit 14. 6) are as follows:

Exhibit 14. 5

Income statement for the year ended 31 December 20×3		
	£	£
Revenue		293,350
Cost of sales		<u>181,950</u>

Exhibit 14. 5(continued)

Gross profit		111,400
Less expenses		
Rent and rates	9,470	
Light and heat	2,860	
Wages and salaries	30,400	
Motor expenses	4,950	
Professional fees	1,250	
Sundry expenses	2,620	51,550
Net profit		59,850

Exhibit 14. 6

Statement of financial position as at 31 December 20×3		
	£	£
Non-current assets		
Factory	148,000	
Motor vans	31,180	
		179,180
Current assets		
Inventory	28,700	
Accounts receivable	29,480	58,180
Total assets		237,360
Share capital		159,660
Non-current liabilities		
Loan	50,000	
Current liabilities		
Bank overdraft	5,400	
Accounts payable	22,300	77,700
		237,360

You are required to calculate the following ratios:

(1) Gross profit %.

(2) Net profit %.

(3) Wages and salaries as a % of revenue.

(4) Rent and rates as a % of revenue.

(5) ROCE.

(6) Current ratio.

(7) Quick ratio.

14. 13 * Elizabeth runs a small business called Data Services (DS) and her brother runs a small business called Engineering Services (ES). In the year ended 31 March 20×3 they both generated sales of £160,000 and both made a gross profit of £52,500. Their statements of financial position as at 31 March 20×3 were given as Exhibit 14. 7:

Exhibit 14. 7

Statements of financial position as at 31 March 20×3				
	DS		ES	
	£	£	£	£
Non-current assets		52,270		91,160
Current assets				
Inventory	36,480		37,200	
Accounts receivable	42,140		2,520	
Bank balance	10,420	89,040	2,300	42,020
Total assets		141,310		133,180
Capital		111,830		111,830
Current liabilities				
Accounts payable	29,480		16,580	
Bank overdraft	0	29,480	4,770	21,350
		141,310		133,180

You are required to assess the liquidity of the two businesses by:

(1) Calculating the relevant ratios.

(2) Analysing the ratios.

14. 14 Exhibit 14. 8 & 14. 9 are the extracts from the financial statements of Halwyn plc:

Exhibit 14. 8

Income statement for the year ended 31 March 20×9	
	£000
Revenue	6,923
Cost of sales	4,222
Gross profit	2,701
Distribution costs	(630)

Exhibit 14. 8(continued)

Administration expenses	(847)
Operating profit	1,224
Finance costs (debenture interest)	140
Profit before taxation	1,084
Taxation	320
Profit for the year	764

Exhibit 14. 9

Statement of financial position extract as at 31 March 20×9	
	£000
Equity	
Ordinary share capital	1,500
Retained earnings	1,632
Other components of equity	821
Non-current liabilities	
10% debentures	200

(1) You are required to calculate the following profitability ratios:

· Gross profit percentage.

· Operating profit percentage.

· Return on capital employed.

· Pre-tax return on equity.

(2) Halwyn's revenue for the year ended 31 March 20×8 was £6,482,000. Calculate the percentage increase in the revenue.

14. 15 * The financial statements of Lisa are given as Exhibit 14. 10 & 14. 11:

Exhibit 14. 10

	Lisa			
	Income statements for the years ended 30 April			
	20×4		20×5	
	£	£	£	£
Revenue		78,750		88,590
Opening inventory	3,540		4,140	
Purchases	38,280		39,940	
	41,820		44,080	

Exhibit 14. 10(continued)

Closing inventory	4,140		4,330	
Cost of sales		37,680		39,750
Gross profit		41,070		48,840
Less expenses				
Business rates	6,490		6,570	
Light and heat	1,480		1,560	
Motor expenses	1,110		1,480	
Stationery	430		210	
Training	100		100	
Wages	10,380	19,990	13,690	23,610
Net profit		21,080		25,230

Exhibit 14. 11

	Lisa			
	Statement of Financial Position as at 30 April			
	20×4		20×5	
	£	£	£	£
Non-current assets				
Property		82,800		82,800
Motor vehicles		7,900		7,110
Office furniture		1,570		1,250
		92,270		91,160
Current assets				
Inventory	4,140		4,330	
Trade receivables	8,420		12,150	
Bank balance	2,000	14,560	340	16,820
Total assets		106,830		107,980
Capital				
Opening balance		31,270		37,350
Add profit for the year		21,080		25,230
		52,350		62,580
Less drawings		15,000		21,180
		37,350		41,400
Non-current liabilities				

Exhibit 14. 11(continued)

Business loan	60,000		55,000	
Current liabilities				
Accounts payable	9,480	69,480	11,580	66,580
		106,830		107,980

You are required to：

(1) Calculate the following ratios：gross profit percentage, net profit percentage, wages as a percentage of revenue, return on capital employed, current ratio, quick ratio, asset turnover, inventory turnover, trade receivables turnover and trade payables turnover.

(2) Write a short report (maximum 200 words) analysing the changes that have taken place between 20×4 and 20×5.

Reference

1. Jennifer Maynard. Financial Accounting, Reporting and Analysis (2017). Oxford University Press.

2. Parminder Johal and Beverly Vickerstaff, Financial Accounting (2014). Routledge.

3. ACCA FA Financial Accounting/FIA FFA Interactive Text 2020, BPP Learning Media.

4. ACCA FA Financial Accounting/FIA FFA Practice & Revision Kit 2020, BPP Learning Media.

Answers

Chapter 1

1. 1 D
1. 2 C
1. 3 C
1. 4 A
1. 5 A
1. 6 B
1. 7 A
1. 8 A
1. 9 B and C
1. 10 D
1. 11 A
1. 12 D
1. 13 A
1. 14 B
1. 15 D
1. 16 B
1. 17

Lucy Chan

Trading and profit and loss account for the year ended ending 31 December 20×0

	£		£
Purchases	84,665	Sales	133,770
Gross profit c/d	64,190	Closing inventory	15,085
	148,855		148,855
Rent	4,595	Gross profit b/d	64,190
Wages and salaries	28,865		
Printing and stationery	2,940		
Electricity expenses	2,485		
General expenses	1,295		
Net profit	24,010		
	64,190		64,190

1. 18 Please refer to Exhibit 1.

Exhibit 1

I. Lamb		
Statement of profit or loss for the year ended 31October 20×6		
	£	£
Sales		100,250
Less Cost of goods sold		
Purchases	60,400	
Less Closing inventory	(15,600)	(44,800)
Gross profit		55,450
Expenses		
Salaries	29,300	
Motor expenses	1,200	
Rent	950	
Insurance	150	
General expenses	85	(31,685)
Net profit		23,765

1. 19 Please refer to Exhibit 2.

Exhibit 2

E. David		
Statement of Profit or Loss for the year ended 31 December 20×1		
	£	£
Sales		73,848
Less Cost of goods sold		
Purchases	58,516	
Less Closing stock	(10,192)	(48,324)
		25,524
Gross Profit		
Less Expenses		
Wages	8,600	
Motor expenses	2,080	
Rates	2,680	
Insurance	444	
General expenses	420	(14,224)
Net Profit		11,300

1. 20*-1. 23* Solution available from publisher.

Chapter 2

2. 1 C

2. 2 C

2. 3 A

2. 4 B

2. 5 D

2. 6 B

2. 7 C

2. 8 C

2. 9 A and D

2. 10 C

2. 11 B

2. 12 B

2. 13 B

2. 14 B

2. 15 A

2. 16 A

2. 17 * Solution available from publisher.

2. 18 Please refer to Exhibit 3.

Exhibit 3

I. Lamb		
Statement of financial position as at 31 October 20×6		
	£	£
Non-current assets		
Premises		47,800
Motor vehicles		8,600
		56,400
Current assets		
Inventory	15,600	
Accounts receivable	13,400	
Cash at bank	8,200	
Cash in hand	300	37,500
		93,900
Current liabilities		
Accounts payable		(8,800)
Net assets		85,100
Capital		
Balance b/d		65,535
Add Net profit		23,765
		89,300
Less drawings		(4,200)
		85,100

2. 19 Please refer to Exhibit 4.

Exhibit 4

E. David		
Statement of financial position as at 31 December 20×1		
	£	£
Non-current assets		
Buildings		20,000
Motor vehicle		12,000
		32,000
Current Assets		
Inventory	10,192	
Accounts receivables	7,800	
Cash at bank	6,616	
Cash in hand	160	
		24,768
		56,768
Less Current Liabilities		
Accounts payables		(6,418)
Net assets		50,350
Capital		
Cash introduced		48,000
Add Net profit for the year		11,300
		59,300
Less Drawings		(8,950)
		50,350

2. 20*-2. 22* Solution available from publisher.

2. 23 Please refer to Exhibit 5.

Exhibit 5

T. Leung		
Statement of financial position as at 31 March 20×1		
	£	£
Non-current assets		
Buildings		120,400
Equipment		17,028

Exhibit 5(continued)

Motor van		15,050
		152,478
Current Assets		
Inventory	42,828	
Accounts receivables	29,283	
Cash at bank	4,876	
		76,987
		229,465
Less Current Liabilities		
Accounts payables		(13,975)
Net assets		215,490
Capital		
Balance b/d		212,736
Add Net profit for the year		19,748
		232,484
Less Drawings		(16,994)
		215,490

Chapter 3

3. 1 A

3. 2 B

3. 3 B

3. 4 B

3. 5 A

3. 6 D

3. 7 A

3. 8 A

3. 9 A

3. 10 B

3. 11 A

3. 12 C

3. 13 A

3. 14 D

3. 15 Please refer to Exhibit 6.

Exhibit 6

T. Mann		
Statement of profit or Loss for the year ended 31 July 20×1		
	£	£
Sales		110,859
Less Sales returns		(1,029)
		109,830
Less Cost of goods sold		
Opening inventory	11,949	
Add Purchases	65,100	
Add Carriage inwards	3,570	
	80,619	
Less Purchase returns	(1,176)	
	79,443	
Less Closing inventory	(8,883)	70,560
Gross Profit		39,270
Less Expenses		
Salaries and wages	10,521	
Rent	3,066	
Motor Expenses	6,552	
General expenses	882	
Carriage outwards	1,659	
		(22,680)
Net Profit		16,590

3. 16 Please refer to Exhibit 7 & 8.

Exhibit 7

G. Still		
Statement of profit or Loss for the year ended 30 September 20×7		
	£	£
Sales		380,400
Less Returns inwards		(1,540)
		378,860

Exhibit 7 (continued)

Less Cost of goods sold		
Opening inventory	41,600	
Add Purchases	188,430	
Less Returns outwards	(3,410)	
	185,020	
Add Carriage inwards	3,700	
	230,320	
Less Closing inventory	(44,780)	(185,540)
Gross Profit		193,320
Less Expenses		
Salaries and wages	61,400	
Warehouse rent	3,700	
Motor Expenses	1,910	
Office expenses	412	
General expenses	245	
Carriage outwards	2,100	
Insurance	1,356	
Lighting and heating	894	(72,017)
Net Profit		121,303

Exhibit 8

G. Still		
Statement of financial position as at 30 September 20×7		
	£	£
Non-current asset		
Premises		92,000
Fixtures and fittings		1,900
Motor vehicles		13,400
		107,300
Current Assets		
Inventory	44,780	
Accounts receivable	42,560	
Bank	5,106	92,446

Exhibit 8(continued)

		199,746
Current Liabilities		
Accounts payable		(31,600)
Net assets		168,146
Capital		
Balance at 1. 10. 20×6		68,843
Add net profit for the year		121,303
		190,146
Less Drawings		(22,000)
		168,146

3. 17 Please refer to Exhibit 9 & 10.

Exhibit 9

S. Shah		
Statement of profit or Loss for the year ended 30 June 20×1		
	£	£
Sales		178,560
Less Sales returns		(1,968)
		176,592
Less Cost of goods sold		
Opening inventory	22,733	
Add Purchases	113,990	
Add Carriage inwards	2,976	
	139,699	
Less Purchase returns	(3,091)	
	136,608	
Less Closing inventory	(28,320)	(108,288)
Gross Profit		68,304
Less Expenses		
Salaries and wages	37,075	
Rent and rates	2,918	
Insurance	749	
Motor Expenses	4,250	
Telephone and internet	4,198	

Exhibit 9(continued)

Electricity	1,594	
Carriage outwards	1,920	
General expenses	3,014	(55,718)
Net Profit		12,586

Exhibit 10

S. Shah		
Statement of financial position as at the year ended 30 June 20×1		
	£	£
Non-current asset		
Buildings		80,000
Computer equipment		3,360
Motor vehicles		17,280
		100,640
Current Assets		
Inventory	28,320	
Accounts receivables	37,402	
Cash at bank	4,627	70,349
		170,989
Less Current Liabilities		
Accounts payables		(32,618)
Net assets		138,371
Capital		
Balance b/f		137,305
Add net profit for the year		12,586
		149,891
Less Drawings		(11,520)
		138,371

3. 18 Please refer to Exhibit 11 & 12.

Exhibit 11

T. Owen		
Statement of profit or loss for the year ended 31 March 20×6		
	£	£
Sales		276,400
Less Cost of goods sold		

Exhibit 11(continued)

Opening inventory	52,800	
Purchases	141,300	
Less Purchase returns	(2,408)	
Carriage inwards	1,350	
Less Closing inventory	(58,440)	(134,602)
Gross profit		141,798
Less Expenses		
Carriage outwards	5,840	
Wages and salaries	63,400	
Business rates	3,800	
Communication expenses	714	
Commission paid	1,930	
Insurance	1,830	
Sundry expenses	208	(77,722)
Net profit		64,076

Exhibit 12

T. Owen		
Statement of financial position as at 31 March 20×6		
	£	£
Non-current assets		
Building		125,000
Fixtures		1,106
		126,106
Current assets		
Inventory	58,440	
Accounts receivable	45,900	
Cash at bank	31,420	
Cash in hand	276	136,036
		262,142
Current liabilities		
Accounts payable		(24,870)
Net assets		237,272
Capital		

Exhibit 12(continued)

Balance b/d		210,516
Net profit		64,076
		274,592
Less drawings		(37,320)
		237,272

3. 19 * Solution available from publisher.

Chapter 4

4. 1 D

4. 2 A

4. 3 C

4. 4 C

4. 5 C

4. 6 B

4. 7 C

4. 8 D

4. 9 B

4. 10 B

4. 11 D

4. 12 A

4. 13 C

4. 14 C

4. 15 B

4. 16 * -4. 17 * Solution available from publisher.

4. 18 Please refer to Exhibit 13 & 14.

Exhibit 13

Year 1 valuation						
Purchases Units	Sales Units	Balance Units	Unit cost £	Inventory value £	Cost of sales £	Sales £
10		10	300	3,000		
12		12	250	3,000		
		22		6,000		
	8	(8)	300	(2,400)	2,400	3,200

Exhibit 13(continued)

		14		3,600		
6		<u>6</u>	200	<u>1,200</u>		
		20		4,800		
	12	<u>(12)</u>		<u>(3,100)</u> *	3,100	4,800
		<u>8</u>		<u>1,700</u>	<u>5,500</u>	<u>8,000</u>

* $2\times £300 + 10\times £250 = £3,100$

Exhibit 14

Year 2 valuation						
Purchases Units	Sales Units	Balance Units	Unit cost £	Inventory value £	Cost of sales £	Sales £
B/f		8		1,700		
10		10	200	2,000		
		<u>18</u>		<u>3,700</u>		
	5	<u>(5)</u> *		<u>(1,100)</u> *	1,100	2,000
		13		2,600		
12		<u>12</u>	150	<u>1,800</u>		
		25		4,400		
	25	<u>(25)</u> **		<u>(4,400)</u> **	4,400	10,000
		<u>0</u>		<u>0</u>	<u>5,500</u>	<u>12,000</u>

* $2\times £250 + 3\times £200 = £1,100$

* * $13\times £200 + 12\times £150 = £4,400$

Chapter 5

5. 1 C

5. 2 C

5. 3 B

5. 4 C

5. 5 A

5. 6 D

5. 7 C

5. 8 A

5. 9 B

5. 10 A

5. 11 B C

5. 12 C

5. 13 D

5. 14 C

5. 15 A

5. 16 D

5. 17 C

5. 18

Trade Receivables(SOFP)

	£		£
Opening balance b/f	8,600	Cash	49,000
Sales	44,000	Irrecoverable debts	180
		Irrecoverable debts	420
		Closing balance c/d	3,000
	52,600		52,600
Opening balance b/d	3,000		

Irrecoverable Debts Expenses (SPL)

	£		£
Receivables	180	P/L a/c	600
Receivables	420		
	600		600

In the receivables ledger, personal accounts of the customers whose debts are irrecoverable will be taken off the ledger.

5. 19

First, note the requirement's wording 'recognised for receivables in the statement of profit or loss'. This means the total charge (or recovery) for irrecoverable debts and the allowance for receivables in the statement of profit or loss.

Secondly, consider the allowance for receivables.

	£
Closing allowance required (723,800×1.5%)	10,857
Opening allowance	(15,250)
Reduction needed in allowance	(4,393)

Remember that a reduction to the allowance for receivables is a credit to the statement of profit or loss.

Thirdly, the amount received of £540 had already been written off the previous year and now needs to be credited to irrecoverable debts.

Therefore, the total credit to the statement of profit or loss = 540 + 4,393 = £4,933

5.20* Solution available from publisher.

Chapter 6

6.1 B

6.2 A

6.3 C

6.4 C

6.5 B

6.6 A

6.7 C

6.8 A

6.9 B

6.10 C

6.11 B

6.12 C

6.13 B

6.14

(1) Under the straight line method, depreciation for each of the 5 years is:

Annual depreciation = £(17,000−2,000) /5 = £3,000

(2) Under the reducing balance method, depreciation for each of the 5 years is:

Year	Depreciation
1	35%×£17,000 = £5,950
2	35%× (£17,000 −£5,950) = 35%×£11,050 = £3,868
3	35%× (£11,050 −£3,868) = 35%×£7,182 = £2,514
4	35%× (£7,182 − £2,514) = 35%×£4,668 = £1,634
5	Balance to bring book value down to £2,000: £4,668 − £1,634−£2,000 = £1,034

6.15

(1) A car Monthly depreciation = £(20,000−2,000) /(3×12) = £500 pm

Depreciation 1 June 20×6-28 February 20×7 (9×£500) = £4,500

1 March 20×7-28 February 20×8 (12×£500) = £6,000

B car Monthly depreciation = £(15,500−2,000) /(3×12) = £375 pm

Depreciation 1 June 20×7-28 February 20×8 (9×£375) = £3,375

(2)

Motor vehicles

		£			£
1 Jun 20×6	Payables (or cash) (car purchase)	<u>20,000</u>	28 Feb 20×7	Balance c/d	<u>20,000</u>
1 Mar 20×7	Balance b/d	20,000			
1 Jun 20×7	Payables (or cash) (car purchase)	15,500	28 Feb 20×8	Balance c/d	35,500
		<u>35,500</u>			<u>35,500</u>
1 Mar 20×8	Balance b/d	35,500			

Motor vehicles—Accumulated depreciation

		£			£
28 Feb 20×7	Balance c/d	<u>4,500</u>	28 Feb 20×7	Depreciation	<u>4,500</u>
			1 Mar 20×7	Balance b/d	4,500
			28 Feb 20×8	Depreciation	
28 Feb 20×8	Balance c/d	13,875		(6,000+3,375)	9,375
		<u>13,875</u>			<u>13,875</u>
			1 Mar 20×8	Balance b/d	13,875

Exhibit 16

Statement of financial position (working) as at 28 February 20×8					
	A car		B car		Total
£	£	£	£	£	£
Asset at cost		20,000		15,500	35,500
Accumulated depreciation					
Year to 28 Feb 20×7	4,500				
Year to 28 Feb 20×8	6,000		3,375		
		(10,500)		(3,375)	(13,875)
Carrying amount		<u>9,500</u>		<u>12,125</u>	<u>21,625</u>

6.16* –6.18* Solution available from publisher.

Chapter 7

7. 1 B

7. 2 C

7. 3 A

7. 4 B

7. 5 C

7. 6 D

7. 7 B

7. 8 C

7. 9 C

7. 10 A

7. 11 B

7. 12 A

7. 13 B

7. 14 C

7. 15 A

7. 16 A

7. 17

As at 28 February 20×2, no telephone bill had been received in respect of 20×2 because it was not due for another month. However, the accrual principle means we cannot ignore the telephone expenses for January and February, and so an accrual of £24 is made, being two thirds of the final bill of £36.

The telephone expenses for the year ended 28 February 20×2 are as follows:

	£
1 March-31 March 20×1 (no telephone)	0. 00
1 April-30 June 20×1	23. 50
1 July-30 September 20×1	27. 20
1 October-31 December 20×1	33. 40
1 January-28 February 20×2 (two months: £36×2/3)	24. 00
	108. 10

The accrual will be shown in the statement of financial position of the business as at 28 February 20×2, as a current liability. The journal to record the accrual is:

		£	£
DEBIT	Electricity expense	24	
CREDIT	Accrual (current liability)		24

7. 18 Please refer to Exhibit 17 & 18.

Exhibit 17

J. Wright		
Statement of profit or loss for the year ended 31 March 20×6		
	£	£
Sales	127,245	
Less Discounts allowed	(2,480)	
Return inwards	(3,486)	121,279
Cost of goods sold		
Opening inventory	7,940	
Purchases	61,420	
Less Return outwards	(1,356)	
Less Closing inventory	(6,805)	(61,199)
Gross profit		60,080
Other income—Discounts received		62
Less Expenses		
Carriage outwards	3,210	
Rent and insurance (8,870−600)	8,270	
Wages and salaries (39,200+3,500)	42,700	
General office expenses (319+16)	335	
Increase in allowance for receivables	110	
Depreciation—Fixtures and fittings	190	
Depreciation—Van	1,400	(56,215)
Net profit		3,927

Exhibit 18

J. Wright		
Statement of financial position as at 31 March 20×6		
	£	£
Non-current assets		
Fixtures and fitting at cost	1,900	
Less accumulated depreciation	(190)	
Carrying value		1,710
Van at cost	5,600	
Less accumulated depreciation	(1,400)	4,200

Exhibit 18(continued)

Carrying value		5,910
Current assets		
Inventory	6,805	
Trade receivables	12,418	
Less allowance for receivables	(740)	
Prepayments	600	
Cash	140	19,223
		25,133
Current liabilities		
Trade payables	11,400	
Accruals (3,500+16)	3,516	
Bank overdraft	2,490	(17,406)
Net assets		7,727
Capital		
Balance b/d		25,200
Net profit		3,927
Less Drawings		(21,400)
		7,727

7. 19*-7. 25* Solution available from publisher.

Chapter 8

8. 1 D

8. 2 D

8. 3 B

8. 4 C

8. 5 B

8. 6 B

8. 7 D

8. 8 C

8. 9 C

8. 10 C

8. 11 A

8. 12 C
8. 13 C
8. 14 C
8. 15 B

Chapter 9

9. 1 A
9. 2 C
9. 3 D
9. 4 C
9. 5 A
9. 6 A
9. 7 B
9. 8 C
9. 9 D
9. 10 D
9. 11 D
9. 12 A
9. 13 D
9. 14 B
9. 15 A
9. 16 B
9. 17 C
9. 18 C
9. 19 B
9. 20 C
9. 21 A
9. 22 D
9. 23

Machinery-cost

20×7		£	20×7		£
1 Jan	Bal b/d (2× £15,000)	30,000	31 Mar	Machinery disposal	15,000
			1 Dec	Machinery disposal	15,000
		_____			
		30,000			30,000

Machinery-accumulated depreciation

20×7		£	20×7		£
31 Mar	Machinery disposal W2	6,750	1 Jan	Bal b/d W1	12,000
1 Dec	Machinery disposal W3	8,750	31 Mar	Depreciation 3×15,000/60	750
			1 Dec	Depreciation 11×15,000/60	2,750
		_____			
		15,500			15,500

WORKINGS

(1) Accumulated depreciation at 1 Jan 20×7 = $£30,000 \times \dfrac{24}{5 \times 12} = £12,000$

(2) Accumulated depreciation at 31 Mar 20×7 = $£15,000 \times \dfrac{27}{5 \times 12} = £6,750$

(3) Accumulated depreciation at 1 Dec 20×7 = $£15,000 \times \dfrac{35}{5 \times 12} = £8,750$

Machinery disposal account

20×7		£	20×7		£
31 Mar	Machinery	15,000	31 Mar	Receivables (proceeds)	8,000
			31 Mar	Accu depreciation	6,750
			31 Mar	Loss on disposal	250
1 Dec	Machinery	15,000	1 Dec	Cash (proceeds)	2,500
			1 Dec	Accu depreciation	8,750
		_____	31 Dec	Loss on disposal	3,750
		30,000			30,000

9. 24*-9. 25* Solution available from publisher.

9. 26

Machine

(1) Straight Line	£	(2) Reducing Balance	£
Cost	75,000	Cost	75,000
Year 1 Depreciation	11,070	Year 1 Depreciation 20%×£75,000	15,000
	63,930		60,000
Year 2 Depreciation	11,070	Year 2 Depreciation 20%×£60,000	12,000
	52,860		48,000
Year 3 Depreciation	11,070	Year 3 Depreciation 20%×£48,000	9,600
	41,790		38,400
Year 4 Depreciation	11,070	Year 4 Depreciation 20%×£38,400	7,680
	30,720		30,720

Depreciation = (75,000−30,720) /4 = £11,070

Chapter 10

10. 1 B

10. 2 B

10. 3 A

10. 4 C

10. 5 B

10. 6 C

10. 7 A

10. 8 B

10. 9 A

10. 10 C

10. 11 A

10. 12 B

10. 13 D

10. 14 D

10. 15 B

Chapter 11

11. 1 A

11. 2 A

11. 3 B

11. 4 C

11. 5 B

11. 6 C

11. 7 B

11. 8 C

11. 9 B

11. 10 B

11. 11 B

11. 12 C

11. 13 D

11. 14 B and E

11. 15 D

11. 16 D

11. 17 Hope Ltd. movement of retained profit

	20×1	20×2	20×3	20×4	20×5
	£	£	£	£	£
Retained earnings b/d	–	–	1,000	5,500	12,500
Profit for the year	8,500	12,500	23,500	48,500	37,500
Less:					
Preference dividends (5% of £1×50,000)	(2,500)	(2,500)	(2,500)	(2,500)	(2,500)
Ordinary dividends (% of £1 ×300,000)	2%(6,000)	3%(9,000)	5.5%(16,500)	13%(39,000)	7.5%(22,500)
Retained earnings c/d	0	1,000	5,500	12,500	25,000

11. 18 * Solution available from publisher.

Exhibit 19

Canvat plc:	
Statement of financial position at 31 December 20×1	
	£000
TOTAL ASSETS (2,000 + (320×1. 60))	2,512
EQUITY AND LIABILITIES	
Equity	
Share capital (400 + 80 + 160)	640
Share premium (500 − 80+ 352)	772
Retained earnings	300
Total equity	1,712
Total liabilities	800
Total equity and liabilities	2,512

The bonus issue is of 800,000/5 = 160,000 50p shares:

		£	£
DEBIT	Share premium	80,000	
CREDIT	Share capital		80,000

The rights issue is of (800,000 + 160,000)/3 = 320,000 50p shares at £1. 60 each, ie, £512,000:

		£	£
DEBIT	Cash	512,000	
CREDIT	Share capital (320,000×50p)		160,000
	Share premium [320,000×(1. 60 − 0. 50)]		352,000

The ledger accounts are as follows:

Share capital

	Number	£		Number	£
Balance c/d	1,280,000	640,000	Balance b/d	800,000	400,000
			1 for 5 bonus issue	160,000	80,000
			1 for 3 rights issue	320,000	160,000
	1,280,000	640,000		1,280,000	640,000

Share premium

	£		£
Bonus issue	80,000	Balance b/d	500,000
Balance c/d	<u>772,000</u>	Rights issue: cash	<u>352,000</u>
	<u>852,000</u>		<u>852,000</u>

Retained earnings

	£		£
Balance c/d	<u>300,000</u>	Balance b/d	<u>300,000</u>

11. 20 * Solution available from publisher.

Chapter 12

12. 1 C

12. 2 C

12. 3 A

12. 4 C

12. 5 B

12. 6 D

12. 7 B

12. 8 B

12. 9 B

12. 10 C

12. 11 C

12. 12 Please refer to Exhibit 20 & 21.

Exhibit 20

Hobo	
Statement of profit or loss for the year ended 30 September 20×6	
	£
Sales	623,300
Cost of Sales W2	<u>460,485</u>
Gross Profit	162,815
Distribution expenses W3	56,635
Administration expenses W4	<u>44,038</u>
Operating profit	62,142
Interest (7%×95000)	<u>6,650</u>

Exhibit 20(continued)

Profit before tax	55,492
Taxation	22,680
Profit for the year	32,812

Exhibit 21

Hobo			
Statement of Financial Position as at 30 September 20×6			
ASSETS	£	£	£
Non-current assets		Accumulated	
	Cost	Depreciation	NBV
Premises (3,750+2,750)	275,000	(6,500)	268,500
Equipment (1,200+3,600)	12,000	(4,800)	7,200
Vehicles (2,400+6,500)	18,500	(8,900)	9,600
	472,000	(20,200)	285,300
Current assets			
Inventory		19,840	
Accounts receivables	92,360		
Less allowance for receivables	(4,618)	87,742	
Prepayments		500	
Bank		51,810	
			159,892
Total assets			445,192
EQUITY AND LIABILITIES			
Equity			
Ordinary share capital			100,000
Share premium			50,000
Retained earnings (26,000+32,812)			58,812
			208,812
Non-current liabilities			
7% debentures			95,000
Current liabilities			
Accounts payables		111,450	
Tax payable		22,680	
Interest payable		6,650	

Exhibit 21 (continued)

Hobo			
Accruals		600	141,380
Total equity and liabilities			445,192

W1 Depreciation	£	
Depreciation—Premises (1%×275,000)	2,750	
Depreciation—Equipment (12,000×10%)	1,200	
Depreciation—Vehicles [20%×(18,500−6,500)]	2,400	

W2 Cost of Sales	£	£
Opening inventory	18,950	
Purchases	426,500	
Closing inventory	(19,840)	
50% Depreciation—Premises (50%×2,750)	1,375	
50% Depreciation—Equipment (50%×200)	600	
Productive wages(32,300+600)	32,900	
		460,485

W3 Distribution expenses	£	£
Delivery expenses	22,060	
Warehouse wages	30,200	
50% Depreciation—Premises (50%×2,750)	1,375	
50% Depreciation—Equipment (50%×1,200)	600	
Depreciation—Vehicles	2,400	
		56,635

W4 Administration expenses	£	£
Audit fee	1,200	
Irrecoverable debts	5,320	
Administrative salaries	15,200	
Administrative expenses	5,600	
Rents administration(12,600−500)	12,100	
Allowance for receivables (5%×92,360)	4,618	
		44,038

12. 13 * Solution available from publisher.

12. 14 Please refer to Exhibit 22-24.

Exhibit 22

Gerry		
Statement of profit or loss for the year ended 31 March 20×6		
	£	£
Sales		271,700
Cost of Sales		
Opening inventory	14,167	
Purchases	186,000	
Closing inventory	(23,483)	(176,684)
Gross Profit		95,016
Expenses		
Wages and salaries	31,862	
General expenses (15,840−925+1,437)	16,352	
Debenture interest (30,000×8% or 1,200+1,200)	2,400	
Depreciation (210,000×10%)	21,000	
Allowance for receivables (5%×11,000−324)	226	(71,840)
Profit before tax		23,176
Taxation		(9,700)
Profit for the year		13,476

Exhibit 23

Gerry						
Statement of Changes in Equity for the year ended 31 March 20×6						
	Ordinary shares	Share premium	Preference shares	Revaluation surplus	General reserve	Retained earnings	Total equity
	£	£	£	£	£	£	£
Bal. b/d	100,000	9,500	20,000	10,000	12,000	976	152,476
Profit for the year						13,476	13,476
Transfer					3,000	(3,000)	0
Dividend						(1,200)	(1,200)
Bal c/d	100,000	9,500	20,000	10,000	15,000	10,252	164,752

Exhibit 24

Gerry		
Statement of Financial Position as at 31 March 20×6		
	£	£
ASSETS		
Non-current assets		
Cost	210,000	
Accumulated Depreciation (210,000−191,000+21,000)	(40,000)	
Net book Value		170,000
Current assets		
Inventory	23,483	
Accounts receivables (11,000 − 5%×11,000)	10,450	
Prepayments	925	
Bank	9,731	
		44,589
Total assets		214,589
EQUITY AND LIABILITIES		
Equity		
Ordinary share capital		100,000
Preference shares		20,000
Share premium		9,500
Revaluation surplus		10,000
General reserve (12,000+3,000)		15,000
Retained earnings		10,252
		164,752
Non-current liabilities		
8% debentures		30,000
Current liabilities		
Accounts payables	7,500	
Tax payable	9,700	
Interest payable	1,200	
Accruals	1,437	19,837
Total equity and liabilities		214,589

12. 15 * Solution available from publisher.

12. 16 Please refer to Exhibit 25-27.

Exhibit 25

Burn		
Statement of profit or loss for the year ended 31 December 20×9		
	£	£
Sales (83,460−3,750)		79,710
Cost of Sales W3		(40,960)
Gross Profit		38,750
Distribution expenses W4		(14,822)
Administration expenses W5		(17,812)
Operating profit		6,116
Interest—6% (6%×50,000)	3,000	
—5% (5%×10,000)	500	(3,500)
Profit before tax		2,616
Taxation		(1,200)
Profit for the year		1,416

Exhibit 26

Burn				
Statement of Changes in Equity for the year ended 13 December 20×9				
	Share capital	Share premium	Retained earnings	Total equity
	£	£	£	£
Bal. b/d	100,000	20,000	62,000	182,000
Profit for the year			1,416	1,416
Error correction			(10,000)	(10,000)
Issue of shares	40,000	40,000		80,000
Bal c/d	140,000	60,000	53,416	253,416

Exhibit 27

Burn			
Statement of Financial Position as at 31 December 20×9			
	£	£	£
ASSETS			
Non-current assets		Accumulated	

Exhibit 27(continued)

	Cost	Depreciation	NBV
Premise (20,000+4,000)	200,000	(24,000)	176,000
Equipment (15,000+5,000)	50,000	(20,000)	30,000
Vehicles (4,040+792)	<u>8,000</u>	<u>(4,832)</u>	<u>3,168</u>
	<u>258,000</u>	<u>(48,832)</u>	209,168
Current assets			
Inventory		4,560	
Accounts receivables (8,240 − 8,240×5%)		7,828	
Bank		103,520	
Cash		<u>250</u>	
			<u>116,158</u>
Total assets			<u>325,326</u>
EQUITY AND LIABILITIES			
Equity			
Share capital (100,000+40,000)			140,000
Share premium (20,000+40,000)			60,000
Retained earnings			<u>53,416</u>
			253,416
Non-current liabilities			
6% debentures		50,000	
5% debentures		<u>10,000</u>	60,000
Current liabilities			
Accounts payables		7,210	
Interest payables		3,500	
Taxation		<u>1,200</u>	11,910
Total equity and liabilities			<u>325,326</u>

W1 Vehicle	£	£	£
	Cost	Accumulated Depreciation	NBV
Bal b/d	15,000	(6,560)	8,440
Disposal	<u>7,000</u>	<u>(2,250)</u>	4,480
Bal c/d	<u>8,000</u>	<u>(4,040)</u>	<u>3,960</u>

W2 Depreciation

	£
Depreciation—Premises（200,000×2%）	4,000
Depreciation—Equipment（50,000×10%）	5,000
Depreciation—Vehicle（3,960×20%）	792

W3 Cost of Sales

	£	£
Opening inventory	6,230	
Purchases	15,260	
Closing inventory	(4,560)	
50% Depreciation—Premises（4,000×50%）	2,000	
50% Depreciation—Equipment（5,000×50%）	2,500	
Production salaries and wages	12,320	
Production expenses	7,210	
		40,960

W4 Distribution expenses

	£	£
Warehouse expenses	950	
Warehouse wages	10,100	
25% Depreciation—Premises（4,000×25%）	1,000	
25% Depreciation—Equipment（5,000×25%）	1,250	
Depreciation—Vehicle	792	
Loss on disposal W6	730	
		14,822

W5 Administration expenses

	£	£
Admin salaries	14,200	
Admin expenses	950	
Allowance for receivables（5%×8,240）	412	
25% Depreciation—Premises（4,000×25%）	1,000	
25% Depreciation—Equipment（5,000×25%）	1,250	
		17,812

W6 Disposal

	£
Proceeds	3,750
NBV of disposed vehicle W1	(4 480)
Loss on disposal	(730)

12. 17*-12. 18* Solution available from publisher.

Chapter 13

13. 1 D

13. 2 B

13. 3 A

13. 4 C

13. 5 C

13. 6 D

13. 7 C

13. 8 D

13. 9 D

13. 10 B

13. 11 D

13. 12 B

13. 13 B

13. 14 A

13. 15 C

13. 16 C

13. 17 D

13. 18 * Solution available from publisher.

13. 19 Please refer to Exhibit 28.

Exhibit 28

Nobrie		
Statement of cash flows for the year ended 30 May 20×4		
	£000	£000
Cash flow from operating activities		
Net profit before tax	41,738	
Adjustments for		
Depreciation	5,862	
Profit on equipment disposal	(1,540)	
Investment income	(146)	
Interest paid	1,177	
Operating profit before working capital changes	47,091	

Exhibit 28 (continued)

Increase in inventory	(866)	
Increase in receivables	(5,684)	
Decrease in payables	(3,625)	
Cash generated from operations	36,916	
Interest received *	146	
Interest paid	(1,177)	
Tax paid (W1)	(9,191)	
Net cash flows from operating activities		26,694
Cash flows from investing activities		
Purchase at property plant and equipment (W2)	(28,048)	
Proceeds from sale of equipment	3,053	
Net cash flows from investing activities		(24,995)
Cash flows from financing activities		
Proceeds from issue of share capital		
(27,000 + 14,569) − (23,331 + 10,788)	7,450	
Repayment of long term borrowings (24,068 − 17,824)	(6,244)	
Net cash flows from financing activities		1,206
Increase in cash and cash equivalents		2,905
Cash and cash equivalents at beginning of period (2,224−6,973)		(4,749)
Cash and cash equivalents at end of period (3,689 − 5,533)		(1,844)

WORKINGS

(1) Tax paid

Tax payables

	£000		£000
Tax paid (balancing figure)	9,191	Balance b/fwd	7,323
Balance c/fwd	7,989	Profit and loss account	9,857
	17,180		17,180

(2) Purchases of property, plant and equipment

Property, plant and equipment

	£000		£000
Bal b/d (carrying value)	88,466	Disposals (carrying value) (W3)	1,513
Revaluation (15,395−7,123)	8,272	Depreciation	5,862
Purchases (balancing figure)	28,048	Bal c/d (carrying value)	117,411
	124,786		124,786

(3) Disposal

	£000
Proceeds	3,053
Profit	(1,540)
Carrying value of disposals	1,513

Chapter 14

14. 1 A

14. 2 D

14. 3 A

14. 4 D

14. 5 A

14. 6 C

14. 7 B

14. 8 C

14. 9 B

14. 10 A

14. 11 B

14. 12 Justin

(1) Gross profit%   111,400/293,350×100 = 37. 98%

(2) Net profit %59,850/293,350×100 = 20. 40%

(3) Wages and salaries as a % of revenue   30,400/293,350 ×100 = 10. 36%

(4) Rent and rates as a % of revenue   9,470/293,350×100 = 3. 23%

(5) ROCE   59,850/209,660 ∗ ×100 = 28. 55%

(6) Current ratio   58,180/27,700 = 2. 10:1

(7) Quick ratio   29,480/27,700 = 1. 06:1

* (159,660 + 50,000 = 209,660)

14. 13 * Solution available from publisher.

14. 14

Gross profit %   2,701/6,923×100×100% = 39. 01%

Operating profit%   1,224/6,923×100×100% = 17. 68%

Return on capital employed   1,224/4,153 * ×100×100% = 29. 47%

Pre-tax return on equity   1,084/3,953 ** ×100×100% = 27. 42%

% increase in revenue   (6,923 − 6,482)/6,482×100×100% = 6. 80%

(* Capital employed: 1,500 + 1,632 + 821 + 200 = 4,153)

(* * Equity: 1,500 + 1,632 + 821 = 3,953)

14. 15 * Solution available from publisher.